Belonging in Europe - T Diaspora and Work

CW01064344

This publication does not just mark the presence of black people in Europe, but brings research to a new stage by making connections across Europe through the experience of work and labour. The working experience for black peoples in Europe was not just confined to ports and large urban areas – often the place black people are located in the imagination of the European map both today and historically. Work took place in small towns, villages and on country estates. Until the 1800s enslaved Africans would have worked alongside free blacks and their white peers. How were these labour relations realised be it on a country estate or a town house? How did this experience translate into the labour movements of the twentieth century? These are some of the questions the essays in this collection address, contributing to new understandings of European life both historically and today.

This book was originally published as a special issue of *Immigrants and Minorities*.

Caroline Bressey's research focuses upon recovering the historical geographies of the black community in nineteenth century Britain, especially London. Parallel to this are her interests in ideas of race, racism, early anti-racist theory and identity in Victorian society. She has worked as a curator and is a lecturer in the department of geography, University College London.

Hakim Adi's research has focused on uncovering the history of Africans in Britain, as well as documenting the history of anti-colonialism and Pan-Africanism during the twentieth century. His current research focuses on the relationship between the Communist International and Pan-Africanism in the early twentieth century. He is currently an independent scholar.

Belonging in Europe - The African Diaspora and Work

Edited by
Caroline Bressey and Hakim Adi

- PF → rla of circus ent
- 18c Ab — ending slave trade
- 19c Anti slavery — B sense of movil ✓
- 5Tc — merging clancia
- Making man C₁ — Jubilee
  — PF
  — Aldridge
- Making high c — Funny Eylon
- chilhm th

Routledge
Taylor & Francis Group

LONDON AND NEW YORK

First published 2011
by Routledge
2 Park Square, Milton Park, Abingdon, Oxon, OX14 4RN

Simultaneously published in the USA and Canada
by Routledge
711 Third Avenue, New York, NY 10017

Routledge is an imprint of the Taylor & Francis Group, an informa business

© 2011 Taylor & Francis

First issued in paperback 2013

This book is a reproduction of *Immigrants and Minorities*, vol. 28, issue 2-3. The Publisher requests to those authors who may be citing this book to state, also, the bibliographical details of the special issue on which the book was based.

Typeset in Times New Roman by Taylor & Francis Books

British Library Cataloguing in Publication Data
A catalogue record for this book is available from the British Library

ISBN13: 978-0-415-48870-9 (hbk)
ISBN13: 978-0-415-84621-9 (pbk)

Disclaimer
The publisher would like to make readers aware that the chapters in this book are referred to as articles as they had been in the special issue. The publisher accepts responsibility for any inconsistencies that may have arisen in the course of preparing this volume for print.

Contents

Notes on Contributors

Kathleen Chater is an independent scholar and writer, mainly on historical and genealogical subjects. She is the author of a number of historical publications including *Untold Histories: Black People in England and Wales during the Period of the British Slave Trade, c. 1660–1807* (Manchester University Press, 2009).

Dienke Hondius is Associate Professor of history at VU University, and staff member of the Anne Frank House, Amsterdam. She is co-director of the summer school Black Europe: Dimensions of Citizenship, Race, and Ethnic Relations, member of the scientific board of advice of NiNsee, and board member of the international humanitarian student leadership organisation Humanity in Action. She lives in Amsterdam. Earlier monographs include: Dienke Hondius, *Return: Holocaust Survivors and Dutch Anti-Semitism* (Praeger/Greenwood Press, Westport, CT, 2003); *Absent: Herinneringen aan het Joods Lyceum in Amsterdam, 1941–1943* (Memories of the Jewish Lyceum in Amsterdam, 1941–43) (Vassallucci, Amsterdam 2001); and her PhD thesis *Gemengde huwelijken, gemengde gevoelens. Aanvaarding en ontwijking van etnisch en religieus verschil in Nederland sinds 1945* (Mixed marriages, mixed feelings. Acceptance and avoidance of ethnic and religious difference in the Netherlands since 1945) (PhD thesis, University of Amsterdam. SDU Uitgevers, Den Haag 1999. 2nd ed., 2001); Black Africans in Seventeenth-Century Amsterdam (*Renaissance and Reformation/Renaissance et Réforme*, 2008, no. 1. CRRS, Toronto, Canada). Current research projects include a book on the history and impact of the concept of 'Race' in Europe, with a focus on Dutch contributions from 1600 onwards entitled *Race in European History*. A book on the history of education about World War II and the Holocaust: *Oorlogslessen*, forthcoming 2010. She is also preparing an online database, *Bystander Memories, Project Eyewitnesses*, containing oral history interviews and transcripts of the memories of non-Jewish eyewitnesses of the Holocaust in the Netherlands. Website: www.let.vu.nl/staff/dg.hondius.

Jan Marsh was curator of 'Black Victorians' exhibition at Manchester and Birmingham Art Galleries, 2005–06; and editor of the accompanying catalogue *Black Victorians* published by Lund Humphries. She is currently working on the wider representation of 'Black' figures in European art.

Caroline Bressey is a Lecturer in the Department of Geography, University College London. Her research focuses on the black presence in Victorian Britain, particularly London. The aim of her research is to recover the biographies of black Victorians, and develop our understanding of race and racism as experienced by the black community. Recent publications include an edited collection with Dr Claire Dwyer, *New Geographies of Race and Racism* (Ashgate 2008). She is currently researching a biography of Catherine Impey who published *Anti-Caste* in the 1880s.

Sean Creighton is an independent researcher and project worker. His interests range over community, cultural, democratic, labour movement, friendly and mutual society history, Black & Asian heritage in Britain, and slavery and abolition. He is particularly interested in the histories of the London Boroughs of Lambeth, Merton and Wandsworth. He runs History & Social Action Publications publishing pamphlets by friends and in association with organisations. Website: www.seancreighton.com. His recent publications include: 'Battersea and the Formation of the Workers' Educational Association'. In Stephen K. Roberts (ed.). *A Ministry of Enthusiasm. Centenary Essays on the Workers' Education Association.* London: Pluto Press, 2003: 26–40; 'Slavery is Sustained by the Purchase of its Productions': The Slave; His Wrongs and Their Remedy (1851–1856). In (ed.) Ulrich Pallua, Adrian Knapp, Andreas Exenberger, *(Re)Figuring Human Enslavement: Images of Power, Violence and Resistance.* Edition Weltordnung – Religion in – Gewalt 5. Innsbruck University Press, 2009: 169 – 91; *Black People in the North East.* Newcastle: *North East History* 39, 2008: 11–24; 'Paul Robeson's British Journey' in Neil A. Wynn, *Cross the Water Blues. African American Music in Europe.* Jackson: University Press of Mississippi, 200: 125–44; 'Co-operation, Mutuality and Radical Politics'. In *Co-operatives and Mutuals: The New Challenge.* Leeds: Independent Labour Publications, 2005: 7–41.

Robbie Aitken is a Lecturer in German Historical Studies. Key publications: *Exclusion and Inclusion: Gradations of Whiteness and Socio-Economic Engineering in German Southwest Africa 1884–1914.* Oxford: Cultural Identity Studies, Peter Lang, 2007; From Cameroon to Germany and Back via Moscow and Paris: The Political Career of Joseph Bilé (1892–1959), Performer, *'Negerarbeiter'*, and Comintern Activist. *Journal of Contemporary History* (2008) 43, no. 4, 597–616. A larger monograph entitled, *Transnational Lives: Survival, Politics and Identity amongst German-speaking Cameroonians* is in preparation. Areas of research interest:

Africans in Europe, German colonialism, conceptions of blackness and whiteness, constructions of race, modern German history.

Hakim Adi is Emeritus Reader at Middlesex University and Honorary Research Associate at University College, London. Hakim is the author of *West Africans in Britain 1900-60: Nationalism, Pan-Africanism and Communism* (Lawrence and Wishart, 1998) and (with M. Sherwood) *The 1945 Manchester Pan-African Congress Revisited* (New Beacon, 1995) and *Pan-African History: Political Figures from Africa and the Diaspora since 1787* (Routledge, 2003). He has appeared in documentaries and radio programmes, and has written widely on the history of Pan-Africanism, the African Diaspora, and Africans in Britain, including three history books for children.

Gavin Schaffer is Senior Lecturer in Modern European History at the University of Portsmouth. He is author of *Racial Science and British Society 1930–62* and co-editor of *The Lasting War: Society and Identity in Britain, France and Germany after 1945*.

INTRODUCTION

Belonging in Europe

The European myths about identity and nationalism, citizenship and ownership, are the building blocks for Fortress Europe. While the latest wave of African incomers are found washed upon a Sicilian beach when the tide goes out: bloated, breath-less, anonymous.[1]

The aim of this collection is to highlight the possibility of comparative histories of the African diaspora in Europe by assembling research focusing on various European countries that is not usually published in a single volume. The research brought together here owes much to the authors who have confronted the historical myth that there is no history of the African diaspora in Europe before 1945. It also seeks to build on the work of all those who have previously attempted to highlight the history of the African diaspora in Europe such as the pioneering work of Hans Debrunner. Debrunner's *Presence and Prestige: A History of Africans in Europe before 1918* was published over 30 years ago but historians have, for a variety of reasons, found it difficult to follow the path that he charted. Indeed, since its publication there have been few works that have focused on the African diaspora in Europe.[2] Instead, historians have tended to concentrate on deepening the study of the African diaspora in specific countries, such as Fryer's *Staying Power*, on Britain and Ndiaye's recent work *La condition noire*, on France.

In addition the research on the representation of black people in European art has proved fruitful. Allison Blakely's work on *Blacks in the Dutch World: The Evolution of Racial Imagery in a Modern Society* and *the Image of the Black in Western Art* are well-known examples.[3] Exhibitions such as 'Black Victorians' and 'Black is Beautiful' have provided fruitful avenues of research and the exhibitions have acted as successful interventions into European historical narratives.[4] However, aside from studies focused on the history of art, the majority of historical research remains focused within the confines of European national (and their corresponding imperial) boundaries.[5] One obvious reason for this trend is the difficulty associated with translation and the fact that historical research is normally only written and published in one language. However, it is also the case that even the study of the African diaspora within individual European countries is marginalised and pursued with difficulty and this has made wider pan-European research and collaboration even more difficult.

The papers in this collection were brought together as the result of a conference, 'Belonging in Europe: The African Diaspora and Work c1400–1945' convened by The Equiano Centre, University College London as part of the events marking the bicentenary of the parliamentary abolition of the British Slave Trade in November 2007. The conference itself was inspired by an event that had taken place at University College Falmouth earlier in the year. 'Belonging in Britain. New Narratives/Old Stories: "race," heritage and cultural identity' was a symposium that focused on debates around 'race', cultural heritage and belonging. It sought to explore what *belonging* in Britain means through case studies of the work of a range of cultural practitioners including the photographer Ingrid Pollard, the curator Carol Tulloch, heritage critic Jo Litter and Caroline Bressey. The intention of the organisers was to 'confront "old stories," myths and assumptions and sketch out new narratives and possibilities'.[6]

Borrowing from the title of the Falmouth symposium, 'Belonging in Europe' aimed to move the discussion of black Europeans beyond an acceptance of a geographical presence in order to consider an assessment of the extent to which black Europeans shared or experienced a sense of belonging in Europe. The conference sought to gather together those who were investigating the lives of the African diaspora through their experiences of employment and as members of the working population in various European countries. The decision to create this focus was based upon the idea that the everyday experiences of work, unemployment, discrimination, unionisation and the friendships and politicisation that men and women experienced through work might give researchers a sense of the degree to which men and women of the African diaspora experienced a sense of belonging to and in Europe.

The experiences of members of the African diaspora in Europe were made up of 'complex processes, involving diverse populations, political and cultural motivations and movements, as well as ambiguous individual strategies'.[7] Many different personal geographies existed and operated at the same time in the same and parallel places, in small spaces and across regions. As highlighted by high-profile Africans that are the focus of Hondius' research, there were a number of Africans, particularly those who were part of colonial elites, who did not expect, or wish, to remain in Europe. In addition to these more privileged individuals, there were those who were semi-settled including sailors, those who became (settlers) (including colonial and cultural elites and sailors amongst them), and then those who were born to settlers.

Several themes for further research emerge from this collection. The individuals recovered by Aitken and in many, but not all, of Chater's examples, come to our attention because they had for various reasons come into contact with operations of the state. Although the men and women in Bressey's paper are present in the archive for different reasons they too were 'highlighted' in the archive for some reason, rather than having the colour of their skin recorded as a matter of course. Thus the numbers of men and women who remain 'invisible' in the archives could be legion but is very difficult to estimate. As a consequence estimating the size of the African population in Europe in any period and how it changed over time will be very difficult if not impossible to calculate. The extent to which this will impact upon the ability to recover new historical geographies of the African diaspora will vary across Europe, depending upon the different apparatus the State used to record ideas of difference within populations. Comparing these technologies of States should provide us with interesting insights into the governmentalities of difference in operation across Europe. However, this will provide little support for those researchers who will have to finely sift through public and private archives in countries where differences of 'colour' were not systematically recorded. As a result it may be some time before pan-European comparisons can be made effectively.

However, there are also those individuals who stand out in the archives, and in this collection, because they held highly visible positions in society. Amongst them are men like Olaudah Equiano who settled in Britain, unlike the subjects of Hondius' research who were in Europe during a similar period, but returned to Africa. Whether more Africans decided to settle in Britain (or were able to settle in Britain) compared to other European countries, during the eighteenth century, is a potential avenue for further research. Their potential differences in experience also highlights another question for researchers – the extent to which common time periods for the history of the African diaspora in Europe, even Western Europe, can be established, or if it is even desirable to do so. Most historical research has focused on the consequences of European intervention in Africa, such as the trans-Atlantic slave trade and colonialism in the making of a modern African diaspora in Europe. In the future research might focus on the period before 1500 in order to establish the extent of the earlier African diaspora, and in particular the significance for Europe of the African presence in the Iberian peninsular.

A group of men and women who attracted inconsistent and often conflicting forms of attention were those who found themselves fighting in Europe during the two World Wars, the second of which is the focus of Schaffer's paper, as well as those who were caught up in the political events which redefined Europe between the Wars. Here Adi and Aitken illustrate that the decade directly following the end of the First World War is critical for our understandings of the political and cultural transformations that took place amongst the African diaspora. All three papers also highlight the need for greater research to be undertaken on hardening racist attitudes that appear to have developed in Europe after the first world.

Work undertaken by Adi and Creighton suggests that members of the European African diaspora met at international events such as Garvey's Universal Negro Improvement Association convention held in New York in 1924, and the pan-African congresses organised by Du Bois and at meetings held under the auspices of the Communist International during this period. Some of these activists stayed in touch when they returned to their respective countries in Europe but more research needs to be undertaken to establish how such meetings contributed to the development of pan-Africanist politics and culture.

Furthermore, how did the geographies of print cultures attached to these movements impact upon the circulation of ideas? To what extent were journals such as *Continents* (the journal of The Ligue Universelle de Défense de la Race Noire, France[8]), the *Negro Worker* (a Communist journal published in English and French from several European cities), the bilingual *Review of the Black World* (Paris) or *Wasu* (journal of the West African Students' Union published in London) read by a pan-European readership? How important were the experiences and criticisms of racism published within these papers and others, yet to be recovered or fully interpreted, in the development of national and diasporic ideas of human rights, pan-Africanism and anti-colonialism? To what extent did European governments exchange information on activist men and women such as Garan Kouyaté, Jomo Kenyatta and the Nardal sisters who contributed to these debates? How can the (un)successful experiences of using state/national archives be shared by historians, since it is sometimes the case that archives in one country shed light on the history of the African diaspora elsewhere in Europe?

Not all members of the African diaspora had access to such high levels of self-controlled mobility employed by early twentieth-century pan-Africanists, but those with more ordinary experiences of life were also mobile individuals. In this volume Bressey illustrates that ordinary Victorian men and women were employed as nurses and valets who travelled between English-speaking parts of the British Empire. They also found work as entertainers in the pleasure gardens and circuses of nineteenth-century Europe. Amongst the most mobile of the African diaspora were those who worked on the sea. This was a significant form of employment for many black men present in Europe from Equiano and his peers up to (and beyond) the Second World War. The important role of sailors and seamen in the circulation of political ideas is an increasing focus of historians.[9] An important link between Europe and its colonies, seafarers played an important part in several of the political organisations established in the early twentieth century, as Adi highlights in his contribution to this volume.

European Enlightenment debates on race, published by theorists like Immanuel Kant, give a sense that discussions of racial hierarchy shared common origins within Europe. However, the differing historical developments of racism within Europe are reflected in this collection. The difficulties in defining the ambiguity of race is replicated in the diverse use of the term 'black' amongst the authors of this collection. Is this uncertainty a particularly European flexibility? How have different European countries understood 'Blackness'? Researchers working on archives in Britain, including Chater and Bressey in this collection, have found that many 'people of colour' were described as black during the seventeenth, eighteenth and nineteenth centuries. This diversity includes people born in India labelled as Negroes. Certainly, the existence of 'Bombay Africans' means that these people might have been Africans (i.e., 'Negroes') from India, but the records seem to suggest that there was a very imprecise application of racial categorisations by civil servants. A man from Bombay could be described as a Negro because this perhaps reflected an understanding of otherness rather than a particularly racial identity.[10] These complex, and as yet little understood, webs of identity are coupled to the fact that many people appear to have had the colour of their skin recorded as an exceptional intervention by a recorder of information, rather than a matter of course. Does this malleable idea of blackness apply to all European countries? If so, how long did it last? How and when did the alignment of blackness with members of the African diaspora become tied?

As BEST stated in 2005:

> the history of Black Europeans, whose current number is estimated at eighteen million, still remains mostly unknown. This is a consequence

both of the reluctance of many European nations to deal with their colonial history and of the widespread notion that Europe indeed consists of many different ethnicities who however all belong to the same "white race." Black Europeans are thus often consigned to the role of "foreigner" instead of being conceived as part of the plurality of a new united Europe.[11]

We hope this collection will contribute to the call for the development of a network of scholars – academic, creative and community based – to establish more formal forums to support and disseminate research on the history of the black presence in Europe so the research boundaries of Europe can be broken down. Scholars need to be able to exchange sources and arrange for the translation of key texts and archives in order to reconstruct the complex historical geographies that were experienced by black populations in Europe before the outbreak of the Second World War.[12] Belonging in Europe is a small contribution to the establishment of such a network. It is, however, also limited in scope. From those who presented to the conference we have collected papers to give as great a variety of history and geography as possible. Although debates and the research content have developed since the conference many of the papers are made up of fragmentary and incomplete archival material. A more complete picture requires a greater collaboration between nationally and pan-European-focused historians. But the majority of papers here still do reflect histories that are rooted in research in Britain. This reinforces our argument that there is a need for an integrated network of researchers from across the breadth of Europe that will enable scholars to build upon each other's research. We would like to thank all those who contributed to the discussions at the conference from the audience and through the presentation of papers which we were unable to include within this collection.

Caroline Bressey
Lecturer in the Department of Geography, University College London, UK

Hakim Adi
Emeritus Reader in Middlesex University/University College London, UK

Notes

[1] Evaristo, 2008, 6. Evaristo's essay appeared in an issue of *Wasafiri*, a magazine of contemporary writing, which focused on African Europeans. It includes a number of translated essays and reviews.

[2] Van Sertima's edited volume *The African Presence in Early Europe* is a well-known exception.

[3] Blakely, Dutch World, 2001 (first published 1987). Blakely has also published *Russia and the Negro*.

[4] 'Black Victorians: Black people in British Art 1800–1900' curated by Jan Marsh was shown at Birmingham Museum and Art Gallery and Manchester Art Gallery in 2006. 'Black is Beautiful: Rubens to Dumas', in Amsterdam, Nieuwe Kerk, 26 July–26 October 2008. A catalogue is available in Dutch and English, Black is *Beautiful: Rubens to Dumas*, Zwolle. The Netherlands: Waanders Publishers, 2008. The exhibition continues to have a presence through an online research lab available in Dutch and English http://www.blackisbeautifulamsterdam.nl/resea rchlab

[5] For example, see Ndiaye, *La condition noire* on France, Fryer, *Staying Power* on Britain and Oguntoye, *Eine afro-deutsche Geschichte* on Germany.

[6] Details of the Belonging in Britain symposium can be seen on the symposium poster, including an image by Ingrid Pollard http://www.falmouth.ac.uk/ component/option,com_gallery2/Itemid,1168/?g2_itemId=1285. Part of the discussion can also been seen on the YouTube site for University College Falmouth.

[7] Khalfa, 2008, 15.

[8] Khalfa, 2008.

[9] See, for example, Frost, 1995; Linebaugh and Rediker, 2000; Jenkinson, 2009.

[10] An exhibition on 'Bombay Africans 1850–1910' was held at the Royal Geographical Society, London in 2007. The exhibition maintains an online presence: http://www.rgs.org/WhatsOn/Exhibitions/Exhibition/ba01.htm

[11] BEST: Black European Studies in Transition established 2004 at Gutenberg University Mainz, http://www.best.uni-mainz.de/modules/Informationen/index. php?id=13.

[12] The establishment of the project 'Newspapers and Periodicals of the African Diaspora in Europe' which aims to collect, preserve and digitalise journals from the nineteenth century onwards is a welcome example. Several hundred titles in Italian, English, French, German, Portuguese and Spanish have already been collected. The project is directed by James P Danky at the University of Wisconsin-Madison.

References

Blakely, Allison. *Blacks in the Dutch World: The Evolution of Racial Imagery in a Modern Society*. Bloomington: Indiana University Press, 2001.

Blakely, Allison. *Russia and the Negro: Blacks in Russian History and Thought*. Washington, DC: Howard University Press, 1987.

Debrunner, Hans. *Presence and Prestige: A History of Africans in Europe Before 1918*. Basel: Basel Afrikan Bibliographien, 1979.

Evaristo, Bernardine. "CSI Europe: African Trace Elements. Fragments. Reconstruction. Case Histories. Motive. Personal." *Wasafiri* 23, no. 4 (2008): 2–7.

Frost, Diane, ed. *Ethnic Labour and British Imperial Trade: A History of Ethnic Seafarers in the UK*. London: Routledge, 1995.

Fryer, Peter. *Staying Power: The History of Black People in Britain*. London: Pluto, 1984.

Jenkinson, Jacqueline. *Black 1919: Riots, Racism and Resistance in Imperial Britain*. Liverpool: Liverpool University Press, 2009.

Linebaugh, Peter and Marcus Rediker. *The Many-Headed Hydra: Sailors, Slaves, Commoners, and the Hidden History of the Revolutionary Atlantic*. London and New York: Verso, 2000.

Khalfa, Jean. "'The Heart of the Black Race': Parisian Negritudes in the 1920s." *Wasafiri* 23, no. 4 (2008): 15–24.

Ndiaye, Pap. *La condition noire: Essai sur une minorité française*. Paris: Calmann-Lévy, 2008.

Oguntoye, Katharina. *Eine afro-deutsche Geschichte: Zur Lebenssituation von Afrikanern und Afro-Deutschen in Deutschland von 1884 bis 1950*. Berlin: Hoho Verlag Christine Hoffman, 1997.

Van Sertima, Ivan, ed. *The African Presence in Early Europe*. London: Transaction Books, 1986.

Job Mobility amongst Black People in England and Wales during the Long Eighteenth Century

Kathleen Chater

Independent Scholar

The first historians of the Black presence in Britain assumed that, like their colonial counterparts, Black people[1] were enslaved and tied to one master. This view is being modified but has by no means been generally abandoned. Drawing on a database of some 4500 entries, this paper looks at the occupations of first- and second-generation Black Britons. Initial findings suggest the first generation's mobility was comparable to that of the indigenous white population and that there were no differences in the second and subsequent generations.[2]

Introduction

What is called Black history first aroused interest in the 1960s in America, so the first historians of Black British history tended to use studies on slaves in America to explore the experiences of Black people in Britain. Folarin Shyllon called his first book *Black Slaves in Britain* (Oxford, 1974) and asserted that the experiences of Black people in eighteenth-century Britain were the same as those in the twentieth century in the United States of America. This assumption that the treatment in North America and Britain was identical has had an unfortunate effect on subsequent works in which Black people in England and Wales have been regarded through the prism of American slavery, rather than looking at what was normal for indigenous white people.[3] Norma Myers, for example, used studies of slave families in America as her starting point to examine the experiences of Black people in Britain.[4] Until recently, historians have concentrated on published and comparatively easily accessed examples, like advertisements for the sale of Black people and the handful of cases brought to the courts to determine the legality of slavery, which appear in all the general surveys of Black British history that deal with the eighteenth century. These, however, are a tiny proportion of the many thousands of Black people in England and Wales (the best estimate over the long eighteenth century, effectively the period of the British slave trade, is around 10,000) who did not attract this kind of attention. Although advertisements for runaways are usually adduced as evidence of the existence of enslaved Black people in Britain, every eighteenth-century newspaper carried numerous advertisements for runaway white people: apprentices, wives and husbands deserting their families, members of the armed forces, absconding criminals, etc.

In 1772 the Mansfield Judgement in the case of James Somerset finally clarified the law.[5] Lord Mansfield concluded that slavery had not existed in England since the establishment of Common Law in medieval times and that while in England and Wales people were free, though elsewhere they could be slaves, depending on the local laws overseas. James Somerset, like those at the centre of previous cases – Dinah Black, Katherine Auker, John and Mary Hylas, Thomas Lewis and Jonathan Strong – was the slave of a master from the colonies or, in the case of Thomas Lewis, a sea captain. Although the rulers in the colonies had passed legislation on slavery there, Black people had always been free in the mother country but this was not popularly understood. What their masters, and the Black people themselves, believed might have affected their behaviour, but it did not alter their legal status. Even Folarin Shyllon acknowledged that there was a difference between the behaviour of people in the households of those who had lived in the colonies and those who had not.[6] There is apparently no case in the English courts involving the Black servant of a master resident in England or Wales, which I would is suggest further evidence that they were not regarded as enslaved here. However, as Mary Prince's account shows, colonial masters continued to bring slaves to Britain into the nineteenth century.[7]

It is difficult to determine how Black servants were regarded before 1700. The assumption has been that they were seen as slaves, but to use present-day definitions of slavery is an example of temporal parochialism, judging the past by contemporary intellectual fashions. Some of the current definitions would have been regarded as normal in the seventeenth century, for example, being coerced into working under threat of punishment. In 1638, the Quarter Sessions in Blandford, Dorset ruled that a girl, undoubtedly white, who was 'living at home idle with her mother and doth not betake herself into service' should work or be imprisoned in the House of Correction until she did so.[8] Vagrants were whipped and put into workhouses. Even later in the eighteenth century, forced child labour was regarded as unexceptional. Orphans, as Ignatius Sancho was, became the parish's responsibility. They might go into the workhouse or be put out 'to nurse'; someone would effectively act as a foster-carer (although adoption and foster care were not legally formalised until 1926). At the age of seven, they would be 'apprenticed'. Because people were so reluctant to take on a parish child, in some parishes there was a ballot to force people to take them. Very few were taught a real skill – they were just used as cheap labour. They might be, as slaves were in the Americas, forced to work for other people and their wages appropriated.[9] Many were appallingly treated as inquest records and even cases at the Old Bailey attest.[10] Sancho, 'given' to two aristocratic ladies in the Greenwich area, was comparatively lucky. His colour gave him novelty value, so instead of winding up as something like a chimney sweep's boy (and they had notoriously short, miserable lives) he was relatively privileged.

The first sporadic appearances of Black people in English records comes in the late sixteenth century, mainly as servants in the households of the aristocracy and wealthy merchants, either based in Britain or connected in some way to the West Indies or to the parts of North America which later became the United States of America, a British colony until 1785. Later, from the beginning of the eighteenth century, they are increasingly found lower down the social scale. It is difficult to recover information about the lives of servants, partly because the records of a household are private, and therefore have not survived to the extent that official records have, and partly because so few servants left accounts of their lives. What follows is necessarily anecdotal but does seem to show that there was little difference in job mobility amongst Black and white servants during the long eighteenth century. It is, however, difficult to reconstruct the lives of many Black people, especially those who did not have a rare or distinctive name. The major problem is that colour and/or ethnic origin are not always given in official records. A majority of references in the database I assembled come from parish registers, primarily baptisms and, to a lesser extent, burials. The apparent absence of Black people from marriage registers is not because interracial marriage was illegal, as it was in the colonies. Their colour or ethnic origin is just rarely noted there. This is because clerks were recording the status of Black people under the Poor Laws, should this become important to establish who had the responsibility for their entitlement to poor relief later in their lives. Following an Act of 1662, parish authorities were obliged to support people who had what was called 'settlement' in their parish if they became unable to support themselves or their families. Settlement was gained in a number of ways, primarily by birth in a parish or by working for a year for a master who had settlement and in the latter case receiving wages. Later Acts added other conditions, such as serving as a parish official, completing a full apprenticeship and renting or owning property worth more than a particular amount. Under the settlement legislation (which was modified many times until World War One, when the last remnants of it effectively ended) marriage in a parish had no implications for settlement rights so the colour or origin of a Black person was not routinely recorded in marriage registers. It is clear from entries in parish registers and other documents, such as inquest papers, trial transcripts, bastardy examinations, etc. that colour and ethnic origin were usually mentioned only in cases where questions of settlement status might be raised or where a distinction between two people of the same name needed to be made. I have not yet found any wills of Black people in England, for example, which mentions their colour/ethnic origin. In parish registers where the occupations of Black people are given, they are overwhelmingly recorded as servants and the names of their masters entered. This is not because all Black people were servants, it is because of the implications of this job under the Poor Laws, as servants gained settlement through their masters. Other jobs, like shopkeeper, gardener, musician, had no such significance, although there were also settlement implications for mariners, the second most frequently mentioned occupation. The percentage of the total on the database who are recorded as servants is only 6%, although it may be presumed that the majority of Black people in England and Wales during the long eighteenth century at least started their working lives in service because, until World War One, that was how the majority of the indigenous population also spent at least some of their lives.

Domestic Servants

Lacking labour-saving devices, servants were needed at all levels of society above the very poorest to carry out the numerous tasks involved in running a household. Samuel Pepys was a clerk in the 1660s and employed a cook, a boy to do odd jobs, a housemaid and a personal maid for his wife. In 1669 he acquired a Black cook, Doll, 'who dresses our meat mighty well and we mightily pleased with her'.[11] An aristocratic family with an extensive estate, however, might employ up to one hundred people to run its various divisions both inside and outside the house or, since many owned more than one property, houses. As Black male servants were a status symbol, they would be employed in highly visible positions. The pageboy who accompanied the lady of the house wherever she went was one such. The footman, who carried messages for his employers and, when they were travelling, oversaw arrangements and went ahead to book accommodation, was another such post. These were probably the positions that the majority of Black male servants in large households initially occupied. When older, they might be promoted. The valet had the care of his master's clothes and personal accoutrements. The butler was in charge of the household's domestic property, like plate and chinaware, as well as the food both the family and servants ate. On a large estate, the most important person was the steward on whose work depended the family's property and lifestyle. Those who rose to the top of the servants' hierarchy, which was as carefully preserved below stairs as that of their masters above, may well have been more inclined to remain in their powerful and comparatively well-remunerated posts. Tobias Pleasant, servant (probably more specifically valet) to a Mr Lane of Hillingdon in Middlesex, remained with his master for some 35 years.[12] Further evidence comes from monumental inscriptions erected around the country by grateful masters, testifying to the virtues of a Black person who had given them faithful service.

Whether in a small or large household there was a hierarchy of jobs. There were a number of people doing the more menial tasks at the bottom, fewer in the middle ranks of management and one, overseeing the work of a particular domain, at the top. For those who were not promoted, the alternatives were to remain in their lowly position or to leave, either for promotion in another household or to set up in business on their own account. It is clear that many Black servants were not tied to one master but independent and free to arrange their own working lives. Some do seem to have been career servants, moving from master to master. The *Proceedings* of the Old Bailey contain a number of examples of servants whose testimonies give insight into their autonomy. Robert Wadeson, for example, said in 1770 that he had been in England about 26 years and was a gentleman's servant. As he did not give his master's name, as most servants did, he probably moved from employer to employer. Others testified in court that they were 'out of place', that is, between hirings, like John Vernon and William Henry. John Moreton came to London from High Wycombe in Buckinghamshire 'to see after a place'. Not all were career domestic servants. A mariner named Thomas Coffee, worked as a servant between voyages, suggesting that he could afford to be choosy about the ships he sailed with.[13] No one found this mobility odd: none of these men were questioned about it during the trials, suggesting it was a normal occurrence. Entries in parish registers also imply that Black servants were not tied to one master. In 1776 in Chelsea, for example, William 'a Negro a Servant at this time with Major Morrison' was baptised.[14] 'At this time' suggests either that he had not always worked for the Major or that his employment with him was not regarded as permanent.

In portraits of the aristocracy, the figure of a Black servant, usually a child, has often been remarked. Although Shyllon assumed that when these appealing children 'had outgrown their usefulness as chattels, and curios, they were fit only to be returned to the full rigours of West Indian slavery',[15] this is presumably because Black people for the reasons given above seem to disappear from the records but there is little evidence that this was routine practice. Samuel Pepys did arrange for a troublesome Black servant to be kidnapped and taken to the colonies – but he also arranged the same fate for a troublesome white boy.[16] Other servants, most notably Ignatius Sancho, were promoted. As noted above, Sancho began his life in England as a pageboy to two ladies, where he was unhappy. He left them to enter the household of the Duke of Montagu and became his son's valet.[17] This was an enviable position which those who attained it might be reluctant to give up for the uncertainties of outside employment. Sancho, however, left service and with financial help from his master, who had by then succeeded to the dukedom, became a shopkeeper in Westminster in 1773. His colour is not mentioned in the record of his marriage in 1758 to a Black woman, Anne Osbourn, nor in the record of the baptisms of his seven children, nor in the list of voters in the election of 1774.[18] His wife seems to have been from Whitechapel, the third generation of the family to live in that parish but there is no indication from the records there of her colour nor that of her forebears.[19] Had his letters not been published, revealing his origins, there would be no evidence that he was Black. How many other moderately prosperous Black people also appear in records without mention of their colour and/or origins cannot be known.

Peter Earle observed that service was 'predominantly an occupation for young men'. There were elderly retainers but he concludes most men had left service before they were 40.[20] Some Black people did stay with the same master for a long time or for life, presumably because they had developed strong bonds. John Scipio was purchased in Jacquin in Africa by the slave-trader William Snelgrave. When Snelgrave died in 1743, he gave Scipio his freedom and a small legacy. Nineteen years later, Scipio himself died – and his will reveals that he had remained as the family's servant.[21] It might be conjectured that Black people were more likely than white to remain in service – they lacked an extended family in this country to provide support and came from a background, either in the colonies or from parts of Africa where slavery was the norm. As far as I have been able to discover, there are no studies of white servants that reveal what percentage of them remained in lifelong service and what percentage left to do other work. It is difficult to recover this kind of information so as yet no comparisons between Black and white servants can be drawn.

Life after Service

Some servants remained in service after marriage, as Sancho did for some years. In Britain, as in most cultures, marriage is a rite of passage, marking the point at which a person establishes a new household. This is the point at which some Black people seem to have left service. In 1716 John Duck, for example, was the servant of Edward Green in Cheam, Surrey. He moved to London on marriage in 1717 and became a teacher of sword-fighting to gentlemen at the Inns of Court there.[22] He must have learned this skill in his master's service. Because of their experience in dealing with suppliers of food, it was not uncommon for indoor servants to sell food after leaving service. John Cranbrook was baptised in Rochester, Kent in 1764, married in London in 1772 and a few years later moved to Clapham, then in rural Surrey, where he ran a greengrocery until his death in 1797.[23] Another Black man, Affrick Hunsdon, a servant of Mathew Blucke in Hunsdon, Hertfordshire, became a victualler.[24] His occupation (but not his colour) is mentioned in the record of the baptism of his son, suggesting that he had left service on marriage. Others simply left to set up in business. About the time that Duck came to London, William Smith was in service there. By 1722 he was running a sutler's booth (a kind of fast-food stall) in Hyde Park.[25] In 1795 Connor, 'a Black man', was described as the householder of a property in Clerkenwell where an illegal, and apparently fraudulent, private lottery was held. He was not involved in the scam, nor called as a witness, but simply mentioned as the householder.[26] He was probably running some kind of business there but what was not revealed: the authorities had no interest in him, or his colour, which again suggests that he was not exceptional. So far, Cesar Picton seems to be the one who made the most of his opportunities, although he was greatly helped by the legacies left for him by members of the family he served, the Phillipses. He lived in Kingston-upon-Thames, where he had a licence as a coal merchant and, as his will attests, became immensely rich.[27] This might seem an odd occupation for a Black servant to choose, but the Phillips family's seat was at Picton Castle (from which Cesar took his surname) in Pembrokeshire, where there were extensive coal mines.

Apprenticeships

One of the other ways of gaining settlement under the Poor Laws, besides birth and being paid for a year in a parish, was by serving a full apprenticeship in a parish. Identifying Black apprentices is problematic because their colour is probably not always recorded in the records and after they had gained settlement, their colour and ethnic origin became irrelevant. In 1725 a Scipio Affricanus [sic], described simply as 'a poor orphan', was apprenticed to John Highfield, citizen and cordwainer of London.[28] There is no mention of his colour in the apprenticeship records, but given his name he must have been Black. How many other Black apprentices there were with less distinctive names cannot yet be known without considerably more research. Of the ones about whom there is information, George John Scipio Africanus, originally a servant of the Molyneux family near Wolverhampton, completed an apprenticeship as a brassfounder in Nottingham, but seems never to have done the job, or perhaps only for a short while. He ran various businesses in Nottingham, including an employment agency for servants. Bill Richmond, best known as a boxer, had been apprenticed to a cabinet maker in York and after his boxing career became the licensee of a pub in London and also ran a training gym. His later life is what made him famous – if he had remained quietly cabinet making in York it is unlikely any more would be known about him beyond his name and his job. It may never have been realised that he was Black.

There are a few references to those who did not complete apprenticeships. In 1723 John Robinson, the master of Anthony Emmannuell went to court to get rid of the boy (who was Black) because he said he had run away, embezzled money and was 'incorrigible', despite a spell in a House of Correction. Robert Johnson, another Black boy, petitioned to be released from his indentures, which he said he had entered into without understanding what he was doing.[29]

The Armed Forces

The second most frequently given occupation for Black people on the database is mariner (sailor is traditionally used in the Royal Navy and seaman in the merchant service but in the eighteenth-century men would work for both – merchant seamen were liable to be press-ganged). Because seafarers were itinerant and therefore had no claim on any parish, their occupation was particularly specified. A number of men worked their passage to Britain on ships, especially after the 1772 Mansfield Judgement, because they knew they would be freer here than in the colonies but they did not remain as mariners once they had arrived, so again this occupation might be over-represented in records.

Had Olaudah Equiano not written his autobiography, he would probably be simply another foreign-born sailor, a footnote in someone's thesis on the eighteenth-century navy.[30] There are some studies of Black people in the army and navy but again because place of birth rather than ethnic origin are entered in official records it is difficult to know how many were Black. John Ellis has found that Black soldiers in the nineteenth century were not promoted to the extent that their white counterparts were and this seems to be the same in the navy. It is, however, very difficult to recover information about the eighteenth century because colour is rarely mentioned in records, only birthplaces. It is also unknown what most servicemen did on leaving the armed forces. Those who had served in the Royal Navy were entitled to enter Greenwich Hospital as pensioners, or to receive their pension living outside.[31] There was nothing like this for merchant seamen. A few, like Joseph Johnson, turned to begging because they were unable to work. Soldiers might enter the Royal Hospital at Chelsea.

Other Kinds of Work

Today 'servant' means almost exclusively a domestic servant, someone doing household tasks, but in the eighteenth century it had a much wider meaning – employee is probably the closest equivalent. It cannot, therefore, be assumed that every Black person described as a 'servant' was involved in domestic work. Pepys's diary for April to July 1666 contains several references to 'Black Nan' who seems to have been a shop assistant working for the woman who drew lines on his music paper.[32] She may have simply been a dark-skinned woman of European ancestry (the word black was used to describe both complexion and ethnic origin) but he is so insistent on her colour that it seems likely she had at least a proportion of Black ancestry, either from Africa or the Indian subcontinent. The Proceedings of the Old Bailey published accounts of trials include references to people who were apparently employed in similar positions. In Limehouse Edward Thompson, 'a Black', was working in a warehouse. There is also Thomas Wheeler, 'a Black', who burgled the premises of Mr Norris, a druggist for whom he had once worked. Both Thompson and

Wheeler must have been shop assistants – their masters were not likely to be employing Black servants for status or purely domestic purposes.[33]

Quite a few black men worked as musicians and are noted both in written records and pictures. The army employed a number of black people in bands but others worked independently. Joseph Emidy, a Black composer and performer of music, worked in Cornwall where he became well known.[34] James Woodforde, mentions a Black man blowing a French horn, who, along with two other men and a female dwarf, called at his parsonage. The dwarf (in whom Woodforde was far more interested) sang two songs. The Black man said he had been employed by the Earl of Albemarle.[35] Other occupations that Black men are known to have followed are bricklayer, carter, chapman (an itinerant seller of goods), gardener and miner. Most of these references are mentioned in passing at the Old Bailey when another issue was under examination or come from non-parochial records.

A number became ministers of religion, like John Jea, John Marrant and Robert Wedderburn,[36] who all wrote accounts of their lives. Brian Mackey, the son of a slave woman and a white man in Jamaica, became the parish minister of Coates in Gloucestershire, and is the first known Black Anglican minister to work in England. None of the official records – Mackey studied at Oxford, married and had a number of children – nor his father's will mentions his colour. That comes from the private diary of the minister of the parish where his father retired after leaving the West Indies.[37] Other children of plantation owners by slave women came to Britain because of the prejudice, both social and legal, they faced in the Caribbean. Nathaniel Wells is the one who achieved the greatest social status. Around 1789 he came to London to live with his uncle and aunt and in 1800 came into a substantial inheritance. In 1802 Wells bought Piercefield House at Chepstow in Monmouthshire, where he would spend the rest of his life. Once established as a member of the landed gentry, he became involved in the affairs of the county, taking on the duties expected of a man of his wealth and position: churchwarden, Justice of the Peace and member of the committee of the local hunt. In 1818 he became county sheriff and later deputy lieutenant of Monmouthshire.[38]

Another person of mixed race origins from the Caribbean was Robert Laing, who was admitted to Lincoln's Inn and called to the Bar in 1793, although he was not very successful there. When he was discovered living in desperate penury, a public subscription was launched and his children were cared for. His son was sent to Christ's Hospital, a charity school in London, and was later called to the bar. He was no more successful there than his father had been and returned to his old school as a teacher.

His descendants have also heard that he edited a trade magazine, but have not yet been able to confirm this.[39] Again, nothing about the origins of either Nathaniel Wells or Robert Laing can be gained from official records – all mentions of these come from private letters and diaries.

Much lower down the social scale, Thomas Latham was a parish constable in Clerkenwell in the 1740s,[40] so he might be called the first known Black police officer. Working as a parish official was another of the ways of gaining settlement. Parish constables were not paid at this time: they were either volunteers or elected and generally appointed for a year. Although it is often said that they were elderly and incompetent, this was a claim made by the people who wanted to replace them with a paid police force so it was in their interests to represent them badly. Most that I have come across in parish records had respectable day jobs, gardeners and the like. Unfortunately, the parish's vestry minutes of Latham's time in office have not survived so his occupation is not known.

Women

The lives of Black women are harder to recover. Very occasionally the Black wife of a white man is mentioned but there must be many more than the few that have been found so far. Under the Poor Laws on marriage women took their husbands' settlement status so their colour and ethnic origin disappear from the records. Of course, women had to work to contribute to the family income but what they did very rarely appears in records, whether relating to Black or white women. We know about some – mainly the unfortunate. Sylvia Woodcock, for example, described as 'a mulatto' was the wife of a white servant and had been in service herself before marriage. Her husband worked in London while she grew vegetables at her home in Enfield. We know about her only because her husband killed her so he could marry another woman. The case was tried at the Old Bailey and reported in the newspapers, the only sources that give her colour, which was not mentioned in either marriage or burial registers.[41]

It is also from the Old Bailey trials that we learn more about some Black women's lives. A few of them were prostitutes and the temptation is to conclude that Black women were sexually exploited. Some undoubtedly were but it is wrong to assume that a majority were on the basis of a few headline cases. Again, the majority of Black women in this country lived ordinary, unremarkable lives. Others, it must be added, decided to exploit their gender. The woman known as Black Harriott was enslaved in Africa and shipped to Jamaica, where she became the property of William Lewis, a sea captain with an estate on the island. He made her his mistress, taught her to read and write and educated her in social accomplishments. They had two children. Around 1766 Lewis brought her to England and they set up home next to a brothel off Piccadilly in the parish of St James Westminster. Lewis died in 1772, leaving Harriott in such debt that she was put in the King's Bench prison. Sir James Lowther paid off her debts and presumably set her up in business as a madam, initially in her old home. She soon moved from there, taking over the premises of another brothel-keeper nearby. At first she was highly successful. Then, it is said, she made the mistake of falling for one of her clients and neglected her business. In 1776 she was back in the King's Bench prison. Released from there in 1777, she resumed business but the following year again suffered financial problems and returned to the King's Bench. On her release from the prison, she was forced to move to the slightly less prestigious area of Charlotte Street in St Marylebone. Around 1778 she died of tuberculosis.[42]

Ann Duck, the daughter of John Duck previously mentioned, started out her working life just as respectably as her father. She seems to have become a shop assistant – but then she went spectacularly off the rails. She worked as a servant in a brothel, became a prostitute herself and finally joined the Black Boy Alley Crew, a notorious and feared gang of criminals in Clerkenwell. Ann specialised in enticing men into a public house and then robbing them. She always worked with one or more women. She appeared in court a total of 19 times and there were many other incidents, one involving the death of a victim, for which she was not tried. Eventually, she was sentenced to death and hanged. She has the distinction of being the Black person who made most appearances (five in all) at the Old Bailey during the long eighteenth century. One of her sisters was later tried for theft, but acquitted and disappears from the records.[43]

At the more respectable end, appearing at the Old Bailey as a plaintiff, is the Black wife of a soldier from the West Indies who was also Black. Hannah Bowling's occupation is not mentioned but she probably, like most army wives, did laundry or nursed the sick and wounded. How she came to marry him and what she did before marriage were not revealed. Joanna Vassa, the daughter of Olaudah Equiano, married a non-conformist minister and probably did the charitable work of all ministers' wives, as well as running the household. Lord Mansfield's great-niece, Dido Elizabeth Belle, married an estate steward in London. She too had domestic tasks but may also have done odd jobs for her husband's employers as the wives of stewards were expected to do.[44]

Children

So far it appears that most Black people in England and Wales started their working lives as servants. The second generation of migrants generally move into a wider range of occupations that their parents[45] and this appears to be true of Black people in the long eighteenth century. Reconstructing the families of a large number of Black people should produce some interesting results on the social and geographical mobility of their children but this has not yet been possible. It is important to notice that, although in the colonies children inherited their parents' slave status, there are no court cases about the status of any Black servant's child nor has any reference to this possibility yet been found in English records. What proportion followed their parents into service and what proportion when into other occupations is not yet known. A few of the children of Black servants, especially in rural areas where the options were limited, do seem to have followed their parents into service. The few families that have been reconstructed show that the descendants of Black people, like those of the white population, followed a range of occupations, some ascending the social scale and some descending.

It is not yet known what all the children of John Cranbrook, mentioned above, did. His eldest son became a hairdresser, and died a wealthy man, although whether his prosperity came solely from hairdressing remains to be discovered. A daughter married an official in the Bank of England and their son married a doctor's daughter. The descendants of Cranbrook's other children include ministers of religion and cab drivers. James Cranbrook, John's grandsons, became a non-conformist minister in a number of places, ending up in Scotland where his controversial beliefs caused him to be expelled from his position there.[46] His eldest son followed his father into the church but became an Anglican minister. What happened to James's younger children must await further research. Samuel Barber, the son of Francis Barber, Samuel Johnson's Black servant and heir, also chose a religious occupation, becoming a Primitive Methodist preacher.

A similar social spread occurs amongst the descendants of Peter George Florida, a Black man, who was a servant in Buckinghamshire. A witness at his wedding was the wife of James Patterson, an army captain who presumably helped his eldest son George when Peter Florida died young in 1793. In Monmouth (Patterson was in the Welsh Regiment), George married and had a family. References to Floridas in Welsh records are found until the twentieth century. It is not clear whether George Florida actually served in the Army but by 1851 he was a market gardener. One of Peter George's daughters was a lace-maker: women in Buckinghamshire had a long lace-making tradition. Before marriage to a farm labourer she had an illegitimate son, who became a cabinet maker, which required apprenticeship. One branch seems to have had a mechanical aptitude, becoming engine fitters and later working on railway engines for the Great Western Railway, which operated between 1835 and 1947. There is also a blacksmith. Another descendant became a sea captain. Some did not have such skilled jobs: there are general labourers and factory workers. The women mainly went into domestic servants in middle-class households before marrying but one became a milliner and others, the daughters of a factory operative making boots, worked as boot fitters.[47]

Edward Juba was a Black servant of a family in Earl Shilton, Leicestershire, baptized in 1757. He was later apprenticed as a needlemaker in Leicester and became a freeman on the successful completion of his term. Leicester is one of the boroughs where the freedom can be passed to the eldest son – in fact there is a Juba today who has the freedom though descent from Edward.[48]

The names of Black people whose lives I have been able to reconstruct have either the stereotypical names sometimes given to Black people or rare names. This is not because all Black people were given such names – the most common name for a Black person in the long eighteenth century was John Williams – it is just that this kind of name is easier to find in records. Trying to track the movements of an eighteenth-century John Williams and his descendants, whether Black or white, is a virtually impossible genealogical task, unless the person owned land or was extremely rich. Most Black people, of course, were neither – and neither were most white people.

Conclusions

From these examples, it can be seen that the question of social mobility, and occupations are a good indicator of this, in Black people and their families is a complex one, which is only beginning to be explored. This has been necessarily cursory account of job mobility amongst Black people during the long eighteenth century, mainly because there is still a huge amount of research to be done. What has, I hope, been demonstrated is that the old stereotype of the Black servant, enslaved and trapped as a domestic menial, is wide of the mark. Many moved freely from job to job and had a considerable degree of autonomy. This of course raises many questions about the treatment of Black people in Britain, the mother country of colonies where Black people were legally oppressed because of their colour or race, not least why it was so markedly different from the fate of Black people in the colonies.

Notes

[1] There is still no agreement on a definition of a 'Black' person. In the eighteenth century, the word was applied to people of African origin, from the Indian sub-continent, occasionally from the Middle East, and also to dark-skinned Europeans. In general, the word was capitalised when referring to a person from a non-European ethnic minority and with a lower-case initial letter when describing skin colour. I have chosen to follow this practice, not least because it is not possible in many cases to determine from where an eighteenth-century Black ultimately came.

[2] This paper is drawn from a Ph.D. thesis, completed in 2007, since published as Untold Histories: Black People in England and Wales during the period of the British Slave Trade, c. 1660–807 (Manchester, 2009).

[3] The situation in Scotland, which had and still has a separate legal system, was different. There, following an Act of 1597, poor white people could be enslaved and their children inherit this status. This continued until 1799, despite the celebrated case of Knight v. Wedderburn (1778), which ruled that Knight, who was Black, was free. Millar 2002.

[4] Myers, *Reconstructing the Black Past*, 118–35.

[5] Wise, *Though the Heavens May Fall* is the most recent account.

[6] Shyllon, *Black People*, 78. He does, however, call these 'plantation' and 'non-plantation' households thus reinforcing the parallels with America. In England there were no plantations and a large enough indigenous agricultural workforce to make enslaved field hands unnecessary.

[7] Prince, 1831.

[8] Hearing and Bridges, *Dorset Quarter Sessions*, 426.

[9] For example, see Burrows, *Decisions of the Court of Kings Bench*, 330. This work includes other similar examples. The court was the highest in the land. As it was expensive to take a case to this level, it may be presumed there were considerably more cases of this kind resolved in lower courts.

[10] The most notorious cases were those of two inhumanly treated parish 'apprentices' who died at the hands of their masters, a mother and daughter both called Sarah Metyard and another named Elizabeth Brownrigg. Ordinary's *Account*, 19 July 1762 and 14 September 1767.

[11] Pepys, *Diary* V, 510.

[12] *Proceedings* I, no. 3: 1780–1. He died four years later. London Metropolitan Archives (LMA) *Registers of Hillingdon*, burial 6 May 1784.

[13] *Proceedings* 1769–70, nos. 180–83; 1773–4, nos. 146, 640, 609; 1785–6, no. 139.

[14] LMA, *Registers of St Luke Chelsea* 31 January 1776.

[15] Shyllon, *Black People*, 78.

[16] Bryant, 1938; Pepys, *Diary* IV, 382. This might be considered further evidence of the difference between present-day definitions of a slave and how servants, especially minors, were treated in the past. At this period, the treatment of Black slaves, white indentured servants and transported criminals in the Americas was not as stratified as it later became. See Jordan and Walsh.

[17] Sancho, *Letters*.

[18] City of Westminster Archives (CWA), Registers of St Margaret Westminster, 17 December 1758; the same registers record the baptisms of Frances Joanna on

25 January 1761; Anne Alice on 18 September 1763; Elizabeth Bruce on 9 March 1766; Jonathan William on 10 April 1768; Lydia on 29 April 1766; Catherine on 7 November 1733 and William Leach Osborne on 5 November 1810; *Correct Copy of the Poll*, 15. As a householder with property worth more than a certain amount, Sancho qualified for the franchise.

[19] Sancho, *Letters*, 250, no. 14.

[20] Earle, *A City Full of People*, 85.

[21] Chater, 'Where There's a Will', 26. Technically Snelgrave could not manumit Scipio. As the Mansfield Judgement clarified in 1772, slavery had never existed in England and Wales since the establishment of common law in medieval times but this was not generally understood.

[22] CWA, E2574, 242; CWA, *Registers of St Clement Danes*, 12 August 1717; Ordinary's *Account*, 7 November 1744, 6ff.

[23] Society of Genealogists (SoG), unpub. transcript KR/E 159–60, Registers of St Margaret Rochester, 20 November 1764 (when he was noted to be 13 years of age); Guildhall Library (GL) Register of All Hallows Staining 3 March 1772; LMA Registers of Clapham, Surrey, 13 July 1797.

[24] His baptism took place in Hunsdon on 1 April 1711, he was married on 1 December 1724 and their son was baptised on 8 September 1727. Only Affrick senior's baptism records his colour. I am grateful to Dr Jill Barber of Hertfordshire Record Office (RO) for this information.

[25] *Proceedings*, 7–12 September 1722, 5.

[26] LMA, MJ/SP/1795/10/032. I am grateful to Dr Caroline Bressey for drawing my attention to this case.

[27] The National Archives (TNA), PROB 11/1863. A leaflet giving his life history was produced by Kingston Record Office and sent to me by Marion Bone.

[28] SoG, unpublished typescript, APP, *The Apprentices of Great Britain 1710-1762*, I. This index to both apprentices and masters covers records in TNA, IR 10/159.

[29] Hanway *The State of Young Chimney Sweepers' Apprentices* quoted in George *Life in Eighteenth Century London*, 137; LMA, W.SP 1727 Jan/2. Unfortunately, there are no surviving documents that record the outcome of this case.

[30] Equiano, *Narrative*. In all official records and in the letters he wrote to the press his baptismal name, Gustavus Vassa, was used. Olaudah Equiano only appears in his autobiography.

[31] Ellis, 'Black Soldiers in British Army Regiments', 12–5; John Deman, who served under Nelson, for example, is depicted in a picture in Greenwich Hospital's Painted Hall. After the abolition of slavery in the colonies, there are separate lists for 'Negro Pensioners' covering the years 1839–53, TNA W23/153 and WO23/156–7.

[32] Pepys, *Diary*, VII, 101, 104, 110, 115.

[33] *Proceedings* IV, no. 325: 1785–6; *Proceedings* 1 (February 1727/8): 22–5. Wheeler, 'a loose Liver' according to Norris, seems not to have run away from his master's service but how they parted is not explained. Norris seems to have made no attempts to get him back.

[34] McGrady, *Music and Musicians in Early Nineteenth Century Cornwall*.

[35] Woodforde, *Diary*, 306.

[36] Jea, *Life, History and Unparalleled Sufferings of John Jea*; Marrant, *Narrative of the Lord's Wonderful Dealings with John Marrant*; Wedderburn, *The Horrors of Slavery*.

[37] *Alumni Oxonieses 1715—1886* 3 (Oxford 1891) 895; TNA PROB 11/1422; Ayres, *Paupers and Pig Killers*, 106. Although Philip Quaque was ordained before him, he went to Africa as a missionary.

[38] Evans, 'Nathaniel Wells', 91–106.

[39] Information from Lucy Richards, a descendant.

[40] He appears in the *Proceedings* II, no. 100: 1745–6, where his name is not given. This can be discovered from the Middlesex Sessions Papers where a preliminary hearing to commit Catherine Burk to the Old Bailey was held. LMA, MJ/SP/2855 f. 21.

[41] *Proceedings* II, no. 98: 1788–9.

[42] Burford, *Royal St James*, 201–4.

[43] Ordinary's *Account*, 7 November 1744, 6ff; *Proceedings* VII, no. 362: 1744–5.

[44] *Proceedings* VI, no. 362: 1794–5; Osborne, *Equiano's Daughter*; booklet produced by English Heritage in 2007 incorporating the genealogical research of Sarah Minney.

[45] Mascarenhas-Keyes, *British Indian and Chinese Students* is one of a number of studies looking at the experiences of first- and second-generation Asians.

[46] TNA PROB 11/1647; Chater, 'Settling in England'; the *Scotsman*, 2 March 1868.

[47] Buckinghamshire RO, Registers of Radnage 22 October 1769 and 1781; TNA, RG11/5239, f. 20, 34 and RG12/4369, f. 34, 2; RG10/5340, f. 19, 32; RG11/5261, f. 77, 26; RG12/4375, f. 43, 28; RG12/1980, f. 156, 30 and RG13/2375, f. 134, 23.

[48] See <www.leics.gov.uk/the_juba_family_from_servant_to_freeman.pdf> and <www.leicester.gov.uk/about-leicester/lordmayorcivic/freemen/ceremonies/800th-anniversary-1996/>

References

A Correct Copy of the Poll for Electing Two Representatives in Parliament for the City and Liberty of Westminster. London: 1774.

Ayres, John, ed. *Paupers and Pig Killers: The Diary of William Holland, a Somerset Parson 1799–1818*. Stroud: Sutton Publishing, 1984.

Bryant, Arthur. *Samuel Pepys: The Saviour of the Navy*. Cambridge: Cambridge University Press, 1938.

Burford, E. J. *Royal St James*. London: Robert Hale, 1988.

Burrows, James. *A Series of Decisions of the Court of Kings Bench, Vol. I*. London: 1768.

Chater, Kathy. "Where There's a Will." *History Today* 50 (2000): 26–7.

Chater, Kathy. "Settling in England." *Ancestors* 87 (2009): 35–6.

Earle, Peter. *A City Full of People: Men and Women of London 1650–1750*. London: Methuen, 1994.

George, M. Dorothy. *Life in Eighteenth Century London*. 2nd ed. London: Kegan Paul, 1930.

Ellis, John. "Black Soldiers in British Army Regiments during the Early Nineteenth Century." *AAHGS News* (March/April 2001): 12–5.

Equiano, Olaudah. *The Interesting Narrative of the Life of Olaudah Equiano, or Gustavus Vassa, the African, Written by Himself* (1789), edited by Carretta, Vincent. London: Penguin 1995, second edition 2003.

Evans, J. A. H. "Nathaniel Wells of Piercefield and St Kitts: From Slave to Sheriff." *Monmouthshire Antiquary* 17 (2001): 91–106.

Hanway, Jonas. *The State of Young Chimney Sweepers' Apprentices*. London: 1773.

Jea, John. *The Life, History and Unparalleled Sufferings of John Jea the African Preacher Compiled and Written by Himself*. Portsea: c. 1815.

Hearing, Terry and Sarah Bridges, eds. *Dorset Quarter Sessions 1625–1638: A Calendar*. Dorchester: Dorset Record Society, 2006.

McGrady, Richard. *Music and Musicians in Early Nineteenth Century Cornwall – The World of Joseph Emidy, - Slave, Violinist and Composer*. Exeter: University of Exeter Press, 1991.

Jordan, Don and Michael Walsh. *White Cargo: The Forgotten History of Britain's White Slaves in America*. New York: New York University Press, 2007.

Marrant, John. *A Narrative of the Lord's Wonderful Dealings with John Marrant a Black (Now going to preach the Gospel in Nova Scotia)*. 4th ed. London, 1781.

Mascarenhas-Keyes, Stella. *British Indian and Chinese Students, Graduate and Academic International Entrepreneurship*. London: Department for Innovation, Universities and Skills, 2008.

Millar, John. "White Slaves with Black Faces: Scottish Coalminers in the 17th and 18th Centuries." *Family Tree Magazine* 18 (April 2002): 66–7.

Myers, Norma. "In Search of the Invisible: Black Family and Community." In *Reconstructing the Black Past: Blacks in Britain 1780–1830*, 118–37. London: Frank Cass, 1996.

Osborne, Angelina. *Equiano's Daughter: The Life and Times of Joanna Vassa*. Cambridge: Momentum Arts, 2007.

Pepys, Samuel. *The Diary of Samuel Pepys* Vols. I—X, edited by Latham Robert and Matthews, William. London: Bell & Hyman, 1970–83.

Prince, Mary. *The History of Mary Prince a West Indian Slave*, London: 1831, edited by Moira Ferguson. Oxford: Oxford University Press, 1988.

Sancho, Ignatius. *The Letters of the Late Ignatius Sancho, an African* (1782), edited by Vincent Carretta. London: Penguin, 1998.

Shyllon, Folarin. *Black People in Britain 1555–1833*. Oxford: Oxford University Press, 1977.

The Ordinary of Newgate's Account of the Behaviour, Confession and Dying Words of the Condemned Criminals... Executed at Tyburn (titles varied slightly) (1676–1722), http://www.oldbaileyonline.org.

The Proceedings of the King's Commission of the Peace and Oyer and Terminer, and Gaol-Delivery of Newgate, held for the City of London and the County of Middlesex, at Justice-Hall, in the Old Bailey (1674–1834), http://www.oldbaileyonline.org.

Wedderburn, Robert. *The Horrors of Slavery and Other Writings*, edited by McCalman, Iain. Edinburgh: Edinburgh University Press, 1991.

Wise, Steven M. *Though the Heavens May Fall: The Landmark Trial that Led to the End of Human Slavery*. New York: Da Capo, 2005.

Woodforde, James. *The Diary of a Country Parson 1758–1802*, edited by Beresford, John. Oxford: Oxford University Press, abridged ed. 1978.

'No Longer Strangers and Foreigners, but Fellow Citizens': The Voice and Dream of Jacobus Eliza Capitein, African Theologist in the Netherlands (1717–47)

Dienke Hondius

Department of History, VU University Amsterdam, Amsterdam, The Netherlands

In the early modern period, black European lives were and remained highly visible and exceptional. This article focuses on the experiences and reception of Jacobus Capitein and two other African men who came to Europe as children in the eighteenth century. Jacobus Capitein was enslaved when he entered the Netherlands. He came from the Gold Coast, now part of Ghana, entered higher circles and received a privileged education. Capitein wrote a thesis in theology at Leiden University. As an immigrant amongst the Dutch, his texts were attempts to translate his experiences and memories for a Dutch audience. As a theologist, he addressed the international community of scholars, writing in Latin. Capitein's eighteenth-century study in theology can be seen as a consequence of his conversion to Christianity and acceptance in Christian circles. Gratitude and apology are important elements in his personal narratives but a contrast between his positive individual African–European friendships on the one hand, and the harsh limitations he met in his working life are evident. These simultaneous and contrasting experiences marked the ambivalent reception he received, and help explain why his stay in Europe, and that of many other Africans, remained temporary.

Johannes Capitein became a theologist at Leiden University.[1] In portraits made of him in the Netherlands, Capitein is, as art historian Elmer Kolfin writes, 'a somewhat chubby young man, his hair concealed by a wig, wearing the clothes of a clergyman'; in other portraits, he is seated before a bookcase, or pointing at the bible, thus presented in the same fashion as other, white, clergymen'.[2]

Capitein's theology and biography has been studied by church historians and journalists.[3] The full text of Capitein's thesis was translated into English by Grant Parker, whose inspiring volume also provides extensive contextual information.[4] My focus here is on how the autobiographical texts by Capitein give us an insight into the process of entrance and acceptance of Africans into the higher strata of Dutch and European society during the eighteenth century.[5] In many ways Capitein was a pioneer in what would later be called 'race relations', a concept that, significantly, does not have an adequate Dutch translation. Jacobus Capitein has inspired a variety of scientists, journalists and writers. The resulting historiography is dominated by a tendency to interpret his life as surprising and tragic. He is generally regarded as little more than a victim of history, submissive to Dutch 'white', 'protestant' standards.[6] This is in line with the negative, often hateful images of blacks in the Dutch colonial world which have been noted by Allison Blakely and Ernst van den Boogaart in their pioneering studies.[7]

Grant Parker reminds us of Orlando Patterson's sharp characterisation of slavery as 'social death – a deracination of social context' and 'a radical non-belonging and marginality, typically originating in and even sustained by violence'. Parker asks: 'To put it bluntly: to what extent was Capitein's life in the Netherlands a time of "social death"'? The question is justified and the interpretations of victimhood are plausible, but they are also limited, overlooking the voice and agency of the actors concerned. As the Ghanaian theologian Kpobi notices, Capitein was 'the first sub-Saharan African ever to study protestant theology in a European University, and to receive ordination in Europe'.[8] As such, he became quite famous in circles of church historians. The rare and exceptional texts of Capitein, whose own West-African name he could never remember once he started writing and speaking Latin and Dutch in the Netherlands, can be studied and valued as a collection of unique African narratives situated in the Netherlands. As such, Capitein's thesis can be read as an inquiry into the possibilities of a religious life in exile.

Jacobus Capitein and his contemporaries were of course not the first Africans to meet Europeans. Centuries earlier, the first encounters between Europeans and African 'others' were recorded in travel and exploration reports.[9] In these meetings, a border is found, crossed, recognised. Invariably, this leads those involved to wonder about difference as well as similarity and connection. It is an intriguing phenomenon that individual experience is able to somehow exist separated from historical awareness. However repetitive and predictable historically or sociologically various human experiences may be, this does not appear to change the individual perception of the experience. The fact, and even the conscious knowledge that something has happened before, ages ago, appears not to be very relevant in the light of the actual experience. The power of experience is more immediate. The perception of being the first person to experience, for example, the crossing of a border, remains significant and 'new' for every generation. This is particularly true for emotional and unexpected experiences, such as falling in love, loss and mourning, or childbirth, but also for first encounters with 'others'. The reactions to these individual experiences retain a certain freshness, oblivious to time or the experiences of previous generations.

The awareness of asymmetric historiography has increased. History writing is an unequal process, because African, Asian, or slave narratives are far rarer than Dutch, English, or French narratives. However, a second form of historiographical asymmetry is not often recognised within this process: the extent of reciprocity and mutuality of human relations. 'On the imperial frontier Europeans confront not only unfamiliar Others but unfamiliar selves', writes Mary Louise Pratt.[10] Dutch historian Angelie Sens remarks that several modern researchers of race relations are critical about imperialism and inequality, but that is where their criticism ends: they do not recognise the reciprocity in the relationships between 'us' and 'them'. Sens:

> Contacts between "we" and "the other" coincide with mutual images, representations, prejudice, fascinations and fears, with confrontations and adaptations. The characteristic way for an eighteenth-century person to make sense of new impressions, to fit the "other" into his or her own world view and view of humanity, was a process of comparison, with all the in- and exclusion mechanisms that go with that.[11]

This reciprocity may be hidden in existing sources such as correspondence and personal documents that therefore deserve new reading and analysis, as the sources by and about Capitein show.

Several former slaves who came to Europe wrote about their experiences. The German equivalent of Capitein is the former slave Anton Wilhelm Amo, who also came from the Gold Coast, spent some time in Amsterdam, and then lived in Germany where he studied and later taught philosophy at

Halle University. The topic of Amo's 1729 dissertation was 'The rights of an African in eighteenth century Europe'. He became the first African lecturer in the philosophy of law at Jena University in 1739. He returned to the Gold Coast around 1745 and died in or around 1756.[12] A third comparable history is the life of Philip Quaque or Kwaku, also a slave born on the Coast of Guinea in 1741. He was sent to England by the missionary Rev. Thomas Thompson, was christened in Islington, London in 1759, and ordained as an Anglican priest in 1765. That year he also returned to the Gold Coast and he died there in 1816.[13] Graham Parker has compared Capitein's narrative with that of the better known Olaudah Equiano.[14] While his contemporary Amo became an early Enlightenment philosopher in Halle and Jena, the context of Capitein's texts remains firmly Christian, fitting Dutch eighteenth-century Protestantism. It is significant that his 'Politico-theological dissertation concerning slavery, as not contrary to Christian freedom' in 1742 was defended and published under the authority of the most powerful Dutch Calvinist, Joan van den Honert, Professor of Theology at Utrecht and Leiden.[15]

During the eighteenth century it remained highly exceptional for Africans to enter the higher echelons of Northern European societies. Dutch colonialism was first and foremost about trade and commercial traffic. Settlement of Dutch colonials was limited to coastal areas and port towns, and cultural domination was limited as well. Dutch colonisers installed their own Calvinist preachers (*predikanten*), and some school-teachers, only in those places where a substantial Dutch community was formed. Religious services were for the Dutch exclusively and there were no substantial programmes of conversion.[16] The same was true for education; schools were rare, and intended for children of Dutch colonials. As a result, very few Dutch language slave narratives or other forms of indigenous ethnography, either recorded in Europe or in Africa, have so far been discovered.

The most important autobiographical text written by Capitein is the introduction to his treatise, the thesis he wrote to complete his studies in theology at Leiden University in 1742. In this beautifully written text Capitein explains who he is and how he came to the Netherlands. The impression one gains from this text can be characterised in one word: gratitude. Capitein expresses how grateful he is to the various Dutch who took him away from Africa to the Netherlands, liberated him from slavery and helped him to build a life and to study in this country.

> As a boy of seven or eight, orphaned by war or some other cause, I was sold to admiral Arnold Steenhart, who had landed at a certain place in

Africa called St Andrew's River in order to buy slaves. This is what this eminent man has told me himself, when I recently was in Middelburg.... He gave me to his friend, Jacob van Goch, now my greatly revered patron and Maecenas, someone who will have my filial affection right up to the grave. At that time he was a very successful and skillful merchant on behalf of the noble directors of the African Society. He wanted me to be known as Capitein and he doted on me with paternal love thanks to his good character which caused his fame to spread virtually throughout all Guinea. Eventually, when he was about to return to his native land, he promised that he would take me with him and would see to it that after being duly instructed in Christianity, I might practice some trade which was not demeaning and thereby earn a living.[17]

The name he was born with, in 1717 in the immediate hinterland of the Guinea coast, part of modern Ghana, is no longer known. When Van Goch returned to the Netherlands from Elmina on 14 April 1728, he took Jacob – who he named after himself – with him. They arrived in Middelburg and went to Den Haag, 'the birthplace of my most honoured benefactor'. What sort of a relationship there was between Jacob and his master Jacob we do not know. His naming gives us a clearer idea about this, in particular the names he was given when he was baptised at the Kloosterkerk in The Hague by the Reformed minister Johann Philipp Manger on 8 July 1735. His names were now Jacobus, after his patron Jacobus van Goch; Elisa, after Van Goch's sister Elizabeth; and Johannes, after Van Goch's niece Anna (Johanna) Mulder. These three were also witnesses of the baptism. This suggests that Capitein was not merely their protégé, but may have been regarded as part of their (extended) family. The circle Capitein enters is one of the Dutch-reformed protestants, active in church work and theology. In The Hague Jacob learnt Dutch, 'the art of painting, to which I was strongly inclined', and attended classes of theologian Joan Philip Manger. Manger's death was a sad moment for Capitein, and he wrote a long farewell poem for his teacher. The poem reflects his great admiration for Manger, in which he compares him to a god and a saint: 'How I listened to him, seeming like Apollo ... And was heard in the measure of his compassion', and he adds: 'The greater part, if not the whole of the progress I made in my studies can be attributed, by God's providence, to the catechism classes of this great and now sainted theologian'.

Capitein shared his classes with two sons of Mr Willem Henrik van Schuylenburch. He spoke about Capitein to one of the sons of theologian Henrik Velse, suggesting that Jacob might be a theology student as well. The study of theology was an opportunity, but it had not been his own idea, writes Capitein:

> I sincerely admit that I do not know whether I did reveal this intention of mine to anybody. What is certain is that this theologian, following the desire which always drove him to advance the truth of the Gospel, called me to come to him, and asked me if this report was true? To which I answered that I had no objection whatever to that proposal.

Velse contacted Van Goch to suggest sending the teenager to the best Latin school in The Hague. Van Goch agreed and, reflected Capitein, 'from this time one, at his own cost, my benefactor not only committed me to study, but also abundantly provided all that was necessary for me to study successfully. A lady in The Hague, Miss F.C. Roscam, opened her house to him and helped him in particular with Greek, Hebrew and "Chaldean tongues"'. Moreover, she introduced him to Pieter Cunaeus of Leiden University. The Hague school rector Rutger Ouwens accepted him as a student at his Dutch Academy, and he was then able to go to university: 'The honourable administrators of the Hague's schools and the noble and able counsellors of the Dutch Court, kindly honoured me with their beneficent patronage. This enabled me, after finishing my study of the languages, to devote myself completely to Theology'.[18]

The main goal of Capitein's treatise (a thesis, which is not the same as a doctoral thesis, but is more a general text written at the end of a period of study to prove the student's abilities) was to remove the obstacles to Christian missionary work in Africa. His dissertation was written from his urgent belief that Africans had a duty to Christianity, and were entitled to conversion, in spite of what Dutch church officials feared and thought about this in the Netherlands at the time.

> Some Christians fear that through evangelic freedom slavery will disappear entirely from those colonies which Christians own, to the great detriment of the overseers of those colonies. Indeed there were once, and still are, people in the Christian world, and especially in the Netherlands, who, led astray by some unknown spirit, have determined that evangelic freedom cannot coexist with servitude of the body. As I shall demonstrate, my own present situation demands that I prove that such an opinion stems either from ignorance about the nature of evangelic doctrine, or from superstitious anxiety stemming from the customs of the early Christians, or finally from the institutions and morals of these regions.[19]

Capitein was convinced that 'the proclamation of the Gospel must be carried on in our time in all those places to which Christian dominion and power extends'. The main obstacle was the hesitation and refusal to undertake this missionary work by the West India Company (WIC) authorities. Capitein sought to convince his readers that it would not change the powerful positions of slave owners if they allowed their slaves to be converted to Christianity. His style is that of an attack on unnamed readers who are convinced 'that the liberty of the Gospel cannot coexist with what is properly called slavery'. He regards these thoughts as 'the feelings and fantasies of the fanatics'; the 'wrong and absurd fancy' of 'our opponents'.[20] This can be seen as an indication that the slave trade – which was going through a second booming phase – and slavery were becoming less acceptable and required greater justification at the time. As Grant Parker argues:

> Capitein focuses on the institution of *manumissio in ecclesia*, the practice of freeing converted slaves, begun by the Christian emperor Constantine.... Capitein's argument is that this manumissio was inspired not by divine law but rather by specific circumstances, and that hence it carries no implications for the present time. In short, slave-owners have nothing to fear from the conversion of their slaves.[21]

Capitein describes how slavery vanished from the Netherlands during the middle ages. This was a political development, and had nothing to do with the Gospel, he says. Implicitly he assumes that Christian slave owners will treat their slaves better than others; not because they are told so, but spontaneously, out of Christian love.

> Christian love not only inhibited Christians from treating their slaves badly, but it also, with the passage of time, was able to give occasion for the complete abolition of slavery.... Further, it is clear that each Christian is always permitted, should he so wish, to set his slave free. However, we deny absolutely that these conclusions proceed from any explicit command of the Gospel.[22]

It is possible to read this last line as a call for emancipation. Liberation is thinkable, possible, but not compulsory. Capitein is careful to sail between Dutch protestant doctrine on the one hand, and the West India Company slave traders on the other. This results in a discourse that leaves some room, it is not totally hermetic. Remarkably, he then stretches his argument to the Netherlands, arguing that he would have no objection against the reintroducing of slavery there either, provided it would be 'mild': 'in such a way, however, that masters would practice Christian kindness, and use no unreasonable severity'.[23] To underline this point, he explains:

> Not all are born knowing how to control themselves. They need the leadership and direction of another, who is better than they are, to help them, because they are otherwise unable to stop committing evil deeds, just like some animals whose ferocity is always to be feared if they are not brought under control with bonds. In this case, a weaker

personality is led by the power of the masters: the master, on the other hand, lives by the work of his slaves.

Slavery could be a good idea for Dutch society, with regard to the growing influx of empty-handed beggars, who eat the food of their fellow citizens or of other people while wandering to and fro and weaken their powers, which evil would have been countered if to this day slavery proper had kept its hold amongst Christians.[24] All that is required is a certain kindness, 'a very friendly dominion' between masters and slaves. As long as slavery is kind and mild, Capitein thinks it is worthy of pursuing in every society.

Parker characterises Capitein's writings as 'at best, a product of its times, and particularly of the eighteenth-century tradition with which he effectively identifies himself. At worst, it appears conservative at a period of broader change, notably the loss of status by the Dutch trading empire, and the growing impact of Enlightenment thinkers. Certainly, much of the work reaffirms an older, pre-abolitionist tendency to interpret slavery in a non-physical way'.[25] I disagree with Parker's characterisation of the autobiographical text by Capitein as 'merely an apologia'.[26] There is ambivalence in Capitein's writing, and agency, although mostly subdued. In my view, Capitein is driven and motivated by gratitude and a feeling of obligation towards the white Dutch who liberated him, and sponsored his studies. His words about kindness and Christian love of slave owners beg the question to what extent he was aware of what was going on at that moment, on the coast of his birthplace Guinea, in the eighteenth-century transatlantic slave ships made in the Netherlands, and on the plantations.

To Be a Citizen

Capitein's text may be seen as reflection of his isolated and indeed lonely, exceptional position within the Netherlands. The text enabled his employment and subsequent return to Elmina. His conclusions were, unsurprisingly, quite welcome amongst the West India Company's officials. In the year of his dissertation he was invited to give lectures in churches in Muiderberg, The Hague, as well as in Ouderkerk aan de Amstel, near Amsterdam, where he stayed at the mansion 'Nooyt Dor' of Willem Backer, one of the Directors of the Amsterdam Chamber of the WIC. On these occasions, he chose as the basis for his preaching the bible text Ephesians 2:19, which can be read as a vision and a plea to accept strangers as citizens: 'Now therefore ye are no more strangers and foreigners, but fellow citizens', as the King James Version says; the English standard version says 'no longer strangers and aliens, but fellow citizens'.[27]

Significantly, Capitein expresses this dream, a determined and passionate mission, when he has the attention of the powerful directors of the West India Company:

> Me! Who I a blind Heathen! A poor slave was, has the Lord now sent out in that large broad harvest of Moors, so that I was allowed to be the first among the Moors, to offer to my brothers, Christ Jesus, who was crucified, and who offers his merits, his riches, his honour, his goods and his justice, and to share with them that grace that has been offered me by God, out of mercy only.[28]

After the acceptance of his dissertation, Capitein obtained the agreement of the West India Company and the Netherlands Reformed Church authorities to appoint him as a minister in Elmina on the Guinea coast. His return to Elmina becomes a last dramatic part of his life. He described his wish to return to his country of birth as a matter of strong obligation to be of service to my fellow countrymen.[29]

Arriving in Elmina on 8 October 1742, he began his work from the castle, where he also lived. He preached to the Dutch officials, and also established a primary school for 'Tapoejers and negro children', who were being instructed in writing by Abraham Suurdeeg, the reader in Elmina. On Sundays he talks about a free text from the Bible, on Mondays he held a catechism class at his house that few attend 'for most of the people here are either Roman Catholic or Lutheran, and the Reformed (17 persons) are thoroughly occupied with daily activities'. There is no real sense of what Capitein thought of the slave trading at the castle while he was living there. Given the fact that his living quarters were inside the castle, right above the enslaved, this must have been part of his everyday, very immediate experience living in Elmina. However, Capitein does not mention this significant confrontation, compared to his previous life in Europe, anywhere in his writings.

In February 1743 he wrote to the WIC informing them that he would like to marry a young African woman, who had been attending his classes:

> I now find, after long deliberation, that it would not be a bad thing were I to take to wife, through a lawful marriage, a young negress who was not only born here in Elmina, but has also shown herself to be fitter for and better capable of education than most.[30]

Her name is not known, and the WIC in Amsterdam explicitly forbade him to marry the woman, without (a known) explanation. Possibly this marriage was seen as crossing the line, because it could have changed her status of enslaved woman into that of a free citizen. The West India Company then took the extraordinary decision to send a white Dutch woman, Antonia Ginderdros, to Elmina to marry Capitein instead of the woman he had chosen himself, and they were married in October 1745.

Capitein was more successful as a teacher than a preacher. Within a few months, 18 to 20 children attend the school held in the castle every day, mostly 'boys in the service of whites, either as slaves or as freedmen', with two white children brought from Holland and two little Tapoejer girls and yet another with her slave girl. Eventually, he hoped to send two or three of these children over to Holland. By April 1743 the school had grown to 45 children, but his long-term aims for the children were not realised as Jacobus Capitein died on 1 February 1747. Cause of death and the location of his grave are unknown. During the last years of his life he was in debt and had difficulties in relations with the WIC and the religious authorities, the Classis. Parker suggests Capitein may have had an alcohol problem. Director General of the WIC De Petersen writes to Amsterdam that Capitein's 'craving for trade... had dimmed his zeal for religion'. What trade we do not know.[31]

Capitein's full body of writings is consistent in several aspects: his main motivation to study, and to work for the church, springs from his gratitude towards those Dutch who liberated him from slavery and who enabled him to pursue his education. His religious conviction is deep and sincere, and provides his second motivation, to return to his native country to work for the conversion of other Africans. He regards this as a personal obligation: 'I have always thought that the greatest obligation was placed upon me also to be useful to my people at some time. This, I would say, is the greatest obligation, and no injustice. For God, who is to be praised from age to age for the profound richness of his wisdom and foresight, not only led me from Africa to the blessed land of Holland; indeed, he initiated me into a superior religion and endeavoured to hand down to me the rudiments of knowledge'.[32]

It is in this obligation that I see the particularly tragic element in Capitein's life. His own deep faith and missionary zeal was not shared by his Dutch colleagues. His treatise and his work can be seen as attempts to convince the WIC governors and the church authorities of the need to go out and convert others for Christianity. In this respect Capitein was a pioneer, who could not build on existing Dutch missionary activity or even goals. Removing the obstacles for missionary work in Africa and amongst Africans was his main aim during the last years of his short life, and it turned out to be a lonely and unsupported job. Converting Africans to Christianity was not an important element of Dutch policy, and Capitein's plea and active attempts to change this had no great results in his lifetime. His work was at best tolerated, but not seriously supported. My analysis corresponds with that of David Kpobi, who wrote a theological dissertation about Capitein who characterises Capitein as 'a prophet without honour, a minister without empathy, a victim of apathy from above, an ambivalent personality, with two souls in one body, two loyalties in one ministry, and two women in his marriage plans; a victim of his position in society, whose life ends in financial and emotional collapse'.[33]

There appears to be a contrast between the warm and welcoming individual friendships between Capitein and several Dutch on the one hand, and the tough structures of Dutch colonial and commercial society he lived in. On an individual level, Capitein was supported, taken care of, liberated, stimulated, and welcomed in Dutch protestant and liberal circles. This open, welcoming and kind reception was not extended to all Africans: it was individual, exceptional, and limited to the individual relationships between Jacobus Capitein and several Dutch people he met in his lifetime. Despite his relative success at Elmina Castle, Dutch trade and church policy remained as harsh as it had been before: trade was directed towards maximum commercial gain, and church ministers in Africa were appointed first and foremost for the care and the contentment of small Dutch circles in the colony, with no intention to actively spread Christianity amongst the local population. Jacobus Capitein's story remains exceptional and his experiences exclusive. Neither his personal gratitude, nor his merits, or his work in the Netherlands and in Elmina were able to influence or change Dutch policies.

Of course, Capitein's gratitude for his liberation from slavery is clear and strong, but, says Parker, 'this is not the entire story. Was the social proximity expressed by Capitein more a matter of wishful thinking than an actuality'?[34] Parker sees several aspects of Capitein's life that indicate this 'social death' to some extent. He was probably quite isolated and 'much of the kindness he received shaded into patronizing behavior'. His continuing dependency from the WIC and the Classis 'hints that his status of relative privilege and acceptance depended ultimately on his ability to satisfy Dutch mercantile interests'. The example that makes this most clear is the history of his forced marriage to a Dutch woman sent to him by the WIC instead of the African woman of his own choice. It is no exaggeration to state that from early childhood until his days back in Elmina, Jacobus Capitein remained subjected to the considerable power of the WIC. However, Capitein himself does not indicate anywhere that he had similar reflections or second thoughts about his position. Furthermore, as Eekhof makes clear in his church historical approach, Capitein was a 'star' in his own time, praised, famous, and the subject of numerous *laudatio*, highly admiring poems and portraits.[35] But the nature of this praise has always the character of observing the unexpected achievements of the black African who surprises everybody in Europe with his talents. One example was the poem to accompany Capitein's portrait at the age of 25, by his friend Brandijn Rijser in 1742:[36]

> Observer, contemplate this African: his skin is black
> But his soul is white, since Jesus himself prays for him.
> He will teach the Africans faith, hope and charity;
> With him, the Africans, once whitened, will always honor the Lamb.

Almost a century later, in spite of very different circumstances in the beginning of their European lives, Aquasi Boachi's experiences remained similar to those of Capitein. Aquasi Boachi was one of the two Ashanti princes who came to the Netherlands in the nineteenth century; they have recently been immortalised in Arthur Japin's novel *The Two Hearts of Kwasi Boachi*. Gratitude and apology appear to be common elements in the autobiographical texts by both Boachi and Capitein. Next to that, there is frustration. Capitein's feelings of gratitude may well have diminished near the end of his life after his return to the Gold Coast, with regard to what must have been frustrating experiences; but apart from his correspondence with the West India Company no sources for his thoughts or experiences of life in Africa have been found, and so there is no evidence to substantiate this suggestion.

Capitein's history was highlighted at the beginning of the twentieth century, when several books and his own writings were published by church historians in the Netherlands and in the United States. Two orthodox Dutch-American Christian newspapers claimed in 1916 that Capitein's academic career was the best illustration of how different and how much better Dutch race relations were in comparison with the situation in the United States. The article was intended to 'defend our reputation'.[37] At the beginning of the twentieth century, some shame had developed about the Dutch involvement in the slave trade. To counter that shame or uneasiness, the history of Jacobus Capitein proved useful. In 2005, a Dutch play featuring Capitein was produced in the Netherlands which bitingly criticised the idea of Dutch tolerance as revealed by the experience of Capitein.[38]

Philip Quaque and Anton Wilhelm Amo

Although Capitein's experiences were unique they can be compared to two other Africans mentioned, Philip Quaque and Anton Wilhelm Amo, Philip Quaque, born in 1741 on the Cape Coast the son of Cudjo, who worked there as Cabosheer, known as Birempon Cudjo. Wishing his son to be educated, Cudjo sent Philip to England in 1754 together with two other African youths, Thomas Coboro and William Cudjo.[39] They were in the charge of Revd. Thomas Thompson to be maintained and educated at the expense of the Society for Propagation of the Gospel in Foreign Parts. Thompson had founded a school on the Cape Coast as a missionary, and it is likely that the African youths were able to read when they travelled to England. They lived in Islington, London, in the home of school master Mr Hickman, who gave them entrance to his school.

They remained with Hickman for five years, until 1759. We know that on 7 January 1759, Philip Quaque and William Cudjo were baptised in the parish church of Islington. Thomas Coboro had died in 1758, possibly of the effects of a small-pox infection two years earlier. Their families on the Cape Coast were not kept informed of their progress. In 1762 Birempon Cudjo asked, through the agents of the Company of Merchants Trading to Africa how the boys were doing, remarking that he had not had any news for four years. Shyllon informs us that in December 1764, Cudjo died in Guy's Hospital in London 'after a period of confinement occasioned by a mental breakdown'. Philip Quaque did better, first living in the home of the Revd. Moore, then becoming ordained a deacon by the Bishop of Exeter in the Chapel Royal, St James's Palace, in 1765. In that same year he was also ordained priest in the Church of England by the Bishop of London, as well as marrying an English woman, Catherine Blunt – a spouse one hopes he had been able to choose himself, contrary to what happened to Jacobus Capitein. In 1766 Quaque was appointed missionary, catechist, and schoolmaster to the Africans in the Gold Coast. He sailed there together with his wife, arriving in February 1766. Unfortunately, Catherine died within a year. Quaque remarried twice and would remain Chaplain of the Cape Coast Castle for another 50 years, until he died in 1816 at the age of 75.

Quaque continued the school Thompson had started, and thus was slightly less of a pioneer than Jacobus Capitein had been in Elmina.[40] However, opening this school to African children appears not to have been allowed: established as a school for the children of white British military and colonial families, it did accept 'mulatto' children as well as 'children of some very wealthy blacks'. They were educated in religion, reading and writing, as well as arithmetic. As an ordained priest, Quaque could perform baptisms. We know that he had baptised 52 persons by 1774, 'few of them Africans'. Apparently, Quaque had lost the ability to speak his native language when living in England and, like Capitein, he faced indifference if not hostility from the British authorities at Cape Coast Castle regarding his missionary work and his church services.[41]

Black European Philosopher

Anton Wilhelm Amo (ca. 1700–ca. 1759) was born near Axim about 1700. As a child of about four years old he was taken to Holland through Johannes van der Star, a preacher in the then Gold Coast, and given as a present to the Duke of Brunswick, Anton Ulrich. Amo grew up in the Duke's house at Wolfenbütel, Germany, was baptised there in 1721 and named 'Anton Wilhelm Rudolph Mohre'. He received a good education and became a law student at the University of Halle. There he defended his thesis in 1729, *De Jure Maurorum in Europa*: on the Rights of the 'Moors' in Europe. In contrast to Capitein's effort to reconcile the slave trade and Christianity, Amo argued against the purchase and enslavement of Africans by European Christians, and promoted the recognition of their common right to freedom. He based his argument on an original analysis of Roman law and legal history. A recent analysis of Amo's argument summarises it as such: 'African kings, like their European counterparts, had been vassals of Rome. By slave trading, Europeans were violating the common heritage of Roman law, the principle that all the Roman citizens were free, including those who lived in Africa'.[42] What we know of Amo's analysis places him firmly decades ahead of the abolitionist movements in Europe, and he deserves prominent recognition in the history of European legal philosophy. At the first international conference on Black European Thinkers held in 2009, the American philosopher Lewis Gordon argued that Amo's career should be seen as a rival to Emmanuel Kant. According to Gordon, Amo's mentor was Jewish, and his thesis advisor was female, which was certainly rare in the eighteenth century. Unfortunately, crucial texts by Amo are missing, but increasingly his work is being included in volumes by and about Africana philosophers.[43]

During his life in Germany it appears that Amo was well liked and respected, and his reputation grew steadily. In 1733 he led a procession during the visit of Frederick of Prussia to Halle. Moving on to Wittenberg, he gained his doctorate in philosophy in 1734, with a thesis that was published as *On the Absence of Sensation in the Human Mind and its Presence in our Organic and Living Body*. He developed himself as a rationalist and empiricist philosopher, and he may have been influenced by Gottfried Leibniz, who he had met as a boy at the Duke of Brunswick's. Back in Halle he found employment as a lecturer in philosophy, and from then on he consciously used the name that presented him as African:

Antonius Guilelmus Amo Afer. In 1736 he was awarded a professorship, followed by a second book in 1738, *Treatise on the Art of Philosophising Soberly and Accurately*. A year later he moved to Jena, where he continued to teach. In addition to philosophy, Amo knew Hebrew, Greek, Latin, Dutch, French, and German – whether he was able to use his African mother tongue is not known. He was nominated as a Counsellor of the Court of Berlin, and then, despite this successful academic career, he returned to the Gold Coast some time after 1743, possibly in 1747. There have been suggestions that he decided to leave the university following internal conflicts and tensions there. Another issue could have been his wish to marry a German woman, which provoked a racist reaction. Back in Guinea, West Africa, according to John Wright, Amo became a goldsmith and seer, 'honoured Ashanti vocations', in or near a fortress Fort San Sebastian, and a Fort Chama, where it is said that he 'died of boredom' in 1756.[44] The University of Halle's *Annals* describe him as 'the Master Amo, who hails from Africa and more particularly from Guinea, and is a genuine Negro but a humble and honourable philosopher'. It would take two centuries before Amo was honoured again for his original philosophical work. Significantly, this rediscovery happened in the context of the German communist regime of the former German Democratic Republic, at the height of the cold war.[45]

Conclusion

To what extent did Jacobus Capitein and the other African men feel that they belonged in Europe? One way to answer this question is to look at the economic room and the space Africans were able to claim and obtain during their life in Europe. Jacobus Capitein remained dependent economically from white Dutch Christian patrons throughout his life. His employment as a protestant minister in Fort Elmina for the West India Company was most likely his first paid job, although more research is required here. We know that the West India Company had a selective policy regarding the employment of Christian ministers in the colonies. It is unlikely that critical minds would have been welcome on board ships (slave or otherwise), or in the fortress of Elmina itself. Capitein's reassuring tone may have been a strategy chosen by him (or by those around him) as part of an exit route from the Netherlands to Africa. His choice of bible fragments also suggests to me that while he remained graceful and grateful and minded his words, his ultimate aim was freedom, citizenship, and emancipation. However, this remained quite covert, implicit, and guarded. In my view, this tone reflects a highly restricted atmosphere in the

Netherlands at the time; it suggests also a lack of contact with more critical minds and a lack of room for a critical perspective on abolition and the position of Africans in the world. Clearly, William Amo appropriated a much more open and critical intellectual space during his university life in Germany. While German academic life at the time was also highly restricted to an economic, religious, and political elite, some of whom were probably involved in trading slaves, Amo's positions in German universities also made him more economically independent than Capitein ever was. Amo was obviously not so directly tied to the slave-trading companies or families that he would have to watch his every word. Nevertheless, it took an amount of courage to write an academic argument against slavery, when he was the only African employed at the universities where he worked.

Although quantitative historical research is lacking, we can see that of the few Africans who were able to travel to and settle permanently as free citizens in Europe, at least in continental Europe, fewer chose to remain, and instead took the opportunity to return to Africa. This would suggest that privileged eighteenth-century black Europeans may have been puzzled by the individual experiences they had with white Europeans in West Africa and during their first introduction to Europe. They had reason to believe they were welcome and developed long-term friendships with white Europeans. In their texts they stress the enormous positive value of friendship, perhaps as a counterweight for the never-ending curious questions they endured as visible exceptional 'others'. The positive private, individual experiences of friendship they had as Africans in Europe were convincing and appeared to be credible. But these individual networks of friends masked, possibly insufficiently, the harder general social climate in which they lived. Their life stories bring to mind the title of an essay by James Baldwin, *The price of the ticket*, about the conditions for entrance and acceptance of black people into mainstream American society. For Capitein, the price of his ticket into Dutch academic society and in particular of his 'return ticket' to Elmina as a protestant minister, was his active defending of the system of slave trade and slavery by the Dutch. Moreover, when he was finally on his way to independence, on the payroll of the Dutch West India Company, this employer took away his right to choose a marriage partner. We do not know to what extent Capitein's choices were the result of coercion or of free will. By comparison, Philip Quaque had more room and more time to build an independent life in Europe, but his experiences after returning to Africa were similarly disappointing and resulted in isolation. Of these three, William Amo reached the highest, most respected academic position while living in Germany, but even Amo ended his life almost anonymously.

All three men were born in West Africa and taken away from their families, bought, or given to Europeans and sent to Europe as children. Their first relationships with white European men were those of children with substitute fathers. Later there were similarly paternal relations of sponsors and supporters who provided for their housing and maintenance for all three men. When as adults they decided to pursue a career, they obtained permission for this step from their benefactors, but from then on they were on their own. In his protestant minister's office in Fort Elmina, Capitein faced the flipside of paternalism. After being appropriated by European higher circles, surrounded with high hopes and expectations, and after their expected integration into those circles and subsequent distancing from their family background, the sudden silent independence must have been a cold surprise. All three men were trained to fulfil positions in society far more elite than others who feature in this collection. But, their lives remain exceptional, their stays in Europe temporary.

Acknowledgements

I thank Siep Stuurman, Alex van Stipriaan, Karin Willemse, Gijsbert Oonk, Wieke Vink, and Joep a Campo of Erasmus University Rotterdam for their comments to parts of an earlier version of this text. I thank Allison Blakely and Linda Heywood for the opportunity to present part of this paper in their seminar at Boston University.

Notes

[1] All quotes of Jacobus Capitein in this article were taken from the translations of Grant Parker, 2001, and D.P.A. Kpobi, 1993.
[2] Kolfin, in Schreuder and Elmer (ed.), 2008: 270–1.
[3] D.P.A. Kpobi, 1993. A. Eekhof, 1917. Henri van der Zee, 2000. Allison Blakely, 1993.
[4] Grant Parker, 2001.
[5] In this article I use 'black' as referring to visible difference from dominant whiteness; as a black African, Jacobus Capitein was and remained highly visible everywhere he went in the Netherlands, and the same is true for other black Africans entering Europe.
[6] Capitein's thesis was translated with commentary by Grant Parker, 2001. About Capitein, see also J.F. Blumenbach, Beytrage zur Naturgeschichte, 1790. And Capitein's thesis: 'Staatkundig Godgeleerd Onderzoekschrift over de Slavernij als niet strijdig tegen de Christelijke Vrijheid'. Amsterdam, 1742.
[7] See Allison Blakely, 1993; Ernst van den Boogaart, 1982, 33–54; Jan Erik Dubbelman and Jaap Tanja (eds.), Vreemd gespuis. Amsterdam, 1987.
[8] Kpobi, 1993: 16.
[9] See, for example, T.F. Earle and K.J.P. Lowe (eds.), 2005, and Kate Lowe, 2008.

[10] Mary Louise Pratt, 1986: 138–62: 140.

[11] Angelie Sens, 2001; SDU, Den Haag 2001: 7. [my translation, dh] Angelie Sens, 1997: 2–26.

[12] Anton Wilhelm [Antonius Guilielmus] Amo came to Amsterdam in 1707 and was given to Duke Anton Ulrich of Brunswick–Wolfenbüttel, who handed him over to his son August Wilhelm. In 1708 Amo was christened with the names Anton Wilhelm after his patrons. In 1721 he was confirmed, in 1727 he went to Halle University, where in 1729 he graduated in law with his *Disputation De jure Maurorum in Europa*. 'The Rights of an African in Eighteenth Century Europe'. According to Sephocle, 'this text has mysteriously disappeared'. In 1730 he went to Wittenberg University and there in the same year gained a degree as Doctor of Philosophy. In 1733, on the visit of Augustus the Strong, Elector of Saxony and King of Poland, Dr Amo led the students' procession in the monarch's honour. In 1734, after having his Disputation published, he was made Professor of Philosophy. In 1736 he returned to Halle as lecturer and there taught psychology, 'natural law', and the decimal system – a universality which was then customary. . . .. In 1738 Amo's *Tractatus de arte sobrie et accurate philosophandi* (Treatise on the Art of Philo- sophising Soberly and Accurately) was published in Halle; he himself had become quite a bright star in the firmament of Halle's early Enlightenment. The following year moved to Jena University, where he gave his inaugural lecture on 'The Frontiers of Psychology', and no doubt stayed there till May 1740. The two sons of Duke Anton Ulrich had died in 1731 and 1735, respectively; Johann Peter von Ludewig, Chancellor of Halle University, died in 1742; and Amo probably found no other patron in Germany. At any rate we hear no more of him until 1753, when he was back home in Axim, venerated apparently as a [traditional] doctor. When he died is unknown. Jahn, 1968: 35–9). See also: Sephocle, 'Anton Wilhelm Amo', 1992: 182–7. Sephocle writes that he worked in Axim, Ghana, as a goldsmith, and died there in 1754. There is a statue of Amo at the University of Halle Wittenberg in what used to be the German Democratic Republic.

[13] A. Eekhof, 1917: 6. See also C.H. Robinson, 1915: 290–1; and H. Gundert, 1894: 76.

[14] Translated with commentary by Grant Parker. Markus Wiener Publishers, Princeton, NJ, 2001.

[15] Van den Honert was, writes Joris van Eijnatten, 'one of the principal clerical authorities in Holland during the 1730s and 1740s. He was a man who zealously protected the interests of his church and carefully watched over the observance and maintenance of its confessions. Not without reason was he nicknamed the "Pope of Leiden" and even the "Pope of Holland." Van den Honert was an authoritative divine; a preface written by him was looked upon as a great privilege. He was also a devoted controversialist, albeit one who debated rationally in a polite but infuriatingly patronising tone. Van den Honert is best regarded as a clerical regent, an ecclesiastical oligarch who maintained excellent relations with various ruling families in the Republic (including his own), dedicated most of his works to magistrates and other persons of influence, took care to marry women of appropriate stock, and was exceptionally proud of what he believed to be his own noble parentage'. Joris van Eijnatten, 2003: 59.

[16] As Ernst van den Boogaart summarises: 'An occasional clergyman attempted to convert the heathen, but conversion was clearly a sideline in the Dutch African enterprise'. Ernst van den Boogaart, 1982: 33–54; 41.

[17] 'Een kind van seven of agt jaaren hetzy in den oorlog, of door eenig ander toeval, van myne ouders berooft zynde, wierd ik verkogt aan den Wakkeren Scheepsbevelhebber Arnold Steenhart, wanneer hij om den Slaavenhandel, aan eene zekere plaats van Africa, de Rivier van S. Andreas genoemt, geland was: gelijk die Aanzienlijke Man, wanneer ik laatst te Middelburg was, mij zelf verhaalt heeft. Deze [. . .] heeft mij vereert aan zynen Vriend, tegenwoordig mynen ten hoogsten te eerden, en met eene kinderlijke liefde te beantwoorden Weldoener en Beschermheer, Jacob van Goch: die toentertijd een zeer Gelukkig en Ervaren Koopman van de Zeer Edele Bewindhebberen der Afrikaansche Compagnie was. [. . .] Deze heeft mij [. . .] Als een Vader zo bemind, dat hy eindelijk, naar zijn Vaderland zullende keeren, belooft heeft, my met zig mee te zullen neemen'.

[18] Jacobus Capitein, quotes from the introduction to his 'Politico-theological dissertation concerning slavery, as not contrary to Christian freedom', Leiden 1742. Translation: David Nii Anum Kpobi, 'Mission in chains', Utrecht 1993: 187–94.

[19] Parker, translation Capitein, 93. 'Verscheiden onder de Christenen vreezen, dat door de Vryheid des Evangeliums de slavenhandel uyt de volksplantingen door de Christenen opgeregt, tot groote schade van derzelfder bewindhebberen, geheel zoude worden weggenoomen. Daar zijn er namelijk geweest, ja! Menschen die [. . .] gestelt hebben, dat de Evangelische Vryheid met het Lyfeigenschap geensints konde bestaan. De tegenwoordige staat myner zaken eyst van my te bewysen, dat deze gedagte, of uyt onkunde van den aart der Evangely-leer, of uyt eene bijgeloovige bekomering, of eindelijk uyt aanmerking van de instellingen en zeden dezer landen, voortgekomen is' (Capitein, thesis, 1742, 22).

[20] Jacobus Capitein, chapter three of the dissertation, translation Kpobi, 199.

[21] Parker: 64–5.

[22] Capitein, translation Kpobi: 212.

[23] Capitein, translation Kpobi: 214.

[24] Capitein, translation Kpobi: 215.

[25] Parker: 65.

[26] Parker: 18.

[27] *Ephese 2:19*: Zoo zijt Gij dan niet meer vreemdelingen en bywoners, maar medeburgers der heiligen en huisgenooten Gods. King James Version and English Standard Version Bible, *Ephesians 2.19*.

[28] Quote of Albert Eekhof, De negerpredikant, 1917, 167. 'My! Die ik een blinde Heyde! Een arme slaave was, laat de Heere nu uitsenden in dien grooten ruymen oogst der Mooren, opdat ik eersteling uit de Mooren mogte zijn, om mijnen broederen, Christus Jewus ende dien gekruyzigt, ende door syne verdiensten, synen rijkdom, eere, duuragtig goed ende geregtigheid aan te bieden, en hun dier genade mede deelagtig te maaken, die mij hier van God uit louter genade, geschonken is'.

[29] 'Hierom dacht ik altoos, dat 'er eene zeer groote nootzaak op my gelegt was, om te eeniger tijd mijnen Lands-genooten van nut te zijn'.

[30] Letter of Capitein to the Meetings of Ten, WIC, from Elmina, 15 February 1743. Orig. At State Archives, The Hague, Letters and Papers from Guinea, no. 113, fol. 139r–140v. Translation by Kpobi, 1993, 235–6.

[31] Grant Parker: 15–7.

[32] Parker: 85.

[33] Kpobi, 1993: 153–74.

[34] Parker: 74–5.

[35] A. Eekhof, 1917, gives many examples of these poems, and how Capitein is mentioned in church historical journals and books.

[36] Translation Parker: 48–9.

Aanschouwer zie deez'Moor! Zijn vel is zwart: maar wit
zijn ziel, daar Jesus zelf als Priester voor hem bidt.
Hij gaat Geloof, en Hoop, en Liefde aan Mooren leeren,
Opdat zij, witgemaakt, met hem het Lam steeds eeren.

[37] The aim was to counter the 'impression that the Dutch nation is guilty of having introduced the curse of slavery in America', with the well-known Dutch ship that carried 'twenty negars' to Jamestown, Virginia in 1619. This is how The Banner, published in Grand Rapids by the Christian Reformed Church, claimed Dutch superiority in 1916: '[The Dutch] opened their Universities to the black man, recognizing him as the bearer of God's image carved in ebony, long before other nations did so. This is shown by the fact that in 1737 the Negro, Jacob Eliza Johannes Capitein, was allowed to enter the University of Leyden in Holland, from which he graduated in 1742 as doctor of divinity, the first Negro perhaps in modern history, who obtained this degree. Secondly, the Dutch long ago felt at liberty to ordain Negroes to the sacred office of the ministry, since in 1737 the Classis of Amsterdam examined and licensed this same black man as a candidate, and solemnly ordained him as minister with "general consent". Thirdly, the Dutch cared for the spiritual needs of the Negro at an early date, since this same Rev. Capitein, who hailed from the St Andrew's river in Africa, in 1742 was sent to St" George d'Elmina in Guinea, by the Dutch West India Company to serve the church at that place as pastor and to preach the gospel to his heathen kinsmen there.' The Banner, 6 January 1916, vol. 51, no. 998. *Publication Committee of the Christian Reformed Church, Grand Rapids, Michigan.* A Weekly, devoted to the Interests of the Christian Reformed Church and Calvinistic Principles: 40–1.

[38] Gustav Borreman as Jacobus Capitein in a recent play called 'De kleur van droes'/ Colour me evil, written by Mark Walraven, directed by Felix de Rooij. Performed across Europe, as well as in Ghana and the Dutch Caribbean, 2004–06. See: http://www.artunited.nl/generated/4.html

[39] Quaque is pronounced 'Kwaku'. For references to Philip Quaque's correspondence, see: http://www.wheaton.edu/bgc/archives/GUIDES/151.htm Papers of Philip Quaque.

[40] Shyllon, Black People in Britain, 1555–833. Oxford University Press, Oxford 1977: 57–8. See also: F.L. Bartels, Philip Quaque, 1741–818, *Transactions of the Gold Coast and Togoland Historical Society*, 1955, vol. 1, pt. 5: 153–77. Idem, Jacobus Eliza Capitein, in *Transactions of the Historical Society of Ghana*, IV, 1959, I: 3–13.

[41] http://www.wheaton.edu/bgc/archives/GUIDES/151.htm Papers of Philip Quaque.

[42] Unfortunately, the full text of Amo's dissertation was lost, and the analysis of his work has to be based on a summary of it published by the university. See: http://www.kirjasto.sci.fi/amo.htm

[43] Gordon, *An Introduction to Africana Philosophy*, 2008, 35–40. Conference presentation and debates, international conference 'Black European Thinkers and Trajectories of Emancipation', VU University Amsterdam, July 2009. See also: Abraham, '*Anton Wilhelm Amo*', 2003, 191–9. Kwasi Wiredu, 'Amo's Critique of Descartes' Philosophy of Mind', in: idem, 200–6.

[44] Amo was also elected a member of the Dutch Academy of Flushing. This may be connected to his meeting in West Africa in 1753 with David Henri Gallandet, Swiss-Dutch physician and ship's surgeon, 'who noted that Amo lived like a hermit'. Gallandat worked in Zeeland. John S. Wright, 'Amo, Anton Wilhelm (1703–56)', in: Edward Craig 1998, 210–1. Posthumous recognition of Amo came during the communist regime in the former German Democratic Republic in 1965 with a statue in Amo's honour in Halle, and a publication of German and English editions of his texts in 1968 by the Martin Luther University of Halle-Wittenberg. See also: Wiredu et al. (2003); Hallen (2002); *Anton William Amo's Treatise on the Art of Philosophising Soberly and Accurately* (with commentaries) by T. Uzodinma Nwala (1990) first published in 1738 in Latin in the Netherlands, a compendium of his university lectures; *African Philosophy: Myth and Reality* by Paulin J. Hountondji (1983).

[45] For more information, see: Abraham, 1962. W. Emmanuel Abraham, 'Amo', in Robert Arrington (ed.), *A Companion to the Philosophers* (2001). Anton Wilhelm Amo *Antonius Gvilielmus Amo Afer of Axim in Ghana: Translation of his Works* (1968: Halle, Martin Luther University, Halle-Wittenberg). A summary of his work on Apathy was published in Safro Kwame (ed.), *Readings in African Philosophy: An Akan Collection* (1995: University Press of America). H. Brentjes *Anton Wilhelm Amo — Im Halle, Wittenberg, und Jena* (1968: Jena). Monika Firla *Anton Wilhelm Amo* (Nzema, Rep. Ghana) — Kammermohr, Privatdozent für Philosophie, Wahrsager. In: Tribus 51.2002. King, *One Hundred Philosophers*, 2004. See also: http://www.kirjasto.sci.fi/amo.htm. Recently, a play about Amo was performed in Germany. 'Gallandat (Marcell Kaiser) debattiert mit Anton Wilhelm Amo (Komi Mizrajim Togbonou)'. Theatre company 'Freuynde und Gaesdte', 2009, Münster. See: http://www.ivz-online.de/lokales/muenster/kultur/1044738_Die_Suche_nach_der_Wuerde.html

References

Abraham, W. Emmanuel. "Amo." In *A Companion to the Philosophers*, edited by Robert Arrington. Oxford: Blackwell, 2001.

Abraham, W. Emmanuel. "Anton Wilhelm Amo." In *A Companion to African Philosophy*, edited by Kwasi Wiredu, 191–99. Malden, MA: Blackwell, 2003.

Amo, Anton Wilhelm. *Antonius Gvilielmus Amo Afer of Axim in Ghana: Translation of his Works*. Halle: Martin Luther University, Halle-Wittenberg, 1968.

Banner, The. "A Weekly, devoted to the Interests of the Christian Reformed Church and Calvinistic Principles." *Publication Committee of the Christian Reformed Church, Grand Rapids, Michigan* 51, no. 998 (6 January 1916): 40–1.

Bartels, F. L. "'Philip Quaque', 1741–1818." *Transactions of the Gold Coast and Togoland Historical Society* 1 (1955), pt. 5: 153–77.

Bartels, F. L. "Jacobus Eliza Capitein." *Transactions of the Historical Society of Ghana* IV (1959), part I: 3–13.

Blakely, Allison. *Blacks in the Dutch World.* Bloomington, IN: Indiana University Press, 1993.

Boogaart, Ernst van den. "Colour Prejudice and the Yardstick of Civility: The Initial Dutch Confrontation with Black Africans, 1590–1635." In *Racism and Colonialism. Essays on Ideology and Social Structure*, edited by Robert Ross, 33–54. The Hague and Leiden: Martinus Nijhoff Publishers, 1982.

Capitein, Jacobus Eliza. *Staatkundig Godgeleerd Onderzoekschrift over de Slavernij als niet strijdig tegen de Christelijke Vrijheid.* Amsterdam: 1742.

Capitein, Jacobus. *Politico-Theological Dissertation Concerning Slavery, as Not Contrary to Christian Freedom.* Leiden: 1742. Trans. David Nii Anum Kpobi as *Mission in Chains.* (Zoetermeer: Uitgeverij Boekencentrum, 1993), 187–94.

Dubbelman, Jan Erik and Jaap Tanja, eds. *Vreemd gespuis.* Amsterdam: 1987.

Earle, T. F. and K. J. P. Lowe, eds. *Black Africans in Renaissance Europe.* Cambridge: Cambridge University Press, 2005.

Eekhof, A. "De negerpredikant Jacobus Elisa Joannes Capitein. Bijdrage tot de kennis van onze koloniale kerkgeschiedenis." In *Nederlandsch Archief Kerkgeschiedenis*, vol. XIII (The Hague: Martinus Nijhoff, 1917), 138–74.

Eijnatten, Joris van. *Liberty and Concord in the United Provinces. Religious Toleration and the Public in the Eighteenth-Century Netherlands.* Leiden and Boston: Brill, 2003.

Firla, Monika. *Anton Wilhelm Amo - Kammermohr, Privatdozent für Philosophie, Wahrsager*, vol. 51 (Nzema, Rep. Ghana: Tribus), 2002.

Gordon, Lewis R. *An Introduction to Africana Philosophy.* Cambridge and New York: Cambridge University Press, 2008.

Gordon, Lewis R. *Conference presentation and debates, international conference "Black European Thinkers and Trajectories of Emancipation".* Amsterdam, VU University Amsterdam, July 2009.

Jahn, Janheinz. *Neo-African Literature: A History of Black Writing.* New York: Grove Press, 1968.

King, Peter H. *One Hundred Philosophers.* New York, Barron's Educational Books, 2004. http://www.kirjasto.sci.fi/amo.htm

Kpobi, D. P. A. *Mission in Chains: The Life, Theology and Ministry of the Ex-Slave J.E.J. Capitein, 1717–1747.* Zoetermeer: Dissertation, Utrecht University, Boekencentrum Zoetermeer, 1993.

Lowe, Kate (guest editor). special issue "Sub-Saharan Africa and Renaissance and Reformation Europe: New Findings and New Perspectives." CRRS, Toronto, Canada, *Renaissance and Reformation/Renaissance et Réforme* 32, no. 1 (2008).

Parker, Grant. *The Agony of Asar. A Thesis on Slavery by the Former Slave Jacobus Elisa Johannes Capitein 1717–1747.* Princeton, NJ: Markus Wiener, 2001.

Pratt, Mary Louise. "Scratches on the Face of the Country; or What Mr. Barrow Saw in the Land of the Bushmen." In *"Race", Writing and Difference*, edited by Henry Louis Gates, 138–62. Chicago: University of Chicago Press, 1986.

Schreuder, Esther and Elmer Kolfin, eds. *Black is Beautiful, Rubens to Dumas*. Zwolle and Amsterdam: Waanders, 2008.

Sens, Angelie. "Was Adam zwart? Nederlandse bijdragen aan de aap-debatten in de achttiende en negentiende eeuw." *Theoretische Geschiedenis* 24, no. 1 (1997): 2–26.

Sens, Angelie. *Mensaap, heiden slaaf: Nederlandse visies op de wereld rond 1800*. Den Haag: SDU, 2001.

Sephocle, Marilyn. "Anton Wilhelm Amo." *Journal of Black Studies* 23, no. 2 (1992): 182–7.

Shyllon, Folarin Olawale. *Black People in Britain, 1555–1833*. Oxford: Oxford University Press.

Wright, John S. "Amo, Anton Wilhelm (1703–1756)." In *Routledge Encyclopedia of Philosophy*, edited by Edward Craig, 210–11. London: Routledge, Volume 9.

Zee, Henri van der. *'s Heeren Slaaf: Het dramatische leven van Jacobus Capitein*. Amsterdam: Balans, 2000.

Pictured at Work: Employment in Art (1800–1900)

Jan Marsh

National Portrait Gallery, London, UK

This paper was first presented as an illustrated talk following the exhibition of pictures and sculptures featuring figures of African ancestry in art in the nineteenth century, entitled Black Victorians: Black People in Art 1800–1900, curated by the author and shown in Manchester and Birmingham in 2005–6. Amongst other things, this added to our increasing knowledge of the part played by models of African ancestry in the creation of historical art. From the Renaissance to the Modern age, whenever artistic emphasis was placed on representation from life rather than from ideal forms, there emerged an employment niche for models that could not be filled by those of European origin. What follows is a necessarily abbreviated introduction to this aspect of labour history in Britain, largely focussed on the nineteenth century. The information is visual rather than textual and the sources are therefore pictorial and sculptural. The illustrations, thus an integral element of the presentation but costly to reproduce in print form, are referenced where available via websites.

Introduction

The work undertaken by male and female models of African ancestry is seen obliquely in many forms of visual art. Like actors in theatre and film, but almost always anonymously, they generally represent figures in subject paintings. As, for example, in George Morland's famous image *Execrable Human Traffic, or The Affectionate Slaves*, first exhibited at the Royal Academy in London in 1788 as a visual contribution to the emergent Abolitionist campaign. It depicts a family being forcibly separated by European traders for transport to the slave ship waiting offshore.

The imagined slave trade scene is set on the west coast of Africa, but the painting was produced in London.[1] The four African figures were drawn from models – at a guess one male in different poses, one female and one child. The picture's success promoted Morland to a sequel: *African Hospitality* (1791) showing a true-life incident when shipwrecked Europeans were rescued by Africans – again painted in London, probably employing some or all of the same models. We can know nothing of the identity or situation of the models, but can conjecture that the adults had other occupations – modelling for artists was 'casual' employment – and were probably known within the London art world, where artists commonly exchanged information on available models.[2]

On other occasions, the model was the subject of the work. Sir Joshua Reynolds' head study of a young man was most probably painted from a model, who has been speculatively identified as Francis Barber, Samuel Johnson's servant and friend.[3] If this was intended as a study for a large picture, no such link to another work can be established, suggesting that the artist used the model as an example, to practise and demonstrate depicting African skin tones, which require specific pigments and underpainting. Techniques for depicting European skin tones, layered over a green base, were among the essential skills of a professional painter in this period. African complexions required different pigments, careful attention to exact hues and understanding of how light reflects from dark skin. To paint African features well was a display of expertise, and practice in this matter is evidence for the inclusion of Black figures in British picture-making.

John Downman's drawing of *Thomas Williams: A Sailor* has a note detailing the pigments required. Strictly speaking, Williams was an incidental rather than regular model, a seafarer whom the artist must have encountered in Liverpool between voyages (though he bears a Welsh name). He may have agreed to sit for free, or for a small payment in cash or kind.[4]

The pictorial evidence helps to expand our knowledge of the Black population in Britain in past centuries. Reliable information is as yet lacking, but it has been estimated that around 1800 the Black population numbered about 20,000 in London, which is roughly similar to the number of wealthy households, where many footmen, coachmen, nursemaids and cooks of African ancestry were employed. These were perhaps the easiest models to find, but male models were also recruited from the armed services and prize-fighting circles. These yielded many of the 'best' models, according to artists' assessment of physical formation. William Etty's 1840s study of two *Wrestlers* (York City Art Gallery[5]) derives from classical examples and itself illustrates the artistic search for well-muscled models.

One man named Wilson, whom Sir Thomas Lawrence described 'the finest figure he had ever seen, combining the character and perfection of many antique statues' and whom BR Haydon regarded as 'a perfect model of beauty and activity',[6] was employed by George Dawe for the male figure in *Negro overpowering a Buffalo: A Fact which occurred in America 1809* (Menil Foundation 1515) a canvas painted and exhibited in London in 1811.

A drawing by John Bourne from 1807 entitled *A Meeting of Connoisseurs* satirised the fashion for Black models.[7] This shows a tall, well-built fellow posing in the garret of an impoverished artist for a picture of Hercules. By contrast, the poor artist is thin and scrawny. The model, who may indeed represent the man known only as Wilson, sustains his heroic pose with the aid of a broom handle, while gentlemen patrons appraise both art work and model. The model's garments heaped on the floor indicate his regular employment as a coachman.

Other works depict models at work, in the act of modelling. In 1847 as a student at the Edinburgh art school the Trustees' Academy, Thomas Faed made a careful painting of a male model named or known as *John Mongo* who holds his pose with the aid of a rope suspended from ceiling, a piece of art school apparatus.[8] A model commonly expected to hold a pose for around 20 minutes, but anything approaching an 'action pose' is impossible unaided for this length of time – hence steps, ropes, broom handles and other equipment that did not normally appear in the finished painting. From his appearance we'd take 'John Mongo' to be of Indian or maybe East African origin – the sobriquet 'Mongo', which was almost certainly a name bestowed on, not chosen by the young man, indicates that he was thought to come from Africa – was possibly a seafarer who worked at the art school to earn extra money between voyages. Faed's painting, which earned the young artist a school prize, would have taken some time – perhaps a few weeks – to complete, which suggests that 'John Mongo' had a relatively long spell of employment, although he would not have posed on a daily basis. Art schools employed models from a casual pool as and when they were required.

This form of employment continued through the century and well into the next. In 1882 a student named Constance Wood was premiated in the national competitions for her careful study of a model, entitled *A Zulu*, now in the City of London's Guildhall Art Gallery.[9] Possibly the man was Zulu – troupes of African performers were a feature of popular entertainment, and modelling would offer additional or substitute earnings – but the drawing may equally have been given this topical title owing to the presence in London of the defeated Zulu leader Cetswayo.

Models were asked to strike a pose, seldom knowing what subject it was intended for. Cast in an appropriate role, they were costumed accordingly, as in John Simpson's *The Captive Slave*, painted in London and exhibited there and in Liverpool in 1827.[10] First in the 1780s, and then in the 1820s, when slavery again became a political issue in Britain, pictures of enslaved figures, motivated by Abolitionist campaigning, created employment for Black models. In *The Captive Slave* the model is seated with his hands on his knees and his head raised, with an expression as if praying for deliverance. His manacles are likely to have been painted in from studio props, rather than actually worn while posing. If he was the actor Ira Aldridge, as currently claimed, then he was combining modelling with his theatre employment; the 'Captive Slave' pose and costume are comparable with the stage roles he was currently playing. Aldridge, who had migrated to Britain from the United States, where African-American actors were not permitted on 'white' stages, almost certainly sat to James Northcote for the figure of *Othello*, which was Aldridge's 'star role'.[11]

More typical, perhaps, is the unnamed man who posed for the attendant carrying a tray of glasses in the large canvas of *Josephine and the Fortune Teller* by Sir David Wilkie, painted in 1837 for the Houses of Parliament.[12] A careful preliminary study owned by the Duke of Buccleuch demonstrates the model's task. From the study, the figure would be copied into the painting. A similar model was employed in 1882 by Edward Poynter, for an attendant figure in a big picture depicting *The Queen of Sheba meeting King Solomon*. The careful drawing of a man clad in kente cloth, holding a tray, is now in the British Museum.[13]

In the late Victorian era, as knowledge of antiquity progressed, understanding of the geography and ethnicity of the biblical and classical worlds required more 'authentic' artistic depictions, although as with cinema in the twentieth century, the central characters were usually shown as fair-skinned. Despite the common identification of Sheba with Ethiopia, only rarely is its Queen portrayed as African, for example.

One woman who could have modelled for such a Queen of Sheba is seen in Sir John Gilbert's image of an exotic fruit-seller from the late 1840s, see in two fine watercolour studies and a later oil, all in the Guildhall Art Gallery.[14] The figure will have been drawn from a professional model and the fruit obtained in Covent Garden market. Model and fruit were probably drawn at different times, but the model will have posed with the basket on her head – the whole to be an evocation of rich and sensuous colour, in orientalist mode.

The number of Black boys in art probably reflects their presence on the streets; in the nineteenth century lads aged 12–14 commonly worked as messengers and delivery boys. Artists requiring a young man of African ancestry could find a suitable model going about his daily business. The artist William Henry Hunt developed a specialism in the 1830s, depicting young boys and girls in everyday situations, with punning titles; painted in watercolour, these were published as lithographs in the series called *Hunt's Comic Sketches*. Though most were white, a handful of the youngsters depicted were Black. A likely model is drawn as himself, in Hunt's watercolour study in the Victoria & Albert Museum, London, of a boy in his work clothes, with the basket to carry whatever goods he was delivering.[15] The same lad, in identical jacket and kerchief but different trousers, is shown doing sums on a slate, under the title *A Brown Study*, punning on his colour and abstracted mood. A third image, in the Lady Lever Art Gallery, shows a Black boy huddling round glowing coals, a visual version of the perennial joke. In Liverpool, a messenger boy was the direct subject of an oil painting by William Windus.[16]

Another occupational group that occasionally featured as models were the itinerant salesmen known as pedlars. From visual evidence it is known that then as now some of these were members of the African, Indian and Arab diasporas in Europe. One such – who may or may not have been drawn from an actual pedlar, but appears to be based on observation, is shown in William Mulready's *The Toyseller* (1858, the later of two versions) now in the National Museum of Ireland.[17]

Slavery as a theme persisted well after Abolition in British territories, and campaigning against American slavery through to the 1860s increased employment opportunities for dark models. A whole repertoire of paintings and drawings resulted from the huge popularity of Harriet Beecher Stowe's *Uncle Tom's Cabin*, published in 1852 and translated into all languages from Armenian to Welsh. For his 1866 painting of *Little Eva and Uncle Tom* (now in the Russell-Cotes Gallery, Bournemouth), the artist Edwin Long will have employed three Black models – Uncle Tom on the right, Topsy nestling close to him and Rosa listening on the left.[18] All three are pictorially outshone by the dazzling virtue of angelic white Eva. This of course was often the visual role played by Black models, although the iconology of their deployment is outside the scope of this paper.

Another well-known image, Thomas Jones Barker's *The Secret of England's Greatness*, which shows Victoria presenting a bible to an African envoy and is now in the National Portrait Gallery, London.[19] I have written at length about the historical context of this painting but in relation to the present topic, while Victoria, Albert and the attendant figures were painted from photographs (the artist was not granted the favour of portrait sittings), the ambassador was in all probability painted from life, albeit not from the ambassador, since the scene is but loosely based on an incident involving an envoy from Zanzibar said to have taken place many years earlier, and transposed to the 1860 period.[20] The kneeling ambassador, who is finely depicted with impressive naturalism, must be painted from a model dressed in appropriate East African costume. Many artists kept a prop and costume box, some of whose items came from theatrical suppliers; they also lent and borrowed garments and accessories to and from each other.

As in this case, most professional models, whatever their ethnicity, remain anonymous. A few are known by name and from a sketchy biography, but the topic is hard to research as hardly any gave their occupation as artist's model on any national Census. The visual evidence is thus all-important. One model whose life can be partially reconstructed from both visual and documentary sources is Fanny Eaton. She was born Fanny Antwistle or Entwhistle in Jamaica around 1835–6, and by the mid-1850s was married to a London cart- and cab-driver named James Eaton. They had half a dozen children, and lived near Coram Fields in north-central London. Fanny, in a manner typical of her class, worked as a laundress and cleaner, and also intermittently as a model for many artists (one of whom described her as 'mulatto' or mixed race) during the 1860s. As such, her employment is visible in various guises.

In November 1859 she appears to have been employed by a group of young artists working on various subject pictures. Or just possibly, she modelled at one of the informal life classes organised by artists who thereby shared the cost. The three artists we know of through their drawings of Fanny Eaton at this date were Frederick Sandys, Albert Moore, and Simeon Solomon.[21]

Following from these and other studies, Fanny appears, not always recognisably, as Sandys' Morgan le Fay (Birmingham Museum & Art Gallery), as Moore's The Mother of Sisera (Tullie House Museum Carlisle) and as Solomon's The Mother of Moses (1860, Delaware Art Museum), based on the earlier studies. Models' details were shared among artists, and it is therefore no surprise that Fanny Eaton was then employed by Rebecca Solomon (Simeon's sister) and by Joanna Boyce Wells during 1860, by John Everett Millais in 1863, by Ford Madox Brown in 1864, by DG Rossetti in 1865, by Millais again in 1866–7 and by other as yet unidentified artists. She would seem to have given up modelling around 1870; by 1881 she was recently widowed, living in Chelsea with her seven children ranging in age from 24 to 2 years, and working as a seamstress. Twenty years later she was employed as a cook in Oakfield Isle of Wight. In 1911, she was back in London, aged 75. As with most models, working for artists was one phase in a lifetime's occupations. The casual nature of the work makes it very difficult to track; at the same time, sitting to artists for dark-skinned figures was an employment niche that only members of the African diaspora could exploit. At the same time, as Pamela Nunn has observed, 'what is striking about the employment painters made of Mrs Eaton ... is the ambiguity of the ethnic identity they gave [her]'.[22] As with theatrical casting, a model played the role assigned, rather than him/her self. Moreover, with visual art, the viewer should never accept a painted appearance at face value. An intentional portrait has claims to accuracy that do not apply to a face or figure drawn from a model.

All the examples so far are from British art works, but in respect of dark-skinned figures in the 'high' arts of painting and sculpture, British artists followed a pan-European trend. The French sculptor Charles Cordier provides a clear illustration, not least owing to his specialism in depicting a wide variety of ethnic 'types' modelled from individual men and women. Two of his most celebrated pieces were 'Said Abdullah' and the 'African Venus'. The first of these was exhibited at the 1848 Paris Salon as *Saïd Abdallah, of the Mayac Tribe, Kingdom of Darfour* and exists in a number of casts, including one in the British Royal Collection. In this case the model's history is at least partially known.

His name was Seid Enkess and his date of birth was given as 1821. He was recorded as saying he was born in a region variously transcribed as 'Mayak' and 'Maick' which may be that now known as Mayak'elo in Dire Dawa, Ethiopia, and had travelled through Sennar and Darfur. At about age seven he had been captured by a raiding party of Turks, Egyptians and Albanians, and sold in Cairo to an Italian merchant, by him to the Prussian consul in Livorno and finally to Prince Galitzine, in whose entourage he arrived in France around 1838. A year or so later he became an artist's model.[23] His employers included the sculptor Francois Rude and Charles Cordier. According to Cordier, in 1847 'a superb Sudanese appeared in my studio. Within a fortnight I made this bust ... I had it cast and sent to the Salon' (see Musee d'Orsay website 'Facing the Other Charles Cordier 1827–1905 Ethnograhic Sculptor'; in fact Enkess appeared in Rude's studio). The same year Enkess agreed to a life cast of his head and shoulders being made for the Societe ethnologique (now in the Musee de l'homme, Paris) as an example of 'Sudanese' ethnic type.

The cast exhibited at the 1848 Salon was plaster; the bronze version was first shown in Paris in the first quarter of 1851 when 'Mayac' and even Dafur were perhaps deemed too obscure and the work was re-named 'Negro from Tambouctou' and then from May to October at the Great Exhibition in London. The success of the worked shaped Cordier's subsequent career. He promptly sought a young African woman whose head and shoulders he sculpted as a companion piece to Said Abdallah.

The model's name and origin are as yet undiscovered, but she too was presumably working in the Paris studios. Entitled 'African Venus', her bust was shown at the Salon in 1852 and in the same year Queen Victoria commissioned copies of both African Venus and Said Abdallah (in his guise as 'Negro from Timbuctoo') as birthday and Christmas gifts for Prince Albert. When versions were shown in Paris and London in 1860 and 1861, Said was entitled 'Nubian Negro' and Venus was called 'Negro Woman of the African coast' which presumably signals a West African identity.

Later Cordier produced another pair, one variously known as 'Negro from the Soudan' and 'Negro in Algerian costume' (at the Musee d'Orsay[24]) for which the model is said to have been an Algerian who 'played the tam-tam in the festivities of Algiers' Muslim community before Ramadan'; and 'Capresse des Colonies' the model for which is thought to have been a Caribbean woman in Paris.[25] Her bust exhibited in London in 1861 translated the title as 'Negro Woman of the Colonies'.

Finally, but by no means the only remaining example from Europe in this period, one can cite the man named Mohammed (or so-called by his employers) from somewhere in north Africa, who worked as artists' model in Berlin, where in 1877 he was painted by Queen Victoria's daughter Vicky, Crown Princess of Prussia. The fine portrait that resulted was presented to her mother.[26]

Modelling for artists remained a niche occupation for men and women of African ancestry into the twentieth century, and there is scope for further research into this as yet unexplored area of labour history.

Notes

[1] chnm.gmu.edu/revolution/d/228/.
[2] See Bignamini and Postle, 1991.
[3] See Tate Collections NO55843.
[4] Tate Collection T10168.
[5] See also www.artnet.com/.../robinson/robinson9-9-4.asp.
[6] See Honour, *Image of the Black*, 23–7.
[7] Victoria & Albert Museum, London; see also http://www.telegraph.co.uk/culture/film/3675162/Black-Victorians.html?image=7.

[8] National Galleries of Scotland; see Marsh, 2005 # 46.

[9] Catalogue no: 1575.

[10] Art Institute of Chicago; see www.artic.edu/aic/aboutus/press/Captive_Slave_acquis.pdf.

[11] Manchester Art Gallery 1882.2; and see http://www.manchestergalleries.org/the-collections/search-the-collection/display.php?EMUSESSID=e1cbac244aeef7d86428c3379626e9ce&irn=16.

[12] Palace of Westminster; see also www.artinthepicture.com/artists/David_Wilkie/.

[13] British Museum 1919.216.35; see http://www.britishmuseum.org/research/search_the_collection_database/search_object_details.aspx?objectid=73920.

[14] See http://collage.cityoflondon.gov.uk/collage/app?service=external/FullScreenImage&sp=Zjohn+gilbert&sp=10073&sp=X&sp=2 and http://collage.cityoflondon.gov.uk/collage/app?service=external/FullScreenImage&sp=Zjohn+gilbert&sp=9093&sp=X&sp=2 apologies for watermark over the figure's face.

[15] http://collections.vam.ac.uk/item/O70225/watercolour-mulatto-boy/?print=1.

[16] Walker Art Gallery WAG 1601; see http://www.liverpoolmuseums.org.uk/walker/collections/19c/windus.aspx.

[17] NGI see http://www.copia-di-arte.com/a/mulready-william/the-toy-seller-1.html.

[18] See http://commons.wikimedia.org/wiki/File:Edwin_Longsden_Long_Uncle_Tom_and_Little_Eva.JPG.

[19] NPG 4969 and see http://www.npg.org.uk/collections/search/portrait.php?search=ap&npgno=4969.

[20] See Marsh, *Black Victorians*, 2005.

[21] For Sandys, see Elzea, 2001, nos. 1.A.169–71; and http://www.britishmuseum.org/research/search_the_collection_database/search_object_details.aspx?objectid=737096&partid=1&searchText=sandys&fromDate=1859&fromADBC=ad&toDate=1859&toADBC=ad&numpages=10&orig=%2fresearch%2fsearch_the_collection_database.aspx&currentPage=1. For Solomon see Cruise, 2005 #32, #33 and fig.25 and http://www-cm.fitzmuseum.cam.ac.uk/dept/pdp/opac/cataloguedetail.html?&priref=13634&_function_=xslt&_limit_=10.

[22] Nunn, 1993, 13.

[23] Cordier, 2004, 203, my translation.

[24] Musee d'Orsay RF 2997 LUX27 http://www.musee-orsay.fr/en/collections/index-of-works/notice.html?no_cache=1&nnumid=1856.

[25] http://www.musee-orsay.fr/en/collections/index-of-works/notice.html?no_cache=1&nnumid=015060&cHash=6623397d0d.

[26] See http://www.royalcollection.org.uk/egallery/object.asp?maker=12650&object=403642&row=2.

References

Bignamini, Ilaria and Martin Postle. *The Artist's Model: Its Role in British Art from Lely to Etty*. Nottingham: Nottingham University Art Gallery, 1991 (reprinted 1999).

Cordier, Charles. *Charles Cordier 1827–1905: l'autre et l'ailleurs*: Exhibition catalogue, Musee d'Orsay Paris, La Martiniere, 2004.

Cruise, Colin. *Love Revealed: Simeon Solomon and the Pre-Raphaelites*. London and New York: Merrell, 2005.

Elzea, Betty. *Frederick Sandys 1829–1904 – A Catalogue Raisonne.* Woodbridge Suffolk: Antique Collectors Club, 2001.

Honour, Hugh. *The Image of the Black in Western Art,* vol. iv/2. Harvard: Harvard University Press, 1989.

Marsh, Jan, ed. *Black Victorians: Black People in British Art 1880—1900.* Manchester: Lund Humphries with Manchester City Art Gallery, 2005.

Nunn, Pamela Gerrish. "Artist and Model: Joanna Mary Boyce's 'Mulatto Woman.'" *Journal of Pre-Raphaelite Studies* Fall (1993): 12–5.

Bhit vil chapter into

Looking for Work: The Black Presence in Britain 1860–1920

Caroline Bressey

Department of Geography, University College London, London, UK

Focusing on the years between 1860 and 1920, this paper considers how newspaper archives can contribute to our knowledge of the livelihoods of working black men and women. Although the empirical material comes predominately from the classified advertisement pages of digitalised English newspapers, references to Irish, Welsh and Scottish newspapers are also made. The types of advertisements highlighted here form two main areas for discussion. Firstly, men and women advertising their availability to work in a wide range of domestic roles. Secondly, employers who were looking for black men and women to perform particular roles. The adverts are short, no more than a few lines, but they mark out spaces in the archives where black men and women become temporarily visible. The reasons why these men and women appear in these advertisements raise complex questions about race, identity and the ways in which racism may have impacted upon their ability to work.

Black Men and Women and the History of Labour in Britain[1]

Turning to page five on Tuesday 7 November 1876, readers of the *Liverpool Mercury* would have found a familiar page of classified advertisements. The page is neatly divided into columns: Agencies and Commissions, Companions, Housekeepers, etc., House Servants Wanted, House Servants Wanting Places, Employment Wanted, Scholastic, Medical, Apartments to be Let, Apartments Wanted, Miscellaneous Wanted, and Money. The advertisements themselves are densely packed into the columns. They are short. Each word costs money. Over 500 advertisements appear on this page reflecting the everyday and more unusual needs of the city's inhabitants. Although some are direct and specific, others are more open.

> A Good General SERVANT Wanted for a family of three. Wages £10 – Apply at 8, Hope-place, off Hope st.

> WANTED, two SERVANTS, one 18 and the other 14 years of age. – 12, Horne-street, West Derby-road.

> WANTED, immediately, in town by a professional Lady, well furnished DRAWING ROOM and BEDROOM, with good cooking. – Address B 52 Mercury office.

> A Respectable Householder Wants to BORROW £50 for two years, on a house. Rental £35. Repayable half yearly. No Professional lenders. – Address A 30, Mercury-office.

> By a respectable Young Man, a Situation as BARMAN in Cocoa Room or Public House. Total abstainer. Good references. – G. 118, Duke-street.

Readers inspecting the advertisements for a new employee would have found, amongst the advertisements for house servants looking for work, one placed by a man from Canada. It is advertisements such as this which form the focus of this paper.

> A Coloured Man (from Canada) desires a Situation as SERVANT in gentleman's family. Accustomed to horses. Age 50. Miss Cane, 130 Duke-street.

British labour history, indeed British history in general, continues to ignore the black presence in analyses of the nation's working class. In *New Left Review* Eric Hobsbawm recently commented that: 'I noticed a new labour history journal which has an article on blacks in Wales in the eighteenth century. Whatever the importance of this to blacks in Wales, it is not in itself a particularly central subject'.[2] To argue that black histories are of marginal importance and marginal interest is to ignore the role of race and racism in the making of the British working class. For the Victorian period the presence of a 'black community' is questionable and Norma Myers has argued that in England the oppression of black and white workers means that class solidarity through racially mixed communities was the most likely support network used by black workers.[3] As a result understanding where and how black people lived within British urban and rural communities is key to understanding how working class support networks were developed and manifested themselves and why, at times, they broke down, resulting in racial violence such as the riots which broke out in 1917 and 1919.[4] Without researching and acknowledging these sometimes uncomfortable histories our core understandings of British labour history cannot be complete.

Looking for Workers

In undertaking such historiography current researchers, who have access, are aided by recent changes in digital technologies that have altered availability to historical data on the black presence in Britain. Digitalisation has created the ability to undertake detailed keyword searches of archives including national census returns and newspapers such as the 'Times Digital Archive 1785–1985' and '19th Century British Library Newspapers'. The British Library collection includes regional newspapers like the *Liverpool Mercury* and specialist newspapers such as *The Era*, a London-based weekly paper that reported on the world of entertainment. These databases are proving to be significant methodological tools. They allow for needle-in-a-haystack searches that previously have been too time-consuming to undertake. The use of these research tools has created the research evidence for this paper.

Like all research tools there are faults. The methods of scanning these vast archives do not always capture the intricacies of identity. It remains too time-consuming to search around broad terms such as 'black' which result in returns on the colour of commodities, surnames and 'bad days' in politics. A host of racialised search terms were inputted into the databases to recover the results used here. 'Coloured man', 'coloured lady', 'coloured chambermaid', 'negress servant', 'coloured kitchen maid', 'coloured cook', 'West Indian cook', 'African nurse', 'coloured servant', and 'West Indian governess' are amongst the many combinations tried. The results highlighted here were further concentrated by limiting searches to advertisements. This excluded returns from journalistic coverage of news, sport and features on people. Results from these areas will prove useful in the future. For example, knowledge of a tattoo artist known as Professor Johnson comes from a general search for 'coloured man' in the *Liverpool Mercury* on 11 October 1880. Johnson worked out of a public house near the Sailor's Home and amongst his hundreds of customers was James Willey who had died from blood poisoning after having two tattoos. It is only because of the inquest into his death and the fact that Johnson, called as a witness, was identified as a 'coloured man' in the articles that we become aware that a tattoo artist living and working in Liverpool in the 1880s was a black man. However, reports by journalists filter the voices of workers and employers to a greater degree than appears to be the case on the pages of classified advertisements. Thus the advertisements, in an attempt to identify the voices of black workers, remains the focus of this piece.

As is highlighted by the Coloured Man from Canada, this method only reveals those men and women who had the colour of their skin recorded in the archives for some reason. This raises two issues, firstly of fundamental questions of race and racism in Britain. If it was not the normal practice to record the colour of a person's skin why have some people, and not others, been coloured in particular archives? Secondly, this uncertainty raises interesting but difficult issues of 'authenticity'. That is, how do we know someone who is given some identification of blackness is a person with African ancestry? Taking the 1881 census as an example there are a number of entries that reflect the complexities of identity revealed by the racialised records of the British population.

Working Records

The national census is of limited use to researchers of the black presence in Britain because the colour of a person's skin was not necessarily or systematically recorded.[5] In addition, the legacy of slavery means that a majority of men and women from the African diaspora in the census have 'British' surnames and an Anglican religion. Unlike Jewish and Irish individuals who can often be identified through the recording of place of birth and/or religion, these fields are of limited help in recovering the presence of individuals from the African diaspora. However, some recorders did make racialised comments on their census returns and these can also be highlighted through digital searches of the returns. These results can raise more questions than they can answer.

On 3 April, the night the national census was recorded in 1881, Henry Blackman was confirmed as head of the household where he lived at 50 Chesterfield Street, Brighton in the county of Sussex in southern England. He had been born in Lewes, about six miles from Brighton, around 33 years earlier. He lived with his wife Ellen Blackman who had also been born in Brighton. Ellen, aged 23, worked as a Charwoman. Henry's occupation is recorded as 'Nigger Minstrel'. Also living in Brighton was Henry Smith, also aged 33. He was a boarder on Thomas Street and also worked as a 'Nigger Performer'. Another couple, Henry and Annie Albery were also working as performers in Brighton. Henry, aged 25 and originally a Londoner was living with his 20-year-old wife at 16 Thomas Street. The couple are both recorded as working as minstrels, Henry as a 'Negro Minstrall' and Annie as a 'Nigger Minstrel Musician'. Family groups of performers were not only limited to couples. According to the April record, Charles Davies, 34, and his 13-year-old son both worked as a 'Negro Comedian Actor'. The Davies men lived with Clara Davies, wife, mother and an artificial florist maker, at 15 Grosvenor Terrace, Newington, London. On the same night in Leeds, Henry Ward, 23, was boarding at 16 Neville Street in the Yorkshire city. Originally from Paddington in west London he was working in Leeds as a 'Negro Comedian Actor'. Not far from the Scottish border on Rickergate, Carlisle, lived Mary and Charles Ashley. Both worked as a 'Professional Negro Singer Musician'.[6]

Samuel Hill is one of the many men and women in the census who was not born in Britain. Originally from St Louis in the United States some time during his 34 years he had crossed the Atlantic and in 1881 was a boarder at a house on Mill Row, in Birchington, Kent. His occupation is recoded as 'Barber (Nigger)'. Also working in hair dressing was Frank May. A Londoner by birth, in 1881 May lived with his parents in the capital where the family worked as theatrical costume makers. Frank's occupation was specified as a 'Nigger Wig Maker'.[7]

The questions raised by all these returns are difficult to answer. Was Henry Blackman a black man who worked as a minstrel, or a white man who blacked-up? Are there any differences in ethnicity to be gleaned from descriptors of men and women as 'negro minstrels' rather than 'nigger minstrels'? Is it more or less likely that a 'negro singer musician' was a professional singer of African descent when compared to a 'nigger minstrel musician'? Michael Pickering's work on minstrelsy illustrates that companies made up with performers of African descent were popular in Britain. For example, in 1881–2 Haverly's Mastodon Minstrels consisting over 65 African-American performers toured Britain, and a number of them stayed on in Britain when the company returned to the United States.[8] Pickering argues that during the 1880s and 1890s minstrelsy became increasingly racist and that black performers had to deal with hardening racial attitudes. How these attitudes are reflected in the descriptors assigned by census recorders is difficult to ascertain. In the case of Frank May these questions are further complicated by the crossing out of 'Nigger' on the census return. By whom, why or what stage of the data collection this was done is unknown. As a result we do not know whether it was crossed out because Frank protested at such an ethnic identification, or an overly specific definition of his trade, or if it was deemed an inappropriate term by someone at a later date.

Knowledge of a place of birth cannot be taken as 'proof' of ethnicity either. We might be relatively confident that John Phillips, born in Freetown Sierra Leone, working as a Ships Cook and Steward and on the date of the census living at 21 Copenhagen Place, Limehouse, was an African man. Similarly, it is likely that Colin Graham, born in Sierra Leone and aged 37 years at the time of the census was an African man. In 1881 he lived in Camberwell south London, with his Hertfordshire-born wife and worked as a public accountant. But there is very little to suggest that Jamaican-born Caroline Bray, aged 50 in 1881 who lived in Hampshire was a Jamaican of European or African descent, or a woman of Indian, Chinese or Creole descent. India was the place of birth given for William De Lancey, aged 29, who appears in the Great Grimsby returns for Lincolnshire with his wife Laura, aged 22. She worked as a singer/actor, her husband is named a Negro Comedian (Actor). The same ambiguities of 'blackface' entertainment' can be applied to William, but his return also highlights that the term 'negro' was not only used to describe people of African descent. 'Educated guesses' on what the recorders may have meant by their racialised definitions are imbued with assumptions about the intersections of race, class and work in British and imperial societies.[9] What is interesting about the classified advertisements placed in the columns of British newspapers is that identity through registers of various geographical registers such as region (e.g., West Indian), nationality (e.g., Canadian) or 'ethnicity and race' (e.g., the colour of a person's skin) was specified both by black men and women looking for work, and employers seeking to fill specifically racialised jobs.

Looking for Work

The men and women who advertised their availability to work in *The Times* and other newspapers were making a financial investment. Comprehensive scales of charges for placing advertisements in *The Times* do not survive for the entire run of the newspaper. Details that do survive from 1833 to 1835 show that the cost of 3-, 4- and 5-line advertisements was 1s 6d and an 8-line advertisement cost 5s. Evidence from the paper in 1914 states that advertisements cost one penny per word.[10] Similarly, rates published in the *Western Mail* in 1899 (see Figure 1) reflect the importance of sculpting an advert that would fit your budget.

Although this scale illustrates it was possible to have repeat advertisements, most of the men and women in this review appear to have only placed an advertisement once. There are a few exceptions. On Monday 18 December 1876 a 'respectable, well-educated Young Coloured Man' who had recently arrived in England (although he does not say from where) advertised his availability for work in the *Liverpool Mercury*. He was specifically looking for a position in a Mercantile Office to start

Words	Once		Three Times		Six Times	
	s.	d.	s.	d.	s.	d.
12 Words	0	6	1	0	1	6
19 "	0	9	1	6	2	3
26 "	1	0	2	0	3	0
33 "	1	3	2	6	3	9
40 "	1	6	3	0	4	6
Each Extra 7 Words	0	3	0	6	0	9

This prepaid scale was for Situations Offered or Wanted, Apartments, Money Wanted, Partnerships, Lost and Found, Miscellaneous, etc., which would be inserted into the *Western Mail* and the *Evening Express*. This rate did not apply to advertisements placed by business or notices from public bodies.
Adapted from the *Western Mail*, Cardiff 6 January 1899.

Figure 1 Rates Paid for Advertisements 1899.

immediately or in the beginning of January 1877. He advertised himself as having a sound knowledge of bookkeeping and a 'fair legible hand'. He assured future employers that he could produce 'excellent certificates' as to sobriety and honesty. His advert was repeated on Saturday 23 December 1876. The *Liverpool Mercury* also carried two adverts for a 'Coloured Young Man' on Tuesday 18 and Saturday 22 November 1879. He was looking to 'make himself useful' in a situation in a hotel, billiard room or as a messenger for offices or shops. On 10 November 1900 a 'Coloured Young Lady' advertised her desire to find work in a Bazaar or Playhouse as an attendant in *The Era*. The advertisement was also carried on 17 November 1900.[11]

In Service

As for many working people, domestic service was an important form of employment for those of African descent living in Britain. Advertisements do not usually carry the name of the potential employee, but they occasionally provide initials, a domestic contact address (often the offices of the newspaper are given as an alternative) and provide an indication of the kind of work men and women expected, or hoped, to undertake.

For men the adverts primarily reveal searches for employment as indoor servants, butlers, valets, grooms and coachmen. In March 1857 a 'Coloured

Young Man' offered his services as an under butler or footman in the *Liverpool Mercury*. The following year a 20-year-old London-based 'In-Door servant, Coloured' advertised his willingness to work in or out of livery. In 1860 once again a 'coloured young man' was searching for a position as a footman or groom in *The Times*.[12] In the summer of 1872 another advert for an indoor servant was placed by a 'Coloured. Obliging, trustworthy, and good servant'. On 17 April 1878 a 'Man-Servant. Coloured' who spoke English and Portuguese advertised his skills as a waiter in *The Times*.[13] Four months later the *Liverpool Mercury* carried an advert for a highly respectable and well-educated 'Coloured young man' who was looking for a job as an indoor servant or a footman.[14]

For women, the advertisements reflect a long link with the caring professions. In May 1886 a 30-year-old 'coloured woman' with very good references advertised her desire to find a new position as a nurse. The following year a 'West Indian coloured nurse' advertised her services. She was only willing to work with one baby and only for 'a gentleman's family'. In April 1891 another 'West Indian Coloured Nurse' and skilled needlewoman offered her services. Another example comes from September 1899 when an advert for a West Indian 'black nurse' appeared in London's *Daily News*. This middle-aged woman was looking for a new position in a gentleman's family that would start by the end of September.[15]

Men also advertised themselves to work in hotels and clubs, particularly as waiters, including, for example, the 'coloured man, age 20' who was looking for work as a waiter in a hotel or clubhouse in 1863. He could be contacted at 41 Great Castle-Street, Oxford Street, London.[16] An advert in the *Glasgow Herald* on Wednesday 29 August 1866 simply reported: A young Man (Coloured) desires a situation as Waiter'. Both men and women worked as cooks. In August 1880 an advert for 'Cook (Plain), or General servant, Coloured Person' was placed in *The Times*.[17] In 1902 *The Times* announced the opening of a new club in London. The Columbia was to be located at the Avondale Hotel in Piccadilly, its aim to act as a meeting place for British subjects and US citizens 'for the convenience of American visitors, and the furtherance of mutual good feeling between the citizens of the two countries'. In order to provide authentic cuisine, 'a skilled chef from the United States and an "Aunt Sally" negress cook from the South' were to be employed in the club's kitchen.[18] In March 1914 a good 'plain cook' then based in Brixton advertised for a new position that would come with the help of a kitchen maid. Interestingly, she described herself as a trustworthy and superior '*light coloured* West Indian'.[19] Did an increasing hostility towards black people encourage this kind of personal identification?

An awareness of racism in Britain is reflected in some of the adverts placed by future employers. Isaac Green placed one such example in *The Era* in 1880. He was looking for 'a good attraction' for his Sheffield bar. In his advert he made it clear that he would not object to employing 'a coloured woman'.[20] This is different to those employers who sought out coloured women for their bars and pleasure gardens that are highlighted below. An awareness of racism is similarly reflected in a *Times* advert placed in November 1919. The potential employer was seeking a domestic servant who would work in her house in Hampstead but also help look after her 'unspoiled' young son. The position came with its own bedroom and the support of daily help. The woman would have to be good natured, but the fact that it was clearly stated that a 'coloured woman or foreigner' would be made welcome, reflects an understanding that life for black men and women was becoming increasingly difficult.[21]

Wanted to Work

There are a number of examples where those looking to employ people specify the desired skin colour of future employees. They vary from what might be assumed specialities, to racialised 'freaks' and employers' desire for an 'authentic' depiction of race. For example, in October 1880 an advert was place for a 'Coloured Man-Servant' who would make himself generally useful in a professional house. Men who were interested were to apply at 57 Great Russell Street opposite the British Museum in central London. In February 1899 the *Western Mail* carried an advertisement for a stoker to operate a stationary boiler in a factory in Bristol, a 'coloured man used to marine boilers' was preferred. Inserted between adverts for cocoa rooms and pastry girls in the *Liverpool Mercury* from April 1900 a request for a 'coloured lady' to undertake 'light business' appeared. What this might have entailed was not expanded upon.[22]

On the Stage and on Display

The pages of adverts confirm that the world of entertainment provided employment for black men and women as actors, singers and stage 'novelties'. Most of these opportunities reflect a demand for men and women to fulfil racialised and sexualised roles. For women this is particularly reflected in requests for barmaids and for men in roles as 'animal trainers'. The role of the circus as an employer of black men has been noted by historians of the Victorian spectacle. John Turner's work on the British circus has recovered a number of references to black Circus artists. They worked as lion tamers, tight rope walkers, clowns, horse riders and animal trainers. [23] The newspaper advertisements directed specifically at 'coloured' men or noting a preference for coloured men are mostly for animal trainers although an advert from a menagerie in Lockerby suggests that the men were not necessarily being asked to perform.

> WANTED a Steady Man as Animal Keeper. One that will enter the Lion's Den and give a performance if required. A Coloured Man Preferred. [24]

Advertisements similar to these were posted in the *Era* by the East London Aquarium in Bishopsgate (22 September 1883) and circuses and menageries based all over Britain including: Preston (22 April 1893), Pontypool (20 April 1895), Pontypridd (1 June 1895), North Shields (27 June 1896), Chorley, Lancashire (21 May 1898), St Ives (11 May 1899), Northumberland (May 1899), West Hartlepool (3 April 1897), Boness (3 November 1900) and Leeds (1 December 1900).

Black women were also seen, by some, as a fashionable addition to their entertainment staff. In April 1885 an advert appeared in the *Liverpool Mercury* for a woman to entertain guests at a hotel and pleasure gardens. A 'young coloured woman' who could sing and play the piano was preferred, but she had to be 'attractive'. [25] In July 1887 The Old Ship in Worksop also wanted a 'coloured lady' to perform as a pianist and vocalist. Five years later two positions for 'coloured' women appeared in the same column of *The Era* in August 1892. The first offered suitable 'coloured lady vocalists' comfortable and permanent situations. Those interested were asked to attend rehearsals at the Assembly Rooms at Crewkerne in Somerset. The second advert came from the Lyric Theatre in west London which required a 'coloured lady singer' as a lead performer. Four years later the Rotunda Theatre, Liverpool advertised for 'coloured people' to perform on their stage. [26]

Black women were also encouraged to apply for jobs as barmaids. Although not in the realm of domestic service, bar work was an important form of employment for Victorian women, with over 27,000 working behind the bar at the time of the 1901 census. [27] It was also a relatively well-paid job and Peter Bailey has highlighted reports of women who served upper- and middle-class patrons preferring it to work as a clerk or governess. In September 1885 an advert was placed in the *Era* for a barmaid in Stockton which specifically asked for a 'coloured lady'. She did not have to have any experience but a professional was preferred. In Birmingham in June 1895 a position as a barmaid at the Manchester Hotel came up. Again no experience was necessary, but only a 'coloured lady' would be successful, and all applicants were asked to enclose a photograph with their references.[28] While working-class women in working-class pubs were not held in high esteem, women who worked in high-class salons were often employed to be handsome, showy and attractive additions to the pub.[29] Although the specificity of requesting a woman of colour implies a landlord's desire to employ a barmaid that would be an alluring addition to his or her staff, how this desirability compared to that of white women is as yet unclear. That Isaac Green's previously featured advertisement for a 'good attraction for a bar' in Sheffield included a 'coloured woman' implies that women of colour were considered attractive and desirable in a similar manner to her white sisters. However, without knowledge of the kind of public house the women were being invited to work in, it is again difficult to know whether they were seen as part of an attractive and alluring idea of the Victorian woman (with all the problematic ideas of femininity attached to that), or part of a marginalised lower working-class group of barmaids.

While the degree of inclusively held within these requests can be debated, other advertisements clearly locate black men and women within the realms of the exotic or freak. In May 1891, the Volunteer Inn in Salford placed an advert for 'all kinds of bar novelties and attractions' as well as for a 'coloured lady or Zulu man'.[30] In addition to novelty roles in bars, a complex range of stage roles were available for both men and women. In 1890 the Coliseum Music Hall in Sheffield advertised for 'novelties' to perform on dates in April and beyond. Particularly desired was a 'Giant, dwarf or coloured lady'.[31] An illusionist based in Newcastle-on-Tyne in February 1886 urgently needed a 'coloured lady and a negro boy' for his act.[32] Both these opportunities seem closer to positions of bar novelties than acting roles that were sometimes available.

The stage version of Harriet Beecher Stowe's 'anti-slavery novel' *Uncle Tom's Cabin* remained popular in late Victorian England and supported numerous performances across the country which also sustained an Uncle Tom's Cabin Company. In December 1884 the company advertised for 'coloured lady and gentleman vocalists or dancers' for an immediate start and a long engagement at the Theatre Royal Cheltenham, and again in October 1885 when the company was based at the Theatre Royal Canterbury.[33] In October 1892 another 'young lady (coloured)' was wanted for the role of Topsy in Uncle Tom's Cabin then on at the Theatre Royal, Doncaster with a run in Grimsby to follow.[34]

How men and women felt about taking these parts or the opportunity they had to take non-racialised roles is hard to ascertain. There are advertisements in *The Era* from men and women who were eager to work in the theatre industry in any capacity. In 1886 a 'coloured young man' who had just finished a provincial tour with Wilson Barrett and company sought a new engagement for a small stage part or general services. A similar position was sought by a 'respectable coloured man' the following year. This man sought any situation and promised to make himself generally useful. In November 1900 a 'coloured young lady' placed an advert requesting a job as an assistant in a bazaar or playhouse. [35]

It is not clear how often advertisements for non-racialised roles would have presented equal opportunities for black and white performers. The singer Amy Height was a respected soprano and 'semi-comic' vocalist. She was described in the Cardiff *Western Mail* as a 'beautiful Octoroon' and 'the only coloured lady on the music-hall stage' in 1891. [36] The adverts featured here suggest this was an exaggeration, but it may be one that accurately reflects the limited roles available to performers of African descent.

Geographies of Workers

A substantial number of domestic servants of African descent are likely to have been born in Britain, but the advertisements reveal that those who were looking for work included men and women who had travelled to Britain from across the Atlantic and around the empire. As well as the Coloured Man from Canada and the Young Coloured Man recently arrived in England who advertised in the *Liverpool Mercury* in 1876, there were a number of men and women who reveal something of their geographical biographies in their advertisements. Some present subtle indications, such as one man's declaration that he had been in English service for 13 years. [37] Others give clearer indications of their past geographies and passages from Africa, the United States, Canada, the West Indies and Australia.

The Times carried a number of these advertisements. In 1879 a 30-year-old 'Coloured man (Egyptian)' who spoke English, Italian, Arabic and a little French was looking for work as a valet or in-servant although he was happy to travel. [38] On Monday 15 March 1880 a 'Coloured man from Africa' published his need for a new job as a valet or in-door servant. Age 25 and standing 5ft 7inches he came with 12 years good personal character and spoke Italian, German and English. His current position was coming to an end on 1 April 1880. He was able to repeat his advert on 16 and 23 March 1880. Three years later a 'coloured young man' of 20 who spoke French and English marketed his skills as an indoor servant. He described himself as a 'Half-cast Anglo-American' with good references. [39] Another 'young coloured young man. Just arrived from the States' hoped to find work as a valet or butler in October 1894. [40] The *Liverpool Mercury* carried advertisements for a 'Young Coloured man from the States' in June 1899 and a 'Young Coloured Man (American)' in June 1900. In May 1900 a 'Coloured Lady from Africa' had advertised her need for a sitting room and bedroom in the Huskisson Street area of Liverpool for a few weeks in June.[41] The following month the *Western Mail* carried an advert for a young 'coloured man' who was 'just from Australia' and looking for work as a handy man.[42]

Wanting to Travel

These advertisements display a certain degree of mobility. The advertisements do suggest that, unsurprisingly, men and women had different reasons for travelling. On Tuesday 26 May 1874 a 'Coloured man' who spoke four languages promoted his availability to work as a valet or travelling servant.[43] In May 1882 a 'young coloured man' announced his desire to find work as a valet and he had no objection to yachting. Nor did the 'coloured man' who was seeking work as a valet or butler in April 1885.[44] The following month a 'middle-aged coloured woman' advertised for a position as a nurse with a baby, but she was very specifically looking to work for a family who were travelling to Australia. In July 1885 a 'coloured woman' who worked as a nurse at 35 Linden Gardens in Bayswater, west London, placed an advert. She was looking to continue working as a nurse and hoped to find a position caring for an elderly lady or one child. She did not object to travel as part of the job. In the autumn of 1898 The *Glasgow Herald* posted a situation wanted by a 'young experienced coloured man as traveller'. In May 1907 another nurse, a 'West Indian. Coloured' who could take care of a young baby placed an advert. Aged 40, she was also prepared to travel if required.[45]

Longings to return home are also subtly revealed in these advertisements. In 1887 a 'coloured' woman, then working at Oakhill Road in Putney, south west London, advertised for an engagement that would enable her to return to the West Indies. She would work as a maid or nurse. The following decade, in October 1899, 'a young negress, from Jamaica, anxious to return home' advertised for a position as a nursemaid 'to any lady' who would pay for her passage home. Women's employers would sometimes place similar adverts on their employee's behalf. One such recommendation was placed by Mrs Caulfield, of Sunninghill in April 1881. She wished to recommend a 'nurse (West Indian)' with a 'view to sending her out to her native country'.[46]

European Geographies of Work

Employment that involved touring and performing, such as the circus, deserves pan-European research in order to unearth the networks of employment that existed across the continent. In 1879, the circus performer Miss LaLa, also known as the 'African Princess', appeared in Britain.[47] She performed in Manchester and in London at the Westminster Aquarium, displaying her skills as a strongwoman, wirewalker and trapeze artist. She also performed in Paris at the Cirque Fernando where she was painted by Degas. Miss LaLa was born in 1858 in Stettin (then in Germany, now in Poland) and was a popular performer. John Turner's work on the British circus has also revealed links to broader European connections. For example, Joseph Hiller described by Turner as 'reputedly black or a mulatto', toured Britain between 1829 and 1842. He set up his own company which toured to the Cirque de Champs-Elysees, Paris in 1844. Hiller had a daughter, Grace Hillerm, who also became a horse rider in the circus, but she is believed to have remained in Paris. George Christoff a tight rope performer and vaulter was the son of Christopher, a black man who was 'one of the finest rope dancers of the world'. Christoff ran a company under his own management in Birmingham in 1856, but his son performed in Lisbon and Moscow. George's career ended badly and he was seen in Dublin in 1873 'blown out with beer and gout'.[48]

The experiences of LaLa, Hiller and Christoff hint at the geographies of mobility that existed for men and women who were part of touring shows. Although Miss LaLa was known as the 'African Princess', her identity did not shape her role within the circus. As we have seen above, certain roles, such as lion tamers were racialised and this seemed to remain the case throughout Europe, or certainly as British companies toured around the continent. In March 1883 Powell and Clarke's circus was in need of a 'coloured man or woman, to perform with the serpents' in Ireland. A similar advert was placed by a circus in Trillick, Tyrone, Ireland in 1895. They required a man who was used to performing animals and they preferred a coloured man for the role. In September 1900 Bostock and Wombwell's Menagerie advertised for an animal trainer. Based in the north of France the successful candidate would have their passage paid for from London. The trainer did not have to be a coloured man, but they hoped to hear from 'Davis, Coloured Man'.[49] There is a need for British black history to connect far more closely to the European experience. An understanding of the experiences and links between race, racism and everyday living, everyday forms of survival and resistance undertaken by black people throughout European histories needs to be developed. Mapping the historical geographies of the European circus could be an interesting way to examine (for example, through reviews) differing attitudes to race across the continent.

Occasionally, black women would be specifically requested for posts which included travel. In October 1892 an advert was placed in *The Era* for a 'good-looking coloured lady to travel'. This particular position was permanent with 'good wages' and housing.[50] Further details would be sent on receipt of a photograph, but no more about the position or where the travel destinations might be was revealed. Usually employers were more forthcoming about the employment opportunities and their location. In April 1893 an International Agency in St Petersburg was keen to employ 'Dancers, Lady Gymnasts, American Coloured Lady Vocalists and Dancers and Novelties of every description' for the 'most brilliant Variety Establishment and Pleasure Gardens in Europe'. For a woman interested in spending time in Belgium there was an opportunity in Ghent for 'a coloured woman to sing and make herself useful in plays and concerts' in 1892. The position came with board, lodging and a salary for three months – perhaps not a bad option for someone who wanted to try out a new place at the start of their career.[51]

The role of doorman may have also been one which black men found themselves able to access across Europe. Advertising for a position in Ireland in 1895, although this time through the *Era*, James' Waxwork exhibition on Henry Street in Dublin promoted their need for a 'smart coloured man' as a doorman. Again applicants were required to send details of their age, height and salary with a photograph. A permanent position was on offer for a suitable employee, but the job was available again the following summer.[52] The London-born artist Glyn Philpot painted a number of Africans during his career in the 1920s and 1930s including a doorman of African descent holding open the Entrance to the Tagada, Paris in 1931. The extent to which men and women found themselves fulfilling stereotypical roles across Europe requires the establishment of cross-cultural research networks across the continent.

Future Work

These brief insights on men and women's work highlight some of the questions of race, racism and labour that need to be better integrated within histories of work in Britain. Although research on occupations associated with black workers, particularly seamen, has been undertaken, new research technologies mean that assumptions that black men and women were not present in a variety of labour markets can no longer be maintained.[53] Black men and women were employed in a range of working-class trades from domestic servants to barmaids, nurses to valets. The advertisements also reveal that a number of British jobs were racialised in a variety of ways, some requiring greater 'authenticity' than others. The degree to which black workers were disadvantaged by their racialisation would have varied, both among individuals and between types of work. Clearly, racial inequality affected all workers. Presumably a white woman could not apply for a job that specified a woman of colour. Did men and women, and later unions, protest against the racialisation of jobs in Britain, if so, why? Did they argue for equality of employment for all or through debates of xenophobia? How did these debates feed into the discussions of international solidarity and the eventual support for white labour rather than inclusive unionisation that developed in Britain at the end of the nineteenth century?[54]

The men and women highlighted here are visible because they or future employers deliberately brought attention to the colour of their skin in an advertisement. This paper has drawn attention to their presence in the archives, but raises a number of questions that are difficult to answer at present. Of greatest interest is why men and women, both employees and employers, used 'race' as a criterion of employability. For employers there are clearly a number of reasons: the desirability of the exotic; a need for 'authenticity'; a belief in appropriateness for a job and a desire to advertise their inclusively. The reasons why workers highlighted the colour of their skin are more difficult to assess. Was it a way to make themselves stand out from the crowd? Were there certain, positive, attributes associated with black female nurses, perhaps a legacy of the Jamaican Victorian nurse Mary Seacole? Did the legacy of slavery leave a residual fashion for black male accessories as footman, doormen and valets? Or do the adverts reflect the experiences of men and women who could afford to save themselves the humiliation of turning up for another interview when a door would be opened and then slammed shut?

The research tools used here deliver scant personal information about these men and women. Personal reflections on everyday forms of racism or how they were challenged and resisted are difficult to surmise. There is still little sense of the social and economic positions these men and women held within working-class communities. Their presence does, however, reflect how a better understanding of their senses of belonging can give a greater comprehension of the diversity of working people's lives and the communities in which they lived. The experiences of the black presence should be of interest to all historians of labour, not because they are exceptional, but because their presence, which may only amount to a small but critical fracture, prompts us to change our core understandings of the histories of working people in Britain.

Acknowledgements

I would like to thank all those who contributed to this paper through discussion at the Belonging in Europe conference and colleagues who commented on earlier drafts.

Notes

[1] The term 'black' in this paper is taken to mean people who belonged to the African diaspora. However, as outlined in the paper, British nineteenth century archives do not use consistent definitions of 'ethnicity' and so it is possible that a 'person of colour' or a 'black' person could be of African or Asian decent. There is certainly a need for further research both on the experiences of Asian people at work and the employment networks that they developed within working class communities, see Rozina Visram, *Asians in Britain: 400 Years of History* (London, 2002).

[2] Hobsbawm, 'Interview: World Distempers' 2010, 149.

[3] See Chater, Black People in England, 2007 and Myers', The Black Presence through Criminal Records' 1987 and *Reconstructing the Black Past*, 1996; also see Fryer, *Staying Power*, 1984.

[4] Jenkinson, *Black 1919*, 2009; Marika Sherwood, 'Lynching in Britain' 1999.

[5] For a more extensive discussion of the implication of this on institutional British archives see Bressey, 2006.

[6] Census returns: Blackman RG11/1080 folio 39, 23; Smith RG11/1080 folio 28, 1; Albery RG11/1080 folio 31, 7; Davies RG11/0541 folio 39, 33; Ward RG11/4537 folio 129, 6; Ashley RG11/5157 folio 140, 52.

[7] Census returns: Hill RG11/0983 folio 87, 21; May RG11/0336 folio 28, 3.

[8] Pickering, *Blackface Minstrelsy in Britain* 2008.

[9] Census returns: Phillips RG11/0469 folio 62, 4; Graham RG11/0675 folio 24, 42; Bray, RG11/1160 folio 9, 12; De Lancey RG11/3270 folio 65, 28.

[10] Private correspondence with Nick May, Deputy Archivist, News International.

[11] An important issue of referencing arises with new digital archives of newspapers – they often do not include page numbers. This means they will have to be accessed online rather than original paper form. Where page numbers are known they are given.

[12] Liverpool Mercury, 23 March 1857; *The Times* 24 March 1858, 15; *The Times* 15 May 1860, 14.

[13] *The Times* Wednesday 24 July 1872, 15; 17 April 1878, 20.

[14] *Liverpool Mercury* 17 August 1878.

[15] *The Times* 4 May 1886, 15; 14 April 1887, 16; 23 April 1891, 16; *Daily News* 5 September 1899.

[16] *The Times* 21 October 1863, 16.

[17] *The Times* 10 August 1880, 15.

[18] *The Times*, 29 May 1902, 12.

[19] *The Times*, 25 March 1914, 15 my emphasis.

[20] *The Era* 20 and 27 June 1880.

[21] *The Times* 22 and 24 November 1919, 3. The location of the advertisement reveals that Situations Required cost 1s per line.

[22] *The Times* 19 and 21 October 1880, 3; *Western Mail*, Cardiff 27 February 1899 2; *Liverpool Mercury* 18 April 1900.

[23] With thanks to The Circus Friends Association of Great Britain for this information which was sent to BASA (the Black and Asian Studies Association) as part of private correspondence in 1999. For further information on the John Turner Collection, visit the National Fairground Archive, at the University of Sheffield www.nfa.dept.shef.ac.uk/holdings/collections/turner.

[24] *The Era* 19 October 1889.

[25] *Liverpool Mercury,* 29 April 1885, 4.

[26] *The Era* 9 July 1887, 21; 27 August 1892; 11 July 1896.

[27] Bailey, 'Parasexuality and Glamour', 1990.

[28] *The Era* 19 September 1885 and 8 June 1895.

[29] Bailey, 1990.

[30] *The Era,* 2 May 1891.

[31] *The Era,* 26 April 1890.

[32] *The Era,* 27 February 1886.

[33] *The Era,* 27 December 1884 and Theatre Royal Canterbury 10 October 1885.

[34] A number of theatres also advertised for 'coloured people' for runs of Uncle Tom's cabin, e.g., 'Coloured People' wanted for a performance of Uncle Tom's Cabin at the Lyric, Hammersmith, *The Era* 2 May 1896.

[35] *The Era* Saturday 25 September 1886; 17 July 1887; 10 and 17 November 1900.

[36] *Western Mail* 25 August 1891, 4.

[37] The advert reads: BUTLER, Single-handed. Coloured man. Age 27. Been in English service 13 years....*The Times* Wednesday 23 June 1886, 19.

[38] The contact name provided is Abdool. *The Times* 30 December 1879, 12.

[39] *The Times* 15 March 1880, 3; *The Times* Friday 23 November 1883, 16.

[40] *The Times* 22 October 1894, 16.

[41] *Liverpool Mercury* 28 June 1899; 20 June 1900; 15 May 1900.

[42] *Western Mail,* Cardiff, Wednesday 25 July 1900.

[43] *The Times* 26 May 1874, 15.

[44] *The Times* 22 May 1882, 19 and 20 April 1885, 15.

[45] *The Times* 22 May 1885, 14; 2 July 1885, 14; 10 May 1907, 15; *Glasgow Herald* 1 October 1898.

[46] *The Times* 28 October 1899, 19; 23 July 1887, 15; April 1881, 3.

[47] Marsh, *Black Victorians,* 2005.

[48] Turner, c/o the Circus Friends Association of Great Britain as above.

[49] *The Era* 17 March 1883 and 16 March 1895; 29 September 1900.

[50] *The Era* 29 April 1888.

[51] *The Era* 29 April 1893; 20 February 1892, 21.

[52] *The Era* 20 July 1895 and 27 June 1896.

[53] For examples for research on seamen see Jenkinson, 2009 and Frost ed. *Ethnic Labour and British Imperial Trade,* 1995.

[54] Kirk, *Comrades and Cousins,* 2003.

References

Bailey, Peter. "Parasexuality and Glamour: The Victorian Barmaid as Cultural Prototype." *Gender and History* 2, no. 2 (1990): 148–72.

Bressey, Caroline. "Invisible Presence: The Whitening of the Black Community in the Historical Imagination of British Archives." *Archivaria* 61 (2006): 47–61.

Chater, Kathleen. "Black People in England. 1660–1807." *Parliamentary History* 26, no. 2 (2007): 66–83.

Duffield, Ian. "Skilled Workers or Marginalised Poor? The African Population of the United Kingdom 1812–1852." *Immigrants and Minorities* 12, no. 3 (1993): 49–87.

Frost, Diane, ed. *Ethnic Labour and British Imperial Trade: A History of Ethnic Seafarers in the UK.* London, Routledge, 1995.

Fryer, Peter. *Staying Power: The History of Black People in Britain.* London, Pluto Press, 1984.

Gibson, Robin. *Glyn Philpot, 1884–1937: Edwardian Aesthete to Thirties Modernist.* London, National Portrait Gallery, 1986.

Hobsbawm, Eric. "Interview: World Distempers." *New Left Review* 61 (2010): 133–50.

Marsh, Jan. *Black Victorians: Black People in British Art 1800–1900.* Hampshire, Lund Humphries, 2005.

Myers, Norma. "The Black Presence through Criminal Records 1780–1830." *Immigrants and Minorities* 7, no. 3 (1987): 292–307.

Myers, Norma. *Reconstructing the Black Past: Blacks in Britain 1780–1830.* London: Routledge, 1996.

Jenkinson, Jacqueline. *Black 1919: Riots, Racism and Resistance in Imperial Britain.* Liverpool, Liverpool University Press, 2009.

Kirk, Neville. *Comrades and Cousins: Globalization, Workers and Labour Movements in Britain, the USA and Australia from the 1880s to 1914.* London, Merlin Press, 2003.

Pickering, Michael. *Blackface Minstrelsy in Britain.* Hampshire and Burlington, Ashgate, 2008.

Sherwood, Marika. "Lynching in Britain." *History Today* 49, no. 3 (1999): 21–3.

John Archer and the Politics of Labour in Battersea (1906–32)

Sean Creighton

Independent Researcher, Black & Asian Studies Association, Mitcham, UK

Born in Liverpool in 1863, John Archer spent time in the Americas before returning to Britain to become a well-known local politician within the emerging labour movement in Victorian and Edwardian London. This paper sketches his personal and political biographies highlighting the moments where his concerns about race, racism and the politics of Pan-Africanism and labour converged. Despite his pioneering role in London labour politics his biography remains fragmented. As such this paper reflects the problems inherent in investigating the role of black people in labour politics and the resulting troubles we have integrating their impact on broader political geographies of race and labour.

Introduction

Describing himself as 'a man of colour' and a Negro John Archer linked black and labour movement politics to demonstrate that Black people were capable of ruling themselves.[1] It must have been his parents who took him as a boy to see a 'famous company of American Negroes' perform 'that soul-stirring Negro tragedy Uncle Tom's Cabin' in Liverpool. As he told the African Progress Union (APU) in 1918 'from that moment the seeds of resentment were planted within me that have resulted in making me the race-man I am'.[2]

His election to Battersea Council in south west London in 1906 for the Progressive Alliance of socialists, labourites, radicals and Liberals was seen as a practical demonstration of the 1900 Pan-Africanist demand for the colonies to be given 'the rights of responsible government'. Archer went on to be Mayor of Battersea between 1913–4, and after the reorganisation of the Battersea labour movement in 1918 a leading local Labour Party activist. Although not a member of Battersea's large manual working class, he identified with it supporting improved working, social support and living conditions and fighting unfairness. He robustly expressed his views. While this essay sketches out his activities, there is still much we do not know about him and his role in the evolution of Labour politics in Britain.[3]

Growing Up

John Archer was born into a working-class family in Liverpool on 8 June 1863. His father, Richard Joseph Archer, was a ship's steward from Barbados. His mother Mary Theresa, nee Burns was an Irish Catholic. By the time of the 1871 Census his sister Mary and brother Albert had been born. The family lived in Blake Street a poor working-class road densely populated with labourers and trades people from a variety of backgrounds, predominantly Irish as well as Jewish families. Long demolished, it was situated in the heart of old Liverpool, at the bottom of Mount Pleasant.[4] As the family does not appear in the Census records for 1881 and 1891 it seems likely that Richard took it to Barbados. In which case John would have seen colonial rule and exploitation against which to judge his experiences of growing up in Liverpool. He is known to have travelled the world so perhaps he followed in his father's footsteps witnessing the hard life and dangers of being at sea.[5] He met Margaret a black woman born in Halifax on the Canadian east coast. They married and came to Britain.[6]

Living in Battersea

By 1894 John and Margaret had settled in Battersea on the south side of the Thames.[7] Four years later they were known to be living at 55 Brynmaer Road. According to the 1901 Census, John worked as a professional singer, but there is no other supporting evidence for this. After becoming a Councillor in 1906 he established a photographic studio at 208 Battersea Park Road. Some of his photographs of municipal facilities and members of its Executive Committee are in the 1908 and 1911 Annual Reports of the Battersea Trades & Labour Council.

Battersea was an exciting part of London for political activists. John Burns, the local socialist leader, and the local labour, radical and socialist organisations movement, had played leading roles in the New Unionist trade union explosion of 1889–92 overseeing the successful dockers and gas workers' strikes and the rapid growth of trade unionism especially amongst the less skilled and lower paid.[8] Battersea's Nine Elms district in the north-east of the area had a very large Irish Catholic population with a strong campaigning record on Irish self-determination.

Formed in 1894 Battersea Trades & Labour Council played a key role in the strengthening the Progressive Alliance between socialists, trade unionists Liberals and Radicals, which had got Burns elected as MP in 1892. The Alliance was necessary to ensure the defeat of the conservative Municipal Reformers. In 1894 the Alliance took control of the machinery of local government, the Battersea Vestry, implementing a municipal socialist agenda, and keeping control from 1900 when the Vestry was replaced by Battersea Metropolitan Borough Council.[9]

Progressive Politics

Coleridge Taylor chap

From his return to Britain Archer engaged in black politics. During her tours in 1893 and 1894 he met Ida B Wells 'rousing the people to the highest pitch of indignation against the lynching of Negroes'. His 'hero in American history' was John Brown.[10] He attended the first Pan-African Conference held in London in 1900 which demanded an end to colour and race prejudice. It also called on Britain in particular to give 'as soon as practicable, the rights of responsible government to the black colonies of Africa and the West Indies'. The Conference set up the Pan-African Association, with Archer elected to the Executive. The organisation was not long-lasting.[11] As well as being a keen activist of Pan-Africanism, Archer was closely involved in the politics of all working people in Britain.

There were connections between political activity for the interests of working people regardless of race. At the end of the Boer War, which the Battersea Progressives had opposed, Chinese indentured labourers were employed in the Rand gold mines.[12] In Britain both the Liberals and the labour movement were opposed to this. The local Progressives organised a demonstration in Battersea Park against the proposal. The specially made banner stated 'Battersea protests against the introduction of SLAVERY in the British Empire'.[13] While we do not know what Archer's view was he may well have shared Sylvester Williams's opposition to the nature of indentured labour, particularly if he had seen the conditions of Indian indentured workers in the West Indies.[14]

By 1906 he was a member of Battersea Labour League, the key organisation supporting Burns within the Progressive Alliance. The League was not affiliated to the Labour Party. This had been established in 1900 as the Labour Representation Committee (LRC). Having attended its launch Conference Burns had rejected the new organisation as being too narrow, preferring to continue to promote the Progressive Alliance approach. Although part of the Alliance Battersea Trades & Labour Council joined the LRC in mid-June 1902.

Consistent with his Progressive approach Burns accepted the invitation to join the Liberal Cabinet in December 1905 to the delight of some sections of the labour movement including the Trades Union Congress. He continued in the Cabinet after the success of the Liberals in the General Election on 8 February 1906. This also saw a big increase in the number of LRC-supported MPs. In February 1906 the Committee became the Labour Party. In April the national Party expelled the Battersea Trades & Labour Council from membership because of its involvement with Liberals in the Progressive Alliance.

In 1906 Archer was selected for a winnable seat in the Latchmere Ward for the Battersea Council elections. Clearly, the Progressives did not think his colour would be an electoral disadvantage. In the lead up to the elections that September he spoke at a large public meeting held in Battersea Park, and chaired an open air election meeting organised by the League on 14 October. He topped the Ward poll with 1051 votes. As a Councillor Archer was a member of the controlling group of a service delivery employer organisation that saw itself as part of the wider labour movement. This was not without difficulties in the relationship between the Council and the trade unions of its direct labour force. John went on the Council Committees overseeing the public baths, health and public works.[15]

Progressive politics was not restricted just to Parliament, the Council or the Poor Law Board of Guardians and issues relating to them. One of the most contentious issues in Battersea that took place in 1907 and 1908 was the attack by medical students on a statue of a brown dog that had been erected by the anti-vivisection movement, which had a strong local following because of the work of the Battersea Anti-Vivisection Hospital. A public meeting in support of the Brown Dog Memorial was held on 13 January 1908. Archer moved the resolution refusing to remove either the statue or the anti-vivisection inscription on it.[16]

Changing attitudes, especially the increasing attraction of ideas about independent labour representation and more militant socialist ideas, created splits within the Progressives. The local branches of the Social Democratic Federation and the Independent Labour Party co-operated through the Battersea Socialist Council. Some of the organisations in the Trades Council split off and formed Battersea Labour Party in 1908. At this time membership of the national party was only for organisations not for individuals.[17]

The August 1907 issue of the Socialist Council's newspaper *Battersea Vanguard* contains a sarcastic comment about Archer's interest in the writings on India of the SDF national leader HM Hyndman. This was part of a running campaign of belittling Burns and his Progressive supporters, and seems to have had no racist overtones.

In the November 1909 Council elections the Progressive Alliance, the Labour Party and the socialist organisations fielded separate lists of candidates. As a result the Conservative Municipal Reformers won control of the Council for three years. Archer failed to get re-elected. He remained a member of the Board of Guardians. The loss of municipal control in 1909 was such a shock that some of the factions dropped their differences.

At the 1912 Council election Archer was re-elected for Latchmere Ward. The controlling Progressive group elected him as Mayor for the period November 1913 to November 1914. The press were obsessed by the news of his nomination as a 'coloured' man and besieged him. He told a reporter 'This question of colour is a surprising attitude in a nation which prides itself on its liberty and equality, and which fifty years ago expended £20,000,000 to effect the liberty of the negro slave in America'.[18]

In his acceptance speech Archer said:

> My election to-night marks a new era. You have made history tonight. For the first time in the history of the English nation, a man of colour has been elected as mayor of an English borough. That will go forth to all the coloured nations of the world and they will look at Battersea, and say 'It is the greatest thing you have done. You have shown that you have no racial prejudice, but recognise a man for what you think he has done'.[19]

His election was noted in the city of his birth. Commenting on the increasing number of black children there, the *Liverpool Mercury* states: 'let us remember Battersea and speculate on their possible future!'[20]

One of the main reasons Archer stood for Mayor was the forthcoming Anglo-American Exhibition at White City in West London. He 'knew that it would be food for thought for those of the American whites, when they arrive here, to find that a Metropolitan Borough of London permitted a man of colour to be its Chief Magistrate'. His Mayoral election made him an important figure within international black circles. The news of his success was telegraphed across the Atlantic and reported in black newspapers in the United States.[21]

He received letters of congratulation from France, Germany, the United States and the West Indies. One of the first was from John Edward Bruce, the President of the Negro Society for Historical Research in New York. In his reply Archer hoped that news of his election would 'encourage you over in America where for so many years you have been suffering the injustice of inequality and not because of lack of brains but because of the racial prejudice that predominates the generality of the whites of your country'.

He continued:

> I am afraid that I would not have a very long life in the U.S.A. because I seem to be peculiarly formed, in other words, I have more of the fighting than peaceful quality within me and I could not put up with the indignities that our people have to put up with in the land of their birth.

He hung a picture calendar that he had been sent from the United States in his room at the Town Hall for Councillors, for officials and visitors to see: 'What Cheer. Dedicated to our 50th Anniversary of Freedom. Factors in our Progress'. He also displayed photographs of 'Members of our Race – Americans and others'. He was proud to be Mayor in the 50th Anniversary year of American negro emancipation.[22]

We know virtually nothing about Archer's detailed involvements in black politics and connections with other black people in London between 1906 and 1913. He was friends with the composer Samuel Coleridge-Taylor, regarding his death in 1912 as a blow to the race. When completing the 1911 Census return he recorded as visitors staying with him, Jane Rose Roberts, wife of the former President of Liberia (she is recorded as born in America, with 'Liberian' crossed out,) and Caroline Ternedes, a widow aged 41 who had been born in the West Indies.

In early January 1914 he attended 'Granny' Roberts's funeral. How she got to know the Archers and became their guest is not known. She had visited Britain on several occasions, met Queen Victoria, and raised funds to build a hospital in Liberia's capital. Visiting her at the Archers in 1910 a journalist noted that she looked like Queen Victoria. Archer explained to Bruce: 'She was very dear to us, and we feel her loss very acutely'. Jane is buried in Streatham Cemetery on Garratt Lane in Tooting, south London, in a grave purchased by Archer's wife Margaret.[23]

The Mayoral Role

Because Battersea Progressives did not believe in lavish expenditure by their Mayors, they gave Archer a budget of £150 which meant he could not afford the level of hospitality by Mayors elsewhere. His friend James Wilson, who helped him reply to the many letters he received, took it upon himself in a private and confidential letter to appeal to Bruce in the States for money to support Archer financially during his Mayorship. Bruce consulted a New York-based West Indian friend Dr York Russell who advised that he could 'not see how' Bruce could do anything without Archer's knowledge.[24]

Mayoral duties included attending events organised by local organisations. After an official visit to Battersea Chapel in York Rd on 21 December 1913, he broke with tradition by refusing to accept invitations to church services. The motives behind such invitations were causing wider concern, because a visit might be thought to confer dignity on a particular church or chapel. Neighbouring Wandsworth Council had a Committee examining the issue.[25]

Archer's refusal was not due to a religious objection. He was a practising Catholic. He attended functions of many charitable organisations along with the local Anglican Vicar Rev. Foster Pegg. They moved the vote of thanks to the Bishop of London at the Sunshine League Festival at Nine Elms Baths in early December, at which tea had been provided to 800 sick and needy children. Later they jointly handed out on behalf of local charities great coats, coal, bread, groceries and money to 321 people.[26]

Despite the success of his election, Archer was aware that racial prejudice was in operation and believed that at times it impacted upon his ability to lead in Battersea. This came to the public fore at a Council meeting in early 1914. On 15 January he had chaired a Town's Meeting about the problems with the way the London County Council (LCC) administered the scheme for feeding needy school children. The Meeting had appointed a deputation to see the LCC, and had wanted the Mayor to be a member. At the next Battersea Council meeting Archer explained that he had declined the invitation because he did not think that his involvement would help gain its objective. In the debate the Municipal Reform leader Haythornwaite called Archer prejudiced. This clearly hurt Archer because after an adjournment he told the Council that since he had become Mayor he had received letters calling his 'mother some of the foulest names that it is possible for a mother to be called'. He 'could not understand why there should be this opposition to' him. 'My dead mother has been called in question because she married a coloured man. ("Shame.") Am I not a man, the same as any other man? Have I not got feelings the same as any other man?' He suggested that opposition to him in the Council Chamber was 'because of his colour'. Haythornwaite denied it. The Council decided that as Mayor Archer should not be a member of the deputation.[27]

The last period of Archer's Mayoral office saw the beginning of the First World War. He launched an appeal for funds to relieve local distress amongst families of men who had volunteered for the front. Despite drenching rain, a large procession marched through the main streets of Battersea to promote it. Archer's period of office as Mayor ended in November 1914. Councils elected a new Mayor every year. Clearly expecting that the War would end quickly, Archer hoped that his successor 'would preside over a meeting to celebrate the declaration of peace' and urged him campaign 'to obtain money for the distressed in Battersea'. Archer returned to life as an ordinary Councillor, although he had obviously made his mark as he and Margaret were invited to join the King in February 1917 visiting hospitals around London. At some stage during the War he and Margaret moved to 214 Battersea Park Road presumably living above his photography studio.[28]

His attitude to the war came out clearly at the May 1918 Council meeting which considered a Committee recommendation to refuse a request for the payment of war bonuses to officers of the Council on military service. Archer successfully moved referral back to the Committee for reconsideration saying while 'he would never have gone to France', 'there were men who thought it was their duty to go, and amongst them were some of the men who it was now proposed to exclude from receiving war bonuses'.[29]

Pan-Africanism

On 21 May 1919 a Grand Fancy Costume Peace Carnival Dance was held at Battersea Town Hall. The music was provided by 'Pollard's Famous Coloured Jazz Band'. The leader Hughes Pollard had fought with the American army during the War and stayed in Europe afterwards.[30] It is possible that the African Progress Union (APU), of which Archer was now President, had made contact with Black American servicemen and ex-servicemen in Britain. It is therefore possible that Archer arranged for Pollard's engagement for the Dance.

Archer had been elected President of the APU at its inaugural meeting on 18 December 1918. Its aims were 'to promote the general welfare of Africans and Afro-Peoples', to set up a social and residential club in London as a 'home from home'; to spread 'knowledge of the history and achievements of Africans and Afro-Peoples past and present'; and to create and maintain 'a public sentiment in favour of brotherhood in its broadest sense'. He remained President until 1921.[31]

His inaugural speech was radical. Referring to the role of Africans, West Indians and African Americans on the battlefields of France and Flanders, he said:

'A war, we have been repeatedly told, for the self-determination of small nations and the freedom of the world from the despotism of German rule. The truth of that statement will be proved by the way' the different countries deal with their 'Negro subjects'. 'That if we are good enough to be brought to fight the wars of the country we are good enough to receive the benefits of the country'. One of the objects of this association is to demand - not ask, demand; it will be 'demand' all the time that I am your President. I am not asking for anything, I am demanding.[32]

In February 1919 he attended the Pan-African Congress in Paris. On 16 June he led an APU deputation to meet the Deputy Lord Mayor of Liverpool to discuss the race riots that had broken out in Liverpool, Cardiff and East London earlier in the month.[33]

In 1921 Archer was at the Westminster Central Hall session of the second Pan-African Congress. Chairing the debate on colonial freedom, he introduced the Indian socialist Shapurji Saklatvala giving a message of support. The Congress Declaration to the World demanded 'the recognition of civilised men as civilised despite their race and colour' and upheld 'the ancient common ownership of the Land and its natural fruits and defence against the unrestrained greed of invested capital', and contained forthright criticism of British colonial rule. It was unanimously adopted. He does not appear to have attended the third Pan-African Congress held on 7 and 8 November 1923.

Battersea Labour Party

During the War the Liberals had split off from the Progressive Alliance and in 1918 the Trades & Labour Council, the Labour Party, the Labour League, and the socialist groups set up the Battersea Trades Council and Labour Party under the new Labour Party constitution which allowed individual members as well as affiliated organisations like the trade unions. Archer became a leading figure in the Party.

The new Party organisation was faced with fighting the General Election in November 1918. The Party wanted to adopt John Burns as its candidate for the Battersea North constituency. Burns had resigned from the Liberal Cabinet in 1914 in protest at the declaration of War. At first he accepted nomination, but then withdrew rejecting the idea of being subject to the discipline of the Parliamentary Labour Whip. Instead, the Party fielded Charlotte Despard, the suffragette and Irish nationalist. Archer was one of her nominators and chaired at least one of her election meetings.[34] Her manifesto included the demand for justice for Ireland and India, and the replacement of Empires by Federations, each member possessing its own domestic autonomy. Given that the Conservatives and the Liberals were fielding a joint candidate as part of the National Coalition Despard was not elected.

With funding from Despard, the Party improved its organisation, and swept into control of Battersea Council in the municipal elections in November 1919. During the campaign Archer chaired a meeting at which he argued that:

> 'Labour was fighting as a combined force, with unity of action. The people had been told that the war was over, but he asked: "How had it benefited the working man?" Had the war benefited anyone in Battersea in regard to land and housing? The price of food was up 130 per cent. As a student of history he could say that there never had been a war that had been beneficial to the labouring classes'.

Topping the poll for Latchmere Ward with 1463 votes Archer 'beemed beneficently'. The Labour Group elected him as its Leader. In the following month he spoke in Council meetings on such matters as the control of local prices, the reform of rates system so that they be '"levied on the capital value of land irrespective of the use to which it was put," and the withdrawal of British troops from Ireland'. Given the British Government's intervention in Russia against the Bolshevik Revolution, he also spoke in support of 'the immediate cessation of the blockade' against, 'and the resumption of food trade facilities' to Russia.[35]

On the Board of Guardians he was instrumental in ending the practice of requiring orphan boys at the North Surrey School 'who had volunteered for training in the school band' to be required to join army bands when they left the school. As 'a lifelong abstainer' he successfully argued against giving beer at Christmas to those living in its institutions. They had already been given beer for the peace celebrations, even though as he commented 'While they's killing people in Russia'.[36]

He does not seem to have been re-elected as Party Leader in November 1920. No reasons are given for the change. Instead he joined the Council's Finance and the Joint Industrial Workshop Staff Committees. He served on the Special Council Committee formed during the coal crisis of 1921. Although he did not stand for election to the Council in November 1922, he continued to be active in Council affairs through appointment on specialist Committees. In 1925 he was agent for Labour's North Battersea candidates in the March LCC Election and stood again for the Council in November, this time for Park Ward but was not elected. As a mark of respect by his colleagues he was made an Alderman, a non-elected seat not linked to an electoral ward.[37]

The Saklatvala Years 1921–26

John Archer's continuing engagement in black politics was articulated through his support for the Indian Shapurji Saklatvala who was selected as North Battersea Labour's Parliamentary candidate in 1921.[38] The years between 1921 and 1926 were a period of intense political activities in Battersea and conflicts with the national Labour Party over the issue of whether Communists should be members of the Labour Party.

Archer was a key advocate of Saklatval's selection along with two Battersea Party colleagues who were active with Saklatvala in the Workers' Welfare League for India: Arthur Field and Duncan Carmichael. In 1920 two local socialist organisations, the Battersea Herald League and the Battersea Socialist Society, which were affiliated to the Battersea Labour, were represented at the foundation of, and dissolved themselves into the newly formed, Communist Party. Many activists, including Saklatvala, became members of the new Party, while retaining their Labour Party membership. On the basis that he accepted the Labour Party constitution and was prepared to abide by the Whip and rules of the Parliamentary Party, his adoption in Battersea was endorsed by the Labour Party's National Executive Committee.

Saklatavla was elected to Parliament in 1922, but lost the 1923 General Election which had been called about the Conservatives' tariff reform proposals. The first Labour Government led by Ramsay MacDonald came to power on a minority basis. Another General Election was held on 29 October 1924 because of the collapse of the Government due to its decision not to prosecute the Communist JR Campbell for incitement to mutiny. The pressure on Labour mounted with the publication of what turned out to be a forged letter said to have been written by Grigory Zinoviev of the Communist International in Moscow calling for an intensification of propaganda in Britain. Saklatvala was re-elected. Archer chaired the final rally at Nine Elms Baths on 27 October.[39]

After rejecting the application of the Communist Party to affiliate to the national Labour Party, the latter introduced a ban against Communists being members of the Labour Party. Saklatvala was therefore refused the Parliamentary Whip. He retained the continuing support of Battersea Labour Party, which campaigned against the ban. When he spoke at Nine Elms Baths in support of the Labour's LCC candidates for North Battersea, he is reported to have said: 'We want the London County Council converted into an instrument of Communist propaganda'. As election agent Archer told the press that Saklatvala had not said this.

> We are not Communists. I do not think there are 30 Communists in Battersea. I am not a Communist myself. We did not return Mr. Saklatvala as a Communist but as a representative of the views of the people of North Battersea. Neither of the Labour candidates is a Communist.[40]

The press devoted large amounts of space to the American ban on Saklatvala going to the United States as part of a Parliamentary delegation to an international Conference. At a Battersea protest meeting Archer 'proposed a resolution deploring America's policy of banning entry to a delegate of a constitutional conference to be held at Washington, and repudiating the "false charges made by an American official against the member for North Battersea."' The resolution also expressed the hope that Mr Saklatvala would ultimately be permitted to go to America 'to face his accusers and to fight out the great principle involved in the unjust ban placed upon his present meeting'.[41]

Battersea Labour Party was finally expelled by the national Party in February 1926 for not applying the ban on Communists as members. It continued its normal activities without further action being taken by the national Party. In the lead up to the General Strike that same year Saklatvala was arrested on a charge of preaching sedition urging British troops not to act against workers in a speech he gave in Hyde Park on May Day. Refusing to be bound over he was sent to prison.[42] The Strike was called by the Trades Union Congress to support the miners who were in bitter dispute with the coal owners. Started on 3 May its collapse 10 days later would have been very demoralising to Labour activists. Battersea's Labour Mayor publicly spoke about the local Party 'passing through deep and troubled waters'.[43] Disagreements were put to one side to welcome Saklatvala back on his release from prison, including a social on 27 June. Shortly afterwards plans were announced for Saklatvala to address a meeting on 2 July 'for all workers in Battersea who sympathise with the work and policy of the Communist Party', although the police did not allow it to go ahead.

The Rift with Saklatvala

The national Labour Party moved to establish new Labour organisations in Battersea. The London Organiser called 'A Conference of loyal supporters in Battersea', the invitation being conditional upon branches accepting the constitution and rules of the Party and its conference decisions. On 29 and 30 June trade unions and other Labour organisations held preliminary meetings to form Divisional Labour Parties for the North and South Constituencies. The *South Western Star* intervened in the process by publishing on 2 July the text of a letter written by Saklatvala on 7 October

1925. The letter had been seized by the police when they had raided his and other Communist leaders houses in the period leading up to the General Strike. While publicly accepting the support of Battersea Labour, he was privately advocating that the Communist Party should adopt a strategy of 'merciless measures to fight the Labour Party', of inviting trade union branches to affiliate to the CP, and suggesting that approval be obtained for this from Moscow.

The publication of the letter must have confirmed to activists like Archer that their action in finally accepting the anti-Communist bans and proscriptions was correct. The hall-mark of Battersea Labour was its understanding of what could be achieved through a 'municipal socialist' approach. Although it had been hostile to the national Party's ban on individual Communists being members of the Labour Party, what they would have seen as Saklatvala's betrayal and increasing hostility of the Communist Party, led them to chose the only option that they thought could guarantee them municipal control.

Archer was elected as Secretary of the new Divisional Labour Party in North Battersea. In 1927 it adopted as its new Parliamentary candidate William Stephen Sanders. His selection and election had symbolic significance. He had played a leading role in the late 1880s and early 1890s in creating the Progressive Alliance. From 1928 to 1929 North Battersea Labour Party shared John's premises at 214 Battersea Park Road. His Party workload was probably heavy. Saklatvala continued to be the MP for Battersea supported by the disaffiliated Labour organisations which remained in existence. After a bitter election campaign with Archer as his agent Sanders was decisively elected as MP in 1929.[44]

Welfare and Unemployment

Alongside this political activity and difficulties Archer continued to play an important role in the activities to improve the quality of working-class lives through action on health and welfare and against unemployment. He took a special interest in these issues including active support for the Nine Elms Swimming Club and as a school governor. He represented the Council at several national and international public health conferences, including in Belgium and Germany. As a member of the Board of Guardians he was a champion of the unemployed. During the Poor Law funding crisis of 1921, the unemployed occupied the workhouse in protest at the decision of the Wandsworth Board of Guardians decision to withdraw payments which enabled people to stay in their homes, thus forcing them into the Workhouse.[45]

At the time Labour members on the Board were in the minority. Archer argued that 'Wandsworth and Battersea cannot stand the financial strain of dealing with the unemployed problem, and it may probably result in action similar to that adopted by Poplar'. The Labour Councillors in Poplar had refused to levy the poor law rate and been imprisoned. He angrily pointed out that the occupiers included men 'wearing silver badges and wound stripes which a grateful country had presented to take with them into the workhouse'. Board meetings became very heated leading to all the Labour members being suspended in 1923 and Archer being physically carried out.[46]

Final Years

Archer was agent for Battersea Labour's North Battersea candidates for the March 1931 LCC election. He had continued to be annually re-appointed as Alderman until he was re-elected to the Council in November 1931 for the Nine Elms Ward. The Labour Group immediately elected him as Deputy Leader. Illness prevented him from attending the Council meetings in April and June 1932. At the latter the Council agreed to send him its best wishes for a speedy recovery. His health deteriorated and he was admitted to St James Hospital, where he died on Thursday 14 July 1932. His death certificate records him as aged 68 dying of cardio-renal failure. His brother Albert was at his bedside when he died.[47]

The funeral was held at the Church of Our Lady of Carmel in Battersea Park Road on Tuesday 19 July. The *Dies Irae* was sung by children from local church schools. Mass was taken by four priests. The mourners included Albert, 21 members and several chief officers of the Council, and representatives of the Nine Elms Swimming Club, and of the Hearts of Oak Benefit Society, his insurance society. There were wreaths from Burns and Sanders and their wives, various Labour organisations and trade unions. He was buried in the Council's cemetery at Morden. His death was noted in Liverpool.[48]

Apart from his brother, there is no mention by the press of any black people attending the funeral or sending flowers. At its meeting on 20 July, the Council expressed its deepest sympathy to Archer's relatives. The Council Labour Group Leader remembered Archer as 'a very ardent worker for the benefit of coloured races and particularly of the negro races...' 'There was always a streak of humour in whatever he said'. William Sanders said that Archer: 'was one of the largest hearted men I have ever had the pleasure of knowing. The poor had no better friend; he spared neither himself nor his substance in giving help to those in need'.

Albert Archer wrote on 6 August thanking the Council for sending him its resolution of sympathy. Later the Council honoured John by naming one of the blocks after him on its new St. John's housing estate near the Thames.[49]

Concluding Thoughts

From the end of 1921 Archer seems to have remained content to stay at the municipal level. He does not appear to have used his membership of the Labour Party to campaign within the national Party on black issues. Nor does he appear to play a major role in black organisation and campaigning. When he addressed the Progress Union in 1918 he said that it and he would be 'demanding'. He appears to have stopped demanding in respect of black rights.

While he had received letters of congratulation on his election as Mayor from people in France and Germany, we do not know who they were whether they were Africans from the French and German colonies, nor whether he kept in contact with them. We therefore do not know the extent of Archer's connections into Europe. While he attended the Pan-African Congress in Paris in 1921 and the Royal Institute for Public Health in Ghent in Belgium in June 1927, we do not know which black and white Europeans he met on these trips nor whether he kept in contact with them. His Labour Party colleague William Sanders was an expert on Germany and friends with leading German Social Democrats. It is not known whether Sanders introduced any of these and other European socialists visiting London to political colleagues like Archer. Archer may also have met Europeans at the various health Conferences held in Britain which he attended on behalf of Battersea Council: the Imperial Congress on Sanitation, the Congress of the Royal Institute of Public Health, and the Annual Conference of the National Association for the Prevention of Tuberculosis in 1926, and the World Dairy Congress and the Congress of the Royal Institute of Public Health in 1928.

Given that it seems that from 1921 he put his faith in Saklatvala to champion Indian and black rights at national and Parliamentary level, he must have felt betrayed in 1926 by Saklatvala's behind the scenes advocacy of a strategy to destroy the Labour Party. From then on his priority seems to have been the re-building of official Labour organisation in Battersea. The split with Saklatvala opened up a fault line within the Battersea labour movement not resolved until Saklatvala's defeat as MP in 1929. It may also have opened up a fault line for Archer's engagement in wider black politics, given the attraction of Communism to many of the activists.

As a Catholic Archer may also have had some difficulties with those who were freemasons like the American WEB Du Bois. Even without these differences new younger activists may have regarded him as an old has-been, compromised by his adherence to the anti-Communist Labour Party.

In the light of the continuing absence of substantial new material shedding light on these matters, Barry Kosmin's evaluation appears to remain relevant.

> 'Archer's identities whether of colour, class or religion were all openly acknowledged. The Battersea working-class movement did not see anything strange in a coloured man's interest in Pan-Africanism on Colonial affairs. It did nothing to detract from his devotion to the Labour Party or to the well-being of his fellow citizens of Battersea'. 'Archer's political philosophy was that of a self-confident, worldly citizen and most emphatically not an immigrant. His blackness added to his insight and experience of life and fuelled his egalitarianism and democratic socialism'.[50]

Areas for future research include continuing to try and ascertain whether Richard Archer moved the family to Barbados, what John Archer did before arriving in Battersea, information about his brother and sister and about his wife in Canada and what happened to her. It has been suggested that there may be material about his political activities in other people's papers, like those of John Burns. On my behalf Dr Shaun McDaid has looked in the Charlotte Despard papers and diaries in the Public Record Office Northern Ireland but found virtually nothing about Archer. If Archer was in contact with black and white Europeans there may been material about him in archives, particularly in France and Germany, including personal papers and police and intelligence reports. Until a breakthrough is made in finding substantial new material about him, John Archer will remain a tantalisingly elusive figure whose influence in labour and black politics may as yet not be fully understood.

Notes

[1] In addition to 'black' the terms 'coloured' and 'negro' are also used reflecting the terminology used by black Americans, West Indians and Britons at the time.

[2] Fryer, 1984, 410.

[3] The following biographical sketches have been published: Kosmin (1978–9), Fryer (1984), Webb (1987), Creighton (1995/6), Green (1998), and Wadsworth (1998). Despite this material Schneer (1999) claims there is no biography of Archer (fn. 27, 300). Pennybacker (2000) expresses surprise that Schneer does not discuss Archer. Since 2000 additional biographical material has been made available: Phillips, Fryer (2004). Archer appears to fall through the gaps in specialist analyses of the labour movement in the 1920s and of the extent of racism in the labour movement. Because these analyses are not sufficiently rooted

in the experience of black men like Archer, I take a very cautious view about the general conclusions about racism within the labour movement. My own researches suggest a much more complicated picture. Wadsworth (1998) and Beliard (2009) illustrate the complexity. Similarly, Battersea's pioneering of municipal socialism is often neglected, for example, Stromquist (2009). This essay therefore does not seek to address theoretical aspects of race and labour during the period of Archer's life.

[4] John Archer's birth certificate 13 June 1863. Information provided by Marij von Helmond. National Museums and Galleries on Merseyside (1995).

[5] *Battersea Vanguard*, the newspaper of the Battersea Socialist Council, refers to his travels; August and December 1907.

[6] Little is known about Margaret. By 1929 she is no longer in the public record. The 1929 electoral register lists a Bertha Elizabeth Archer. No information has been found as to who she is.

[7] There are references in the local papers and speeches about his election as Mayor in November 1913 to him having been in the area for 20 years.

[8] Creighton, 1989; Kapp, 1989.

[9] Creighton, 1999; Wrigley, 1974.

[10] Archer speech to African Progress Union (APU) in Fryer, 1984, 413–4.

[11] The contemporary press coverage of the Pan-African Conference does not detail contributors in the debates. The best analysis and discussion about the conference is in Schneer, 1999. Frank Colenso, a white campaigner for black rights in Natal and Zululand also attended the Conference. He refers to Archer as 'my colleague'. Archer sent a message of sympathy on Colenso's death in 1910, see Colenso and Saunders, 2008, 91, fn. 18 and 101, fn. 74). Thanks to Gwilym Colenso for this information. In his speech to the APU in 1919 Archer paid tribute to Colenso: 'He was my guide and helped me through many thorny paths and I cherish the fact that he numbered me among his friends, Fryer, 1984, 414.

[12] Price, 1972; Wrigley, 1993.

[13] *South Western Star (SWS)*, 1 April 1904. While for many there was racial hostility to Chinese people, this needs to be assessed in the light of broader histories like the African reaction to Indian indentured labourers – see Hughes, 2007.

[14] Hooker, 1975, 83.

[15] *SWS*, 5 and 19 October and 2 and 16 November, 1906.

[16] Ibid., Advert 10 January; *The Daily Graphic*, 15 January; *British Medical Journal*, 18 January, 1908; Lansbury, 1985.

[17] Creighton, 1988.

[18] *Evening News*, 7 November 1913. Given Archer's knowledge of black history the reporter must have confused comments by him about the 80th Anniversary of the decision to spend £20m on freeing the slaves in the British West Indies with comments on emancipation by Lincoln during the American Civil War.

[19] *Wandsworth Borough News*. 14 January 1913. National press coverage of the pending and actual Mayoral election included the *Pall Mall Gazette*, *Daily Graphic*, *Daily Telegraph*, *Daily Chronicle*, *Daily Mail*, *Evening News*, *The Globe*, *The Illustrated London News* and *Punch*. The *Evening News* contains a picture of Archer in formal dress and top hat (7 November 1913). Later the *Daily Graphic* has a photograph of London Mayors including Archer in their official robes at a charitable event (7 January 1914).

[20] *Liverpool Weekly Mercury.* 15 November. Other coverage included: *Liverpool Weekly Post.* 15 November; *The Catholic Times and Catholic Opinion.* 14 November 1913.

[21] *New York Age,* 4 December; *Chicago Defender,* 15 and 29 November; 13, 14, and 20 December 1913; *The Crisis,* January 1914; *Negro Year Book,* 1914.

[22] Bruce Collection. Letter Archer to Bruce, 26 November 1913 and 17 January 1914. There is an advertisement for the calendar *The Crisis,* December 1913, 97. Thanks to Marika Sherwood for the details from the Collection.

[23] Bruce Collection. Letter Archer to Bruce, 17 January 1914. A child emigrant from the United States to Liberia, Roberts had married and was widow of the first President of Liberia; Green, 1998, 211–2.

[24] Bruce Collection. Letters Archer to Bruce, 17 and 28 January 1914; Wilson to Bruce, 28 January 1914; and Russell to Bruce 17 February 1914.

[25] Programme in Battersea Cuttings book 1911–5, 125. Wandsworth Heritage Service; *SWS,* 12 December 1913.

[26] *SWS,* 5 and 24 December 1913.

[27] Ibid., 13 February 1914.

[28] *Daily Graphic,* 14 September 1914; *SWS,* 13 November 1914; Archer appears at this address in the 1918 Electoral Register.

[29] *SWS,* 23 May 1918.

[30] Ibid., 16 May 1919. Thanks to Howard Rye for the information about Pollard.

[31] For further information see Green, 2009.

[32] Peter Fryer, 1984, 415.

[33] For the latest analysis of the riots see Jenkinson, 2009.

[34] *SWS,* 6 December 1918.

[35] Ibid., 24 October, 7 and 14 November and 19 December 1919.

[36] Ibid., 12 December 1919.

[37] Ibid., 19 November 1920, Battersea Metropolitan Borough Council (BMBC) Minutes 27 April 1921, 7 and 9 November 1925, 138.

[38] Squires, 1980; Saklatvala, 1991; Wadsworth, 1998.

[39] Saklatvala General Election meeting leaflet for the rally. Battersea Labour Party Archive.

[40] *Evening Post,* 20 February 1925.

[41] *Daily Telegraph,* 21 September 1925.

[42] *SWS* & *Daily Express,* 7 May 1926.

[43] *SWS,* 11 June 1926.

[44] Creighton, 1988.

[45] Ward, 1992.

[46] Prichard, 1938.

[47] LCC Election Manifesto for Douglas and Ganley. Battersea Labour Party archive; BMBC Minutes. 9 November 1931, 119; 27 April 1932, 1 and 22 June 1932, 57. Nothing is known about Albert apart from the fact that he was living at 5 Stourcliffe Rd, Wallasey in Cheshire at the time.

[48] *SWS,* 22 July 1932; *Liverpool Echo,* 18 July 1932.

[49] *SWS,* 22 July 1932; BMBC Minutes. 29 September 1932, 130. The estate is now called Battersea Village.

[50] Kosmin, 1978–9, 435.

References

Beliard, Yann. "Imperial Internationalism? Hull Labour's Support for South African Trade-Unionism on the Eve of the Great War." *Labour History Review* 74, no. 3 (2009): 319–29.

Bruce Collection. Letters #1640. The Schonburg Center for Research in Black Culture (New York Public Library). Thanks to Marika Sherwood for locating the letters.

Colenso, Gwilym. "Colenso, Francis Ernest (Frank) (1852–1910)", in *Dictionary of National Biography*. Oxford: Oxford University Press, 2006.

Colenso, Gwilym and Saunders Christopher. "New Light on the Pan-African Association." *African Research & Documentation*, 107 and 108 (2008): 27–45 and 89–109.

Creighton, Sean. "Battersea and New Unionism." *South London Record* 4, 1989.

Creighton, Sean. *From Exclusion to Political Control. Radical and Working Class Organisation in Battersea 1830s – 1918*. London: Agenda Services, 1999.

Creighton, Sean. "'I am a Lancastrian Bred and Born...' The Life and Times of John Archer, 1963—1932." *North West Labour History* 20 (1995/6): 73–85.

Creighton, Sean. *Not For Me, Not For You but for Us*. London: Battersea Labour Party Booksales, 1988.

Creighton, Sean. *Stephen Sanders. 1871–1941. Battersea Socialist & Labour MP*. London: Battersea & Wandsworth Labour & Social History Group, 1979.

Fryer, Peter. *Staying Power. The History of Black People in Britain*. London: Pluto Press, 1984.

Fryer, Peter. *Archer, John Richard (1863–1932)*. Dictionary of National Biography. Oxford: Oxford University Press, 2004.

Green, Jeffrey. *Black Edwardians*. London and Portland: Frank Cass, 1998.

Green, Jeffrey. "The African Progress Union 1918–1925. A Black Pressure Group." Paper to Institute of Commonwealth Studies 5 February 1991; reprinted in *Black & Asian Studies Newsletter* 54 and 55 (July and November 2009): 12–28 and 17–22.

Hooker, James R. *Henry Sylvester Williams: Imperial Pan-Africanist*. London: Collings, 1975.

Hughes, Heather. "'The Coolies Will Elbow us Out of the Country': African Reactions to Indian Immigration in the Colony of Natal, South Africa." *Labour History Review* 72, no. 2 (2007): 155–68.

Jenkinson, Jacqueline. *Black 1919: Riots, Racism and Resistance: Imperial Britain*. Liverpool: Liverpool University Press, 2009.

Kapp, Yvonne. *The Air of Freedom: The Birth of New Unionism*. London: Lawrence & Wishart, 1989.

Kosmin, Barry A. "J. R. Archer: A Pan Africanist in the Battersea Labour Movement." London: *New Community* VII (1978–9): 430–6.

Lansbury, Coral. *The Old Brown Dog. Women Workers and Vivisection in Edwardian Britain*. Madison: University of Wisconsin Press, 1985.

Pennybacker, Susan. "Review." *Social History* 25, no. 3 (2000): 361–2.

Pennybacker, Susan. *From Scottsboro to Munich: Race and Political Culture in 1930s Britain*. Princeton: Princeton University Press, 2009.

Phillips, Mike, and John Archer. "Black Europeans. British Library." Online Gallery: www.bl.uk/onlinegallery/features/blackeuro/archerbackground.html

Price, Richard. *An Imperial War and the British Working Class*. London: Routledge Kegan Paul, 1972.

Prichard, A. G. "The Story of My Life. Rev. A.G. Prichard's Autobiography." *Islington Gazette*, November 23, 1938.

Saklatvala, Sehri. *The Fifth Commandment. Biography of Shapurji Saklatvala*. Saldford: Miranda Press, 1991.

Schneer, Jonathan. *London 1900. The Imperial Metropolis*. New Haven and London: Yale University Press, 1999.

Squires, Mike. *Saklatvala. A Political Biography*. London: Lawrence and Wishart, 1990.

Stromquist, Shleton. "Thinking Globally; Acting Locally': Municipal Labour and Socialist Activism in Comparative Perspective, 1890–1920." *Labour History Review* 74, no. 3 (2009): 233–56.

Wadsworth, Marc. *Comrade Sak. Shapurji Saklatvala MP. A Political Biography*. Leeds: Peepal Tree Press, 1998.

Ward, Michael. *Red Flag Over the Workhouse*. London: Wandsworth History Workshop, 1992.

Webb, Roy. "John Archer: Battersea's Black Activist (1863–1932)." *South London Record* 2 (1987): 30–35.

Wrigley, Chris. "Liberals and the Desire for Working-Class Representation in Battersea 1886–1922." In *Essays in Anti-Labour History*, edited by K. D. Brown, 126–58. London: Macmillan, 1974.

Wrigley, Chris. *Republicanism and War in Battersea*. London: Wandsworth History Workshop, 1993.

Surviving in the Metropole: The Struggle for Work and Belonging amongst African Colonial Migrants in Weimar Germany

Robbie Aitken

School of Cultures, Languages and Area Studies, University of Liverpool, Liverpool, UK

This paper looks at the fate of the Africans in Germany during the Weimar Republic in terms of their search for belonging and struggle to find work. In doing so it allows for a discussion of the day-to-day experiences and survival strategies of Germany's African Diaspora, their struggle for political recognition and self-definition as well as economic survival. Their presence was tolerated by German officials only as long as it served the purpose of a German colonial propaganda which sought to regain the lost colonies. In the wider context of economic hardship in Germany and rising racial prejudice, particularly in the late 1920s, many of these migrants faced a continual struggle for economic survival. Increasingly, one of the means of carving out an existence remaining for members of the African Diaspora was to turn to the stage. Here they were asked to 'perform' their blackness – to take on roles of a constrictive nature, reflecting and reinforcing stereotypes of the Black as primitive or exotic.

In January 1930 the Cameroonian Thomas Manga Akwa from the coastal town of Douala wrote to the French Consulate in Berlin describing his precarious economic position.

> I have been resident in Germany for a number of years. For a long time already now I have been unable to find work as a result of the bad

condition of the job market, so that I find myself in great (financial) distress. [...] That is why I have the urgent wish to return to my homeland.[1]

This was one of a number of letters Manga Akwa sent to both French and German officials over a period of several years in which he asked for their help to either find employment or to be repatriated to Cameroon. The French authorities, who exercised mandate control over most of the country, viewed Manga Akwa with suspicion and as a potential pro-German rabble-rouser. On account of his prolonged period of stay in Berlin he was deemed to be thoroughly 'Germanised' and as a result they were reluctant to allow him to return to Douala, both the territory's main port as well as a centre of indigenous unrest. At the same time to German colonial officials, former colonial rulers over Cameroon, he represented a burden on their welfare system that they were unable to get rid of. Manga Akwa's situation was similar to that of dozens of his contemporaries; former German colonial subjects who had entered Germany pre-1914 and who in the interwar era were seemingly stranded in the metropole. Their wish to return to Africa was not only linked to a longing for their homelands, but was also frequently associated with a lack of employment opportunities.

Against a backdrop of continual economic instability and rising racial prejudice and intolerance, particularly in the late 1920s, many of these migrants faced an almost constant struggle for economic survival. This paper illuminates the fate of these former German colonial subjects during the Weimar period. It takes as its focus Cameroonian migrants who, as a group, numerically dominated the African colonial migrant population and it concentrates on the difficulties they encountered in finding employment. This provides an insight into their search for belonging and the survival strategies they utilised. In doing so it reveals the ambivalent relationship of both the German and French authorities towards these migrants and illustrates how their ambiguous civil status impinged upon their ability to carve out an existence in Germany. As will be demonstrated increasingly performing exoticised or racialised roles on the Weimar stage or screen became a central means of making a living.

The presence of men and women of African heritage in German-speaking Europe can be traced at least as far back as the early modern period.[2] Yet, it was following Germany's emergence as a maritime power and the creation of a German overseas empire in 1884 that saw the growth of a permanent, small, but visible black population in Germany. Although no exact figures exist it is likely that in the period prior to the outbreak of the First World War this population was composed of several thousand individuals of African descent from various regions of Africa and from further afield such as Haiti and the United States. A large proportion of these migrants came from Germany's newly established African protectorates of Togo, German East Africa and, to a lesser extent, Namibia. Numerically dominant amongst this population of German colonial subjects were young Cameroonians, in particular young men from Douala.[3] Almost all of the colonial African and Cameroonian migrants who arrived in Germany were men. In part this was due to the gendered structure of many of the African population groups involved in this migration, in which women were afforded only a limited role beyond the domestic sphere.[4]

The means by which Africans reached Germany were many and varied. African seamen arrived at the ports of Bremen and Hamburg; personal servants accompanied colonial officials, missionaries or private individuals on home leave, while others were participants in ethnological exhibitions.[5] Some Africans were trained as missionaries or soldiers and a handful were employed as language instructors at the Hamburg Colonial Institute or the Berlin Seminar for Oriental Languages. In particular, however, an initial impetus for travel came from Cameroonian, especially Duala, colonial elites who sent their children to be educated in Germany. The Duala had a history of sending their sons to be educated in Europe and they envisaged education as a means through which they could win prestige and political influence. As a result dozens of Duala youngsters went to school or served an apprenticeship in towns and cities throughout Germany amongst them was Manga Akwa who came from one of the foremost Duala families. His father, also named Manga Akwa, was the brother of King Dika Akwa as well as being a signatory of the 1884 Treaty of Protection, which helped establish German control over Cameroon, and his cousin was the infamous Ludwig Mpundu Akwa, the future anti-colonial activist, who was similarly schooled in Germany.[6]

Few, if any, of these migrants imagined their stay in Germany as being anything other than temporary and consequently this was a population in constant flux. The various colonial administrations also viewed the presence of colonial subjects in the metropole as being short-term and enacted a number of decrees to control and limit migrants' stays. This was out of concern that migrants were being morally corrupted by their exposure to European society and that upon their return to Africa they were proving to be disruptive and unruly. In the case of Cameroon, migration legislation was passed in 1893 and further tightened in 1910.[7] The legislation determined that migrants had to gain permission from the colonial authorities in order to leave the protectorates and a limit to the length of their stay in Germany was to be set before they left. Further, they were to be placed under the supervision of a white European for the duration of their stay and a deposit covering the cost of the return ticket was to be paid in advance. In spite of the restrictions a considerable number of colonial subjects still successfully reached Germany without ever receiving permission to migrate. Of the Cameroonians who migrated prior to the First World War a majority appear to have returned to Africa before hostilities broke out.[8] Nonetheless, a not insignificant number remained in Germany on a longer-term basis either out of choice or necessity.

The outbreak of war in 1914 effectively ended migration from the protectorates to Germany. During the entire period of the Great War Cameroonian and other African colonial subjects still residing in Germany were cut off from their friends and families in Africa. In addition, shipping connections to the west coast of Africa were interrupted, making it impossible for migrants to return home. Following Germany's defeat and the subsequent peace settlement these colonial migrants were now confronted with changed political and economic circumstances. In particular, their situation was complicated by the fact that they were no longer German colonial subjects. Under the Treaty of Versailles Germany was stripped of its colonies and according to article 127 of the treaty German colonial migrants were to be 'entitled to the diplomatic protection' of the responsible mandate government. Cameroonians, a vast majority of whom were Duala, were now under British, but primarily French protection. At no point, however, was it explicitly specified as to what exactly this meant and frequently they were rendered effectively stateless when the mandate powers reneged upon their responsibilities.

As early as August 1919 the French consul in Berlin reported to the Foreign Office in Paris that numerous Cameroonians had approached him asking for permission to return to Africa and to be provided with the necessary documents to enable them to do this.[9] Other French consulates throughout Germany received similar queries.[10] Often the would-be returnees also required the financial means to return. In general, these migrants were viewed by the French colonial ministry and the mandate administration in Cameroon as being a potentially subversive element that had spent too long in Germany and their repatriation was, therefore, deemed to be largely undesirable. French suspicions of German-based migrants were heightened by post-war Duala-led political initiatives in the metropole. This included the creation of the self-help organisation the African Welfare Association (*Afrikanischer Hilfsverein*) and the sending of a petition to the National Assembly at Weimar by several of its members. The petition's signatories, who included Manga Akwa, protested against French and British influence in Cameroon and instead demanded that Germany and Cameroon be equal partners in the development of post-war Cameroon.[11] Not surprisingly such activities were greeted with concern by the French. Nonetheless, particularly in the years before French mandate authority over most of Cameroon was confirmed in July 1922, the French Foreign Office reluctantly concluded that it was legally difficult to deny repatriation requests.[12] As a consequence in the immediate aftermath of the war a handful of Cameroonians received permission to return after background checks had been carried out for evidence of their loyalty to their former colonial rulers.

Manga Akwa was one of the few permitted to return. He was granted safe passage to Paris by the French Consulate in Berlin and once in the French capital the authorities provided him with subsistence and travel money while he waited to leave for Cameroon.[13] In February 1921 he arrived back in Douala. His stay, however, was short and within months he had fled back to Germany after having been suspected of causing a public disturbance in the district of Akwa by the local French authorities.[14] Not only did this greatly hinder his future chances of being able to return to Cameroon, but it likely helped persuade the French mandate authorities that it was in their interests to prevent any further German-based Cameroonians from re-entering the territory. Indeed, the French Mandate Commissioner complained about friction between the local authorities and the few returnees and by the mid-1920s it appears that he was now successful in forestalling all further decisions on repatriation requests.[15] This effectively stranded colonial migrants still in Germany. Like the French, the German authorities were also unenthusiastic about taking responsibility for their former colonial charges. German policy towards these migrants was shaped by hopes of colonial revisionism – that Germany would one day regain its lost overseas territories. In this respect the presence of these Africans was to be tolerated in order to avoid adverse publicity in the international press. Throughout the Weimar period, however, the long-term goal remained to ensure their return to Africa.

At the end of the First World War African men and women were living throughout Germany and not exclusively in the larger cities, though a majority were increasingly based in working-class areas in Hamburg and Berlin. In both cities many amongst the African population lived an almost nomadic lifestyle, constantly moving from one apartment to the next. This mobility was typical of the German working class and was dictated by the difficulties of paying rent and the search for ever cheaper accommodation.

In the case of colonial migrants it was also due to the unwillingness of many landlords to lease their accommodation to Africans on account of existing social prejudices. Manga Akwa moved at least six times between 1916 and 1925, primarily within the largely working-class Kreuzberg district of Berlin. Increasingly, the German capital became home.[16] Like many of his contemporaries he gradually established roots in Germany and in October 1923 he asked the Colonial Department for a certificate confirming that he was a German citizen in order to marry his partner of four years, the German woman Frau Dunkelmann.[17] Together the pair already had a three-and-a-half-year-old child. Weeks later, however, he received a negative response in which he was told that as a migrant from a former German protectorate he was not a German citizen.[18] During the colonial period German colonial subjects had never enjoyed German citizenship; rather they had occupied an inferior, ill-defined, separate legal position as subjects of a German protectorate (*Schutzgebietsangehöriger*), also described variously by terms such as 'Person under German Protection' (literally, *Deutscher Schutzgenosse*), or simply as 'Native' (*Eingeborene*). Reflecting this Manga Akwa was sent a certificate confirming that he came from a former German protectorate and informed he could apply for German citizenship, should he choose to do so.

In his subsequent citizenship application he appealed to the colonial authorities for support with reference to his family background as well as the influence he claimed to have over his fellow compatriots in Cameroon, which he argued would be of great assistance to the Germans when Germany and Cameroon were reunited.[19] His brief return to Cameroon was dismissed as a mistake and he signed himself off as 'Prince Thomas Manga v. Akwa', adding the distinctive German 'von' as a further sign of his status. Additionally, he presented himself as a German patriot aware of his 'duties' to his chosen homeland, declaring: 'I am German and I want to be German, so when the call comes to fight for the Fatherland I am at every moment ready to do so'. This self-identification as German was not unusual. Colonial migrants who had been in Germany since childhood often developed an affinity with their new homeland and many falsely believed themselves to be citizens. Particularly in their encounters with local authorities such as civil registries and welfare offices much confusion existed over their legal status.[20] It was frequently in situations when they required identity papers from the Foreign Office, such as when wishing to marry, as in Manga Akwa's case, or when documentation had been requested by employers or the local police, that they first discovered that they were not citizens. While there is no record of the authorities' response to Manga Akwa's letter it is clear from later sources that his citizenship application was turned down, though ultimately this did not prevent him marrying his partner. Only a handful of colonial migrants who sought citizenship were ever successful. Under the citizenship law of 1913 naturalisation applications were sent from the local office to the state authority, which then circulated the application to all other German states.[21] The latter then had the right to raise objections and in the few documented cases of African citizenship applications it appears that the states of Bavaria and Thuringia typically expressed concern at the prospects of Africans becoming German citizens.[22] These concerns were linked to a belief that Africans were culturally, morally, and biologically inferior and as such had no right to German citizenship. As a separate consequence of the 1913 law Frau Dunkelmann, upon marrying Manga Akwa, lost her German citizenship and both she and the couple's daughter now inherited his confused civil status as virtually stateless individuals.[23]

Cameroonian and other colonial migrants' lack of German citizenship brought them a number of potential disadvantages in particular with respect to finding accommodation and work. One of the biggest problems that they faced was the constant struggle to secure employment and as non-Germans they were also excluded from receiving state unemployment benefit. During the war a number of colonial migrants had found jobs in munitions factories and a few had entered the army and fought on the front. In the aftermath of the fighting and as a result of the fluctuating fortunes of the German economy that followed Africans, like their German compatriots, were exposed to the economic hardships of hyperinflation and the instability of the employment market. The skills that young Cameroonians had learned during the course of apprenticeships were geared towards them finding future employment in the protectorates, be it as metal worker, shoe maker or tailor, and not in Germany where their opportunities were limited. Some qualified apprentices like the carpenter Joseph Boholle were able to piece together a living in their fields of expertise.[24] Others found temporary employment in unskilled positions as porters, doormen and waiters or more generally as unskilled workers. Frequently migrants were forced to change their occupation one or more times in order to keep working or they had to carry out several jobs at once. A few Cameroonians took advantage of their colonial connections to trade in colonial goods that were often sent to them from Africa by family and friends, but a majority of these enterprises were small-scale and short lived.[25]

Others were less successful in finding work. From the summer of 1911 until the outbreak of war Manga Akwa undertook an apprenticeship in agricultural machine building in Berlin, Alt-Hohenschönhausen with the firm Richard Heike. He hoped to later find a skilled position within the colonial economy.[26] During the war he worked in a munitions factory, but in its aftermath he struggled to find a job, hence his request to return to Douala in 1921. His situation was not unusual and some like the technical engineer Joseph Bilé, himself a war veteran, lost their positions to returning German war veterans, whereas Adamu bin Subeiru became unemployed as a result of the Seminar for Oriental Languages in Berlin suspending its courses in African languages.[27] Like Manga Akwa, both Subeira and Bilé were amongst those seeking repatriation from the French.

Following a prolonged period of unemployment Manga Akwa decided to retrain as a chauffeur and he completed a driving course in 1925. The Berlin police, however, initially refused to grant him a licence on account of an incident in 1923 when he resisted arrest after having been accused of 'pestering' a German woman.[28] The misdemeanour led to a conviction and the police official expressed concern about granting a licence to someone capable of such 'outbursts'. Manga Akwa was upset that this incident which had taken place two years previously and which he dismissed as a 'harmless thing' could potentially prevent him from working.[29] He sought help from the President of the German Colonial Society and former Governor of Cameroon, Theodor Seitz, whom he knew personally. He explained that the incident was a simple misunderstanding and that he had only refused to accompany the police to the station because he could not understand why he was being arrested. Manga Akwa appealed to Seitz that he did not want to resort to begging in order to look after his family, but that the authorities' refusal to issue him with a licence was preventing him from securing employment. To further his cause he referred to his colonial and familial connections and presented himself as a loyal pro-German African who had actively promoted the benefits of German colonialism in Cameroon. In this context he claimed that his reason for fleeing Cameroon in 1921 was because he had been accused by the local French authorities of being a German spy on account of his friendliness towards the Germans. Seitz defended Manga Akwa, referring to him as an 'unassuming' and 'orderly' man and foregrounding his colonial background.[30] He argued that for 'political reasons' it was important to ensure that Manga Akwa was able to work for a living, while at the same time admitting that were Manga Akwa white the incident would have provided sufficient grounds to refuse him his licence. This paternalistic support was not untypical of former colonial officials and was linked not only to hopes of colonial revisionism, but also a sense of duty towards migrants from the former protectorates.[31]

Even with his new driver's licence Manga Akwa was still unable to find work and by the mid-1920s he was just one of an increasing number of colonial migrants who were struggling for financial independence. With no central agency responsible for assisting them an increasing number of Africans in Berlin approached various government departments and agencies such as the Welfare Ministry, the Foreign Office, and the German Colonial Society asking for help. This eventually prompted the Foreign Office to take action. In February 1926 it declared itself willing to look after those from the former colonies whom it deemed, through no fault of their own, found themselves in financial need.[32] The Foreign Office then delegated responsibility to the *Deutsche Gesellschaft für Eingeborenenkunde* (literally German Society for Native Studies, DGfE) under the guidance of Alfred Mansfeld, a former civil servant in Cameroon.[33] The organisation had been created with the purpose of studying and protecting the indigenous populations of the former German colonies along with their traditions. Mansfeld had been approached in November 1925 by the Duala man Wilhelm Edimo Munumé, who on behalf of 17 other Africans, largely based in Berlin and including Manga Akwa, asked him to represent them in their dealings with the various ministries.[34] Drawing on Foreign Office funds, the DGfE provided minimal financial aid in the form of 50 Marks a month for rent and 60 Marks a month for living expenses. Although the DGfE was not the only state organisation to provide aid to poverty-stricken Africans it was soon established as the central organ responsible for the welfare of former African colonial subjects, a role which it carried out up until 1940. Munumé and Manga Akwa were amongst an increasing number of Africans who regularly collected payments from the office of the DGfE in the Martin-Luther Straße 97 in Berlin. Few could survive on these meagre funds, especially those who also had families to support, and often recipients asked for payments in advance which in turn led to considerable tension between the DGfE and the Africans it supported.[35]

The aid provided by the DGfE was envisaged by the Foreign Office as being a short-term solution and it insisted that recipients were not to become dependent on handouts. A further function of the DGfE was therefore to find employment for Africans. In the context of the approaching world economic crisis and at the first steady then rapid growth of unemployment in Germany in the late 1920s and early 1930s this became increasingly difficult. Yet, it was not simply economic factors that hindered Africans' employment opportunities. In February 1928 the DGfE complained that prospective employers often asked about the civil status of former colonial subjects.[36] When informed that those concerned were not German citizens and never had been they frequently lost interest in employing them. Equally, on a day-to-day basis Africans were confronted with prejudice and discrimination. Particularly from the late 1920s onwards this appears to have impinged upon their job prospects. With renewed economic instability the Foreign Office complained that trade associations were known to bully member firms into releasing African employees in favour of taking on Germans. In one specific case the Foreign Office expressed annoyance at the racially motivated dismissal of the Duala man Manfred Kotto Priso from his job with a shoe polishing producer in Dresden in November 1929.[37] Priso, who had previously given presentations in Germany and Austria about the benefits of German colonial rule in Cameroon, was described by the Foreign Office as 'educated', 'skilled' and someone who both feels and thinks German. He was dismissed after the Union of Travelling Salesmen pressurised his employers into letting him go on account of his skin colour. In particular, Foreign Office officials were concerned about news of such incidents reaching the former colonies in the form of letters sent by former colonial subjects in Germany to their family and friends in Africa. Such negative publicity was deemed to be harmful to hopes of colonial revisionism. Further evidence of the increasingly hostile atmosphere towards colonial migrants is provided in one such letter sent by the Togolese migrant Kwassi Bruce to his sister in Ho, Togo. Bruce wrote of the misery and what he called the 'racial hostility' against Africans that he experienced in Germany.[38]

> At this moment now (1932) here in Germany a hostile atmosphere against the Africans prevails regardless as to whether they come from the former German colonies or not. ... This letter to you is a cry for help out of great distress, because things are absolutely terrible.

In spite of the DGfE's considerable efforts it proved impossible to secure a permanent job for Manga Akwa. The stress that this economic dependency and uncertainty placed upon the lives of former colonial subjects and their families is underlined in a letter he drafted in June 1929. He wrote:

> I am married and have a nine year old child and I lost my permanent job in November 1928. Now and again I have had temporary jobs, through which, however, I am not in a position to support myself and my family. Alone the rent for the furnished room in which we live costs 58 Marks a month.

In these circumstances I find myself in great distress and since during this whole time I have also used up my last savings, I am hardly capable of continuing to live with my family.[39]

He ended his letter by asking the German government for financial aid, or better still the opportunity to work for a living. On at least two previous occasions Manga Akwa had been forced to live apart from his family on account of their dire financial situation.[40] Although it is unclear whether these financial pressures were ultimately responsible for the breakdown of his relationship with his wife, whom he was living apart from by January 1930, the family's economic situation undoubtedly placed a strain on the marriage.

While Manga Akwa continued to seek work in his field of training other migrants looked for alternative opportunities. During the post-World War One era increasingly one means of carving out an existence that remained open to members of Germany's African population was to take to the stage and perform. With the emergence of mass popular culture, the rapid growth and development in popularity of the film industry, and popular enthusiasm for North American cultural products such as jazz, black performers were in high demand. Increasing numbers of African-American entertainers toured Europe and Germany from the mid-1920s, often as part of revue shows and the likes of Josephine Baker and the Sam Wooding orchestra enjoyed enormous success. At the same time most of the large European circuses like Sarrasani, Hagenbeck, and Krone also featured African performers. Within this context new employment opportunities, although on a somewhat smaller scale, also opened up for African colonial migrants.

Under the all encompassing title of 'Performer' (*Artist*) colonial migrants and their children took on a wide range of often overlapping jobs such as theatre or film actor, musician, dancer, and circus entertainer, some of which required a rigorous apprenticeship, others less so. Often it was Cameroonians who were unable to find stable employment in their areas of training that entered the artistic arena. For example, Gottlieb Kala Kinger, who had come to Germany pre-war to train as a teacher to later work in Cameroon, instead reinvented himself in 1920s Germany as the dancer and entertainer King Charles. The qualified mechanic Otto Makube found work in Weimar Germany as a jazz band musician.[41] In several cases, the artistic lifestyle became fused with family life and man and wife, sibling or whole family teams of performers were formed.[42]

In general, the roles undertaken by Africans were of a constrictive nature, reflecting and reinforcing existing stereotypes of the Black as primitive or exotic. Circus performers like Hermann Muna Kessern appeared primarily as fire eaters or snake handlers, reinforcing an image of perceived savagery. As jazz musicians the musical ability of colonial migrants was secondary to their appearance and typically they were 'used in dance formations in the manner of a circus attraction – preferably as noisemakers on the drums'.[43] Similarly, stage and film actors like Bebe Mpessa performed in servile roles, such as servant, cook, chauffeur, or seaman or in roles that tended to "demonise black manliness" as something sexually threatening and dangerous.[44] In many ways the difficulties that black entertainers faced in finding positive roles that moved beyond existing racial stereotypes mirrored the experiences of their contemporaries in the United Kingdom, who similarly struggled to be perceived as serious actors.[45]

In interwar Germany black performers frequently represented a generic figure of the racialised exotic other, whose nationality and ethnic background were largely irrelevant. In the context of stage and film it mattered little whether Africans played African Americans or vice-versa, what counted was the performer's skin colour and the authenticity or at least illusion of authenticity of their supposed otherness that this brought. Thus, on several occasions Mpessa appeared in film roles portraying Asian, Arab, and Malayan characters. Mpessa knew to use this changeability to his own advantage and on his calling card he described himself as a 'Representative of all exotic roles on the stage and in film'.[46] The choice of a stage name helped to add to the allure of authenticity. Mpessa was better known as Louis Brody and typically exotic or Americanised stage names were adopted by Cameroonian performers. Thus, amongst others, Alfred Mangundo Köhler was better known as Paprika, Hermann Kessern appeared as Bonambela, and Benedikt Gambe performed as James Dickson.

Performance work often entailed a great deal of moving around and time apart from family while on tour. Here too, colonial migrants' lack of identity papers or citizenship status could prove a hindrance to their ability to work and travel. As part of her ultimately successful citizenship application the dancer Josefa Boholle cited the problems she had travelling outside of Germany as a central reason for her wishing to be naturalised.[47] Previously her employer, Otto Fettin of Fettino's Hawaiian Revue, had written to the Berlin authorities asking that the process be speeded up otherwise Josefa would not be able to tour with the show.[48] The fact that Josefa was earning well certainly helped her application. In 1928 she was able to earn up to 300 Marks a month dancing while her father Joseph

Boholle earned an average monthly wage of only 180 Marks as a carpenter.[49]

Artistic engagements brought colonial migrants and their children a number of benefits, foremost amongst them being the remuneration that they received. Film work, if it could be had, was especially well paid. According to the landlady of Wilhelm Munumé his theatre work afforded him a comfortable lifestyle and he reportedly received 500 Marks for 10 days work in a film production in 1926.[50] Particularly during the early years of Weimar cinema epic film cycles like the Austrian director Joe May's *Herrin der Welt* (1919), which featured [recreated] exotic stage settings and fantastic storylines, provided employment for dozens of African migrants all at once. With the growing instability of the German economy, however, such films were increasingly unrealisable and only a handful of Africans were able to find regular screen jobs. Even the successful Brody, who managed to make a career out of playing the Exotic and was well known to the German cinema going audience, at times worked as a waiter. In general artistic engagements provided only fleeting and unreliable financial relief. Work was frequently seasonal and based on short-term contracts which could be easily broken by both employer and employee alike. Most performers required a second source of income or were reliant on state financial help in order to survive.

Nevertheless, not only did performance work provide an important source of income for former colonial subjects, but it also enabled migrants to come into contact with other men and women of African heritage, helping to foster a sense of community. The '*Filmbörse*' café in Berlin became known as a popular meeting place for Africans looking for work in film productions.[51] Similarly, the circus performer Charley Dünkeloh, grandson of the Barbadian circus impresario Charles Burkett, recalled that it was only natural for touring black performers to establish contact with other Africans in the towns they visited or who were also touring.[52] Similarly, the Diek sisters remarked that when African circus entertainers or individuals came to Danzig their father invited them to his home to eat with his family.[53] Such encounters helped strengthen developing African social and political networks. Equally, in spite of the roles that Africans frequently performed, work amongst the artist community was relatively free from the racial prejudice that Africans otherwise experienced on a daily basis.

A more complex form of performance was linked to complicated criminal schemes. Crimes revolving around forgery and deception were certainly not uncommon during the Weimar period and a handful of Cameroonian and other African men resorted to illegal means as a way to escape poverty and unemployment.[54] Most prominent amongst them were the Duala men Wilhelm Munumé and Peter Mukuri Makembe, whose imaginative fraud and 'tricksterism' self-consciously exploited stereotypes of the African. The men, who were both recipients of funds from the DGfE and occasional stage and film actors, developed an elaborate criminal scheme revolving around forgery and deception in the summer of 1926.[55]

Briefly, the two men wanted to print British 5 pound notes and this required the help of professional printers, paper makers, and equipment suppliers. In their dealings with such businessmen it was necessary not to arouse suspicion. The pair accordingly created roles for themselves, introducing themselves as representatives of the fictitious King Bondongulo from Accra, British West Africa. They claimed that the clichés, logos, and watermarks they required were all part of an advertising campaign organised by the King. Playing on the naivety of their 'audience' and their 'audiences' lack of first hand contact with 'real' Africans, the pair won the confidence of a number of suppliers and successfully produced their own banknotes. The plan unravelled when Munumé was caught trying to exchange a forged note. The prison sentence that the pair received did not deter them from a further attempt as forgers once they were released. Thus, in the winter of 1931 they posed as representatives of the Emperor of Abyssinia again with limited success. One of the consequences of Munumé and Makembe's scams was that the DGfE seriously considered cutting its financial support to the African population. Additionally, Manga Akwa complained that press coverage of the 1926 trial had exacerbated the difficulty that Africans had in finding employment by heightening existing racial tension.[56]

While it would be easy to dismiss Munumé and Makembe as petty criminals it is important to place their activities in the context of the difficult social, political, and material circumstances they faced in Weimar Germany. The exclusion from normal routes of employment and dependency on welfare handouts caused men like Munumé and Makembe to take risks and exercise their resourcefulness and ingenuity to the limits of the law. They openly played upon and subverted existing European representations of the Black and their perceived 'otherness' in order to delude and deceive their victims. Through their skilful use of props and the flexibility of their roles they took on personas of noble and aristocratic black men which challenged existing stereotypes of the Black as a primitive savage.

To conclude, during the interwar period African migrants from the German colonies were faced with numerous challenges in order to establish a space for themselves in Germany. Foremost amongst these was their unclear civil status and the unwillingness of either the French or German authorities to claim responsibility for their welfare. As the example of Manga Akwa demonstrates not only did this affect migrants' chances of returning to Africa, but it influenced their day-to-day experiences of life in Germany through, amongst other things, impeding their ability to find work and accommodation as well as to establish families. In light of the instability of the German economy many of these migrants, like Manga Akwa, were unable to secure long-term employment and were instead dependent on financial handouts from government agencies. This intensified a pattern by which colonial migrants sought a living in performance on the Weimar stage, or as part of elaborate criminal schemes. In this context of effective political, economic, and frequent social exclusion it was difficult for colonial migrants to develop a sense a belonging in Europe, despite their self-identification as Germans. Against a background of changing political climate and rising racial tension in Germany the Foreign Office conceded that it was now practically impossible to find jobs for those Africans still in the country.[57] It had long been decided that the only solution was, where possible, to ensure the return of former colonial subjects to Africa, with the key exception of those married to German or European women. Ever more Africans were petitioning both the French and German authorities to be allowed to return. Such efforts were, however, hindered by the costs involved and had been frustrated by the actions of the French, whom Mansfeld accused of deliberately delaying repatriation applications.[58] As a consequence a handful of Cameroonians migrated to France in the hope of eventually returning to Cameroon. Manga Akwa, after a further failed attempt to gain German citizenship in 1930, was one of the very few Africans who successfully managed to return to Cameroon. By 1938 he was a political refugee in the British mandate.[59] When the National Socialists came to power in January 1933 the situation for Germany's African population deteriorated further and a performance of blackness now became an increasingly important means of earning a living. Whether it was part of the wandering ethnological exhibition run by the Nazis, the Africa-Show, or as performers in colonial propaganda films, glorifying the German colonial past, there was little room to manoeuvre for Africans now living under an explicitly racist regime.[60]

Acknowledgements

I am greatly indebted to the Arts and Humanities Research Council for providing funding for this research. I would also like to thank Eve Rosenhaft, Caroline Bressey,

Hakim Adi, Christoph Laucht and Eveline Meister for their comments on various versions of this article.

Notes

[1] Letter, Thomas Manga Akwa to the French Consulate, 30 January 1930, Bundesarchiv Berlin (hereafter BArch) R1001 4457/7, 249. All translations are my own unless stated.

[2] See in particular, Martin, *Schwarze Teufel, edle Mohren*.

[3] This article is based on a larger project into the lives of Cameroonian migrants and their children in Germany in the period 1884–1960, supported by a grant from the UK Arts and Humanities Research Council. On the basis of this research the names and biographical information about over 800 Africans have been recovered: over a third of these originally came from Cameroon.

[4] On the patriarchal nature of Duala society see, for example, Schler, 'Writing African Women's History'.

[5] Regarding ethnological exhibitions in Germany see, for example, Zimmerman, *Anthropology and Antihumanism*, 15–38; Guaffo, *Wissens- und Kulturtransfer*, 195–241; Thode-Arora, '"Charakteristische Gestalten des Volkslebens"'.

[6] For more on Mpundu Akwa see, von Joeden-Forgey, 'Defending Mpundu'; Eckert, '"Der beleidigte Negerprinz"'.

[7] See, 'Decree of the Imperial Governor of Cameroon Concerning the Emigration of Natives from the Imperial Protectorate, 11 December 1893', *Deutsches Kolonialblatt* 5 (1894), 105 and Decree of the Imperial Governor of Cameroon Concerning Measures for the Control of the Natives, 15 October 1910, BArch R100 4457/6, 54.

[8] Of the over 200 Cameroonians in our database, known to have entered Germany prior to 1914 around two thirds left before the outbreak of war.

[9] Letter, Consul Berlin to the Minister of Foreign Affairs, 18 August 1919, Centre des Archives d'outre-mer Fonds Ministeriels – Série géographique – Togo – Cameroun (hereafter CAOM FM SG), 25–218.

[10] Letter, Minister of Foreign Affairs to the Minister of the Colonies, 6 September 1920, CAOM FM SG, 31–284.

[11] On African political organisations in Germany see among others, Rüger, 'Imperialismus, Sozialreformismus und antikoloniale demokratische Alternative'; Martin, 'Anfänge politischer Selbstorganisation'; Aitken and Rosenhaft, 'Politik und Performance. Deutsch-Kameruner in der Anti-Kolonialbewegung'.

[12] Letter, Minister of Foreign Affairs to the Minister of the Colonies, 22 September 1920, CAOM FM SG, 25–218.

[13] Letter, the Political Department to the Minister of the Colonies, 29 January 1921, CAOM FM SG, 31–284.

[14] From the available documents Manga Akwa's reasons for fleeing Douala remain unclear. He himself claims to have held a pro-German talk with Duala elders, which was discovered by the French authorities. In contrast, a French report suggests that he had embezzled money from local leaders and fled once this had become apparent. See, Letter, Manga Akwa to Unknown, 15 June 1929, BArch R1001 4457/7, 144–5; Letter, Manga Akwa to Theodor Seitz, President of the German Colonial Society, 4 April 1925, BArch R8023 1077a, 98–100; Letter, Head of District, Douala to the Commissioner Cameroon, 17 September 1930, Archives

Nationales du Cameroun, Yaoundé (hereafter ANC) APA 10226. See also Joseph, 'The German Question in French Cameroun, 1919–1939', 83.

[15] Letter, Commissioner Cameroon to the Minister of the Colonies, 30 October 1923, CAOM Fonds Ministeriels Affaires Politiques (hereafter FM AP), 613–1071; Letter, Mansfeld to the President of the German Colonial Society, Theodor Seitz, 16 February 1928, BArch R8023 1077/a, 9–10.

[16] Addresses for Manga Akwa in part from the Berliner Adressbuch as well as various documents found in the Bundesarchiv files R1001 4457/6, 4457/7 and R8023 1077/a.

[17] Letter, Eltester to the Imperial Colonial Department, 17 October 1923, BArch R1001 5149, 140.

[18] Letter, Imperial Colonial Department to Thomas Manga Akwa, 12 November 1923, BArch R1001 5149, 142.

[19] Letter, Thomas Manga Akwa to the Colonial Central Administration, 9 March 1924, BArch R1001 5149, 145–6.

[20] von Joeden-Forgey, 'Nobody's People: Colonial Subjects, Race Power, and the German State, 1884–1945', 469.

[21] Sammartino, 'Culture, Belonging and the Law: Naturalization in the Weimar Republic', 57.

[22] See the response of the state of Thuringia to Joseph Boholle's citizenship application; letter, Thuringian Ministry of the Interior and Economy to the Imperial Minister of the Interior, 14 November 1927, BArch R1001 4457/7, 64. Boholle's citizenship would nonetheless be granted. See also the remarks of the state of Bavaria to Johannes Kohl's citizenship application; letter, Ministry of the Interior to the Imperial Minister of the Interior, 7 November 1928, Staatsarchiv Bremen Senats-Register; Akte btr. den Einbürgerungsantrag des Negers Johannes Kohl und Antrag auf Ehelichkeitserklärung. - 4,13/5 - B.6. Nr. 374, 16.

[23] In legal terms under the 1913 Citizenship law illegitimate children took on the nationality of their mother. It is unclear whether in the case of children born to both African and European parents that this would be respected. During the Nazi period of rule these children were frequently categorised as 'Mischling'.

[24] At times Boholle received financial assistance, but in general he was successful in finding employment. See documents in the file, Landesarchiv Berlin (hereafter LAB) Einbürgerungs-Antrag: A Pr. Br. Rep. 030–06 Nr.6473 Joseph Boholle.

[25] On the trader Mandenge Diek see, Oguntoye, Eine Afro-Deutsche Geschichte, esp. 146–62. See also, Hopkins, 'Zwei schwarze Unternehmer im Deutschland der Weimarer Zeit', 67–72.

[26] Letter, Political Directorate to Minister of the Colonies, 29 January 1921, CAOM FM SG, 31/284.

[27] Regarding Bilé see; letter, Kumpel to the German Colonial Department, 13 December 1920, BArch R1001 4457/6, 134–5. Concerning bin Subeiru see; letter Adamu bin Subeiru to Minister of the Colonies, 7 September 1920, CAOM FM SG, 31/285.

[28] Letter, the Police President, Main Transport Post, to Seitz, 11 April 1925, BArch R8023 1077a, 154.

[29] Letter, Thomas Manga Akwa to Seitz, 4 April 1925, BArch R8023 1077a, 98–100.

[30] Letter, Seitz to Police President, Main Transport Post, 25 April 1925, BArch R8023 1077a, 152–3.

[31] Former colonial civil servants such as Edmund Brückner, former governor of Togo, and Friederich von Lindequist, former governor of German Southwest Africa, showed a degree of paternalistic support towards African migrants residing in Germany during the Nazi period. Forgey 'Die große Negertrommel', 26–27.

[32] Letter, Foreign Office to the Deutsche Gesellschaft für Eingeborenenkunde, 27 February 1926, BArch R1001 7562, 57–8.

[33] The DGfE was the successor organisation to the Deutsche Gesellschaft für Eingeborenenschutz which had been created in 1913, but had ceased functioning in the aftermath of World War One. See in particular the file BArch 6379 Deutsche Gesellschaft für Eingeborenenkunde. Also, Report from D.A.W.Schreiber, The Tasks of the DGfE, 9 September 1927, BArch R8023/a, 34–8 and Möhle, 'Betreuung, Erfassung, Kontrolle Kontrolle', 243–51.

[34] Letter, Mansfeld to the Foreign Office, 24 November 1925, BArch R1001 7562, 44.

[35] Tension came to a head when the Duala man Peter Makembe demanded better conditions before he was willing to take up a job at an exhibition in Düsseldorf that Mansfeld had found for him. The incident ended in a physical altercation and discussions as to whether Makembe could be deported. Letter, Mansfeld to the Foreign Office, 3 May 1926, BArch R1001 4457/6, 204–5.

[36] Letter, DGfE to the President of the German Colonial Society, Dr Seitz, 16 February 1928, BArch R8203 1077a, 9.

[37] On general complaint see; letter, Brückner to the Imperial Finance Minister, 24 February 1930, BArch R1001 7562, 72–4. On Priso specifically see; letter, Eltester (Foreign Office) to the Union of Travelling Salesmen in German National Association of Commercial Employees, 9 October 1929, BArch R1001 4457/7, 162–3.

[38] Letter, Kwassi Bruce to Anny Bruce, 28 June 1932, CAOM FM AP, 613–1071.

[39] Draft Letter, Manga Akwa to Unknown, 15 June 1929, BArch R1001 4457/7, 144.

[40] Letter, Mansfeld to the Foreign Office, 9 June 1926, BArch R1001 4457/6, 230.

[41] For more on Kinger see the testimony of his daughter, Astrid Berger, '"Sind Sie nicht froh, daß Sie immer hier bleiben dürfen?"', 115. On Makube see; letter, Mansfeld to the Foreign Office, 16 May 1928, BArch R1001 4457/7, 121.

[42] Examples include the Duala man Gottlieb Kala Kinger who toured with his German wife Bertha Krebs during the interwar period, the Garber siblings, born to the Togolese migrant Joseph Garber, who performed as trapeze artists during the 1930s, and the Burkett siblings born to the Barbadian entertainer Charles Burkett.

[43] Kater, *Different Drummers. Jazz in the Culture of Nazi Germany*, 18.

[44] Tobias Nagl's research has been influential in recovering the history of African performers in German film and in particular he has focused on the career of Brody. Here, Nagl, '"Sieh mal den schwarzen Mann da!"', 84. See also, Nagl, *Die unheimliche Maschine*.

[45] See Stephen Bourne's impressive account of black performers in Britain, Bourne, *Black in the British Frame*.

[46] 'Der bekannte Negerdarsteller Lovis Brody', Der Film 11 (1921).

[47] Citizenship Application, Josefa Boholle, 7 August 1928, LAB A Pr. Br. Rep. 030–06 Nr.6473, 32–33, here 33.

[48] Letter, Otto Fettin to the Police President in Berlin, 14 July 1927, LAB A Pr. Br. Rep. 030–06 Nr.6473, 19.

[49] First figure from, Citizenship Application, Josefa Boholle, 7 August 1928, 32. Second figure from Citizenship Application, Josefa Boholle, 2 July 1928, LAB A Pr. Br. Rep. 030–06 Nr.6473, 28.

[50] Letter, DGfE to the Foreign Office, 8 December 1926, BArch R1001 4457/6, 255.

[51] Nagl, '"Sieh mal den schwarzen Mann da!"', 82.

[52] Manuela Bauche, '"Im Zirkus gibt es keine Hautfarbe"', 39.

[53] Oguntoye, *Eine Afro-Deutsche Geschichte*, 154.

[54] Among others, the Ghanaians Josef Ackon and Joseph Solomon were also convicted of forgery by a court in Leipzig 1924. Draft, Criminal Proceedings against Josef Benjamin Coblina Ackon and Joseph Samuel Salomon, 21 November 1924, LAB Rep. 58, Acc. 399/No.958, 122–3. See also, Rosenhaft and Aitken, '"König der Abenteurer": Joseph Soppo Muange'.

[55] For more on Munumé and Makembe see, Rosenhaft and Aitken, 'Edimo Wilhelm Munumé und Peter Mukuri Makembe'; Malzahn, 'The Black Captains of Köpenick'.

[56] Letter, German Colonial Society to Alfred Mansfeld, 5 February 1927, BArch R8023 1077/a, 44.

[57] Letter, Foreign Office to the Imperial Minister of Finance, 31 May 1933, BArch R8023/a, 85.

[58] Letter, Mansfeld to the President of the German Colonial Society, Theodor Seitz, 16 February 1928, BArch R8023 1077/a, 9–10.

[59] On Manga Akwa's second citizenship application see; letter, Thomas Manga Akwa to the French Minister of the Colonies, 4 February 1931, CAOM FM AP, 613–1062. On his presence in the British mandate see; letter, Delegate of the Commissioner of the Republic to the French Commissioner at Yaoundé, 4 February 1939, ANC APA 11201/K. In 1930 Manga Akwa was denied permission to return by the French authorities and it remains unclear when and how he managed to return to Cameroon and whether he did so with French consent.

[60] For more information on the Africa-Show see, Joeden-Forgey, 'Die große Negertrommel der kolonialen Werbung: Die Deutsche Afrika-Schau 1935–1943'; Lewerenz, *Die Deutsche Afrika-Schau (1935–1940)*.

References

Aitken, Robbie and Eve Rosenhaft. "Politik und Performance. Deutsch-Kameruner in der Anti-Kolonialbewegung der zwanziger und dreißiger Jahre." In *". . . Macht und Anteil an der Weltherrschaft." Berlin und der deutsche Kolonialismus*, edited by Ulrich van der Heyden and Joachim Zeller, 270–7. Münster: Unrast, 2005.

Bauche, Manuela. "'Im Zirkus gibt es keine Hautfarbe – nur gute und schlechte Artisten.' Die Geschichte der Familie Burkett-Dünkeloh." In *Mündliche Geschichte – Afrika Erinnern. Lebensgeschichten afrodeutscher und afrikanischer BerlinerInnen*, edited by Heike Schmidt. Unpublished Manuscript, Seminar für Afrikawissenschaften, Humboldt-Universität zu Berlin, 2004.

Berger, Astrid. "'Sind Sie nicht froh, daß Sie immer hier bleiben dürfen?'" In *Farbe bekennen. Afro-deutsche Frauen auf den Spuren ihrer Geschichte*, edited by Katharina Oguntoye, May Opitz, and Dagmar Schultz, 114–20. Frankfurt am Main: Fischer, 1992.

Bourne, Stephen. *Black in the British Frame. Black People in British Film and Television 1896–1996.* London: Cassel, 1998.

Brändel, Rea. *Nayo Bruce. Geschichte einer afrikanischen Familie in Europa.* Zurich: Chronos, 2007.

Eckert, Andreas. "'Der beleidigte Negerprinz'. Mpundu Akwa und die Deutschen." *Etudes Germano-Africaines* 9 (1991): 32–8.

Forgey, Elisa. "Die große Negertrommel der kolonialen Werbung: Die Deutsche Afrika-Schau 1935–1943." *Werkstatt Geschichte* 9 (1994): 25–33.

Gouaffo, Albert. *Wissens- und Kulturtransfer im kolonialen Kontext. Das Beispiel Kamerun – Deutschland (1884–1919).* Würzburg: Königshausen & Neumann, 2007.

Hopkins, Leroy. "Zwei schwarze Unternehmer im Deutschland der Weimarer Zeit." In *Zwischen Charleston und Stechschritt. Schwarze im Nationalsozialismus*, edited by Peter Martin and Christine Alonzo, 67–72. Hamburg: Dölling und Galitz Verlag, 2004.

von Joeden-Forgey, Elisa. "Nobody's People: Colonial Subjects, Race Power, and the German State, 1884–1945." PhD diss., University of Pennsylvania, 2004.

von Joeden-Forgey, Elisa. "Defending Mpundu: Dr Moses Levi of Altona and the Prince from Kamerun." In *Mpundu Akwa, der Fall des Prinzen von Kamerun. Das neuentdeckte Plädoyer von Dr. M.Levi*, edited by Leonhard Harding, 84–111. Münster: Lit, 2000.

Joseph, Richard A. "The German Question in Cameroun, 1919–1939." *Comparative Studies in Society and History* 17 (1975): 65–90.

Kater, Michael. *Different Drummers. Jazz in the Culture of Nazi Germany.* Oxford: Oxford University Press, 1992.

Lewerenz, Susann. *Die Deutsche Afrika-Schau (1935–1940). Rassismus, Kolonialrevisionismus und postkoloniale Auseinandersetzungen in nationalsizialistischen Deutschland.* Frankfurt am Main: Peter Lang, 2006.

Malzahn, Manfred. "The Black Captains of Köpenick: A Story of 1920s Berlin." In *Berlin-Wien-Prag: Moderne, Minderheiten und Migration in der Zwischenkriegzeit*, edited by Susanne Marten-Finnis and Matthias Uecker, 91–106. Bern: Peter Lang, 2001.

Martin, Peter. *Schwarze Teufel, edle Mohren: Afrikaner in Geschichte und Bewusstsein der Deutschen.* Hamburg: Hamburger Edition, 2001.

Martin, Peter. "Anfänge politischer Selbstorganisation der deutschen Schwarzen bis 1933." In *Die (koloniale) Begegnung. AfrikanerInnen in Deutschland 1880–1945. Deutsche in Afrika 1880–1918*, edited by Marianne Bechhaus-Gerst and Reinhard Klein-Arendt, 193–206. Frankfurt a.M: Peter Lang, 2003.

Möhle, Heiko. "'Betreuung, Erfassung, Kontrolle – Die Deutsche Gesellschaft für Eingeborenenkunde.'" In *Kolonialmetropole Berlin. Eine Spurensuche*, edited by Ulrich van der Heyden and Joachim Zeller, 243–51. Berlin: Berlin Edition, 2002.

Nagl, Tobias. "'Sieh mal den schwarzen Mann da!' – Komparsen afrikanischer Herkunft im deutschsprachigen Kino vor 1945." In *Zwischen Charleston und*

Stechschritt. Schwarze im Nationalsozialismus, edited by Peter Martin and Christine Alonzo, 81–91. Hamburg, Dölling und Galitz Verlag.

Nagl, Tobias. *Die unheimliche Maschine: Rasse und Repräsentation im Weimarer Kino*. Munich: Text und Kritik, 2009.

Oguntoye, Katharina. *Eine Afro-Deutsche Geschichte*. Berlin: Hoho, 1997.

Rosenhaft, Eve and Robbie Aitken. "'König der Abenteurer': Joseph Soppo Muange." In *Unbekannte Biographien. Afrikaner im deutschsprachigen Raum vom 18. JH bis zum Ende des Zweiten Weltkrieges*, edited by Ulrich van der Heyden, 173–81. Berlin: Kai Homilius, 2008.

Rosenhaft, Eve and Robbie Aitken. "Edimo Wilhelm Munumé und Peter Mukuri Makembe." In *Unbekannte Biographien. Afrikaner im deutschsprachigen Raum vom 18. JH bis zum Ende des Zweiten Weltkrieges*, edited by Ulrich van der Heyden, 153–62. Berlin, Kai Homilius, 2008.

Sammaratino, Annemarie. "Culture, Belonging and the Law: Naturalization in the Weimar Republic." In *Citizenship and National Identity in Twentieth-Century Germany*, edited by Geoff Eley and Jan Palmowski, 57–72. Stanford: Stanford University Press, 2008.

Schler, Lynn. "Writing African Women's History with Male Sources: Possibilities and Limitations." *History in Africa* 31 (2004): 319–33.

Thode-Arora, Hilke. "'Charakteristische Gestalten des Volkslebens': Die Hagen-beckschen Südasien-, Orient- und Afrika-Völkerschauen." In *Fremde Erfahrungen. Asiaten und Afrikaner in Deutschland, Österreich und in der Schweiz bis 1945*, edited by Gerhard Höpp, 109–34. Berlin: Das Arabische Buch, 1996.

Rüger, Adolf. 'Imperialismus, Sozialreformismus und antikoloniale demokratische Alternative. Zielvorstellungen von Afrikanern in Deutschland im Jahre 1919.' *Zeitschrift für Geschichtswissenschaft* 23 (1975): 1293–308.

Zimmerman, Andrew. *Anthropology and Antihumanism in Imperial Germany*. Chicago: University of Chicago Press, 2001.

The Comintern and Black Workers in Britain and France 1919–37

Hakim Adi

Middlesex University/University College London, London, UK

This paper looks at the attempts of the Communist international to organise amongst African and Caribbean workers in Europe, and particularly in France and Britain during the inter-war period. It locates these attempts within the overall objectives of the Comintern to organise all workers, to organise in the colonies and to address what was referred to at that time as the 'Negro Question' – that is the liberation of all those of African descent. The paper particularly highlights the role of communists of African and Caribbean origin and the organisations they formed. It suggests that a sense of belonging was connected with political organising and that for black workers their sense of belonging could also include identifying with other workers and a sense of class allegiance. The role of the communists was to encourage the founding of some of the first workers' organisations amongst the African diaspora in Europe and to provide an ideology to that sought to unite all workers.

Introduction

Workers of African origin had been present in the various countries of western Europe for several centuries but there has been very little research about these workers and even less concerning the organisations they formed, or joined, in order to safeguard and further their interests as workers.[1] Indeed, organised groups of black workers were largely unknown before the twentieth century, although individual workers of African and Caribbean origin did join trade unions and other labour organisations before that time.[2]

The dawning of the twentieth century produced the emergence of the Pan-African movement, which largely originated in Europe, and purported to unite the African diaspora into a movement that could campaign for mutual advancement and an end to racial discrimination, as well as the reform, or even the end, of European colonial rule in Africa and the Caribbean. The first Pan-African conference organised by the British-based African Association was held in London in 1900, and the first three Pan-African congresses, organised from 1919 to 1923 by the African American activist WE B Du Bois, were also held in Europe, in Paris, London, Brussels and Lisbon. Du Bois managed to contact many of the leading political figures from the African diaspora in Europe, such as John Archer in Britain and Blaise Diagne in France, but the Pan-African congresses could not be said to have been specifically concerned with workers, or their interests, and were largely aimed at intellectuals and professionals in Europe, the United States, the Caribbean and Africa.[3]

By the 1920s, however, significant numbers of African and Caribbean workers were also present in Europe and some certainly had family connections with European cities, especially ports, that could be traced back through several generations. There was already a sense of belonging in Europe, if not belonging to Europe, since thousands had participated and many given their lives during the First World War. Perhaps the largest numbers lived in France, where in addition to those who were connected with maritime activities in such ports as Marseilles and Bordeaux, there were also significant numbers of factory workers, as well as soldiers in the armed forces.[4] In Britain there were also significant numbers of workers, especially seamen, mainly living and working in Britain's port cities such as London, Cardiff and Liverpool. In Britain black workers and other residents had been subjected to organised racist attacks in the so-called 'race riots' of 1919, and those employed as seamen were to face many other forms of discrimination in the 1920s and 1920s, including openly racist legislation introduced by the British government.[5] Black workers, particularly but not exclusively seamen, were also to be found in several other European countries in including Belgium, Holland, Germany and Portugal.

In Britain and France, African and Caribbean workers joined trade unions to protect their interests, although even in these organisations they faced discrimination. In Britain, for example, the seamen's union became notorious for its discriminatory policies and its open support for racist measures introduced by the ship owners and government alike.[6] There are few signs that black workers tried to organise themselves independently before the 1920s and, as yet, there is little research in this important field of inquiry. Moreover, there appear to be few signs that black workers in one European country sought organised aid or support from those in other parts of Europe, although for seamen in particular there would no doubt have been many opportunities for on the job co-operation. Such strivings to organise are important as a means of survival but also significant because they suggest that workers had put down roots and felt a sense of belonging, not just in their country of employment but perhaps also a sense of class solidarity, of also belonging in this sense. Yet from 1919 onwards there was an international body that began to take up the question of organising 'Negro workers' in Europe, and particularly in France and Britain, this was the Communist International, or Comintern (CI), which was established in Moscow in 1919 in the aftermath of the Russian Revolution.[7] The aim of this chapter is to detail the attempts of the CI to organise amongst black workers in France and Britain, as part of its efforts to address what was referred to as the 'Negro Question'. The focus is therefore necessarily on workers from sub-Saharan Africa and the Caribbean.

The Comintern's interest stemmed from its general concern with what it referred to as the 'Negro Question', a phrase that originated in the United States but was used to refer to all matters pertaining to sub-Saharan Africa and the African diaspora. The *Manifesto of the Communist International to the Proletariat of the Entire World*, launched in 1919, included a call to the 'Colonial Slaves of Africa and Asia' to rise up against colonial rule and concluded, 'The emancipation of the colonies is possible only in conjunction with the emancipation of the metropolitan working class'.[8] Following the CI's second congress in 1920, it was announced that a 'Congress of the Negro Peoples of the World', would 'be convened in the near future'.[9] In fact such a gathering was not convened for a further 10 years, until the historic First Conference of Negro Workers was held in Hamburg in July 1930. But the founding of the CI and the efforts to hold an international gathering of 'Negro workers' were important decisions that created many of the conditions for developing organisations of black workers in France, Britain and Germany.

At the fourth congress of the CI in 1922 a policy was established in regard to all 'Negroes' throughout the world, in other words for Africa and the diaspora. The 'Thesis on the Negro Question', agreed at the fourth CI congress, declared that 'the penetration and intensive colonization of regions inhabited by black races is becoming the last great problem on the solution of which the further development of capitalism itself depends'. It argued that, 'the Negro problem has become a vital question of the world revolution', and therefore concluded that, 'the cooperation of our oppressed black fellow-men is essential to the Proletarian Revolution and to the destruction of capitalist power'.[10] What was essentially a Pan-African policy for the CI was at least partly a consequence of the view that those of African descent had been the victims of a particular form of racist oppression. It was also based on what seemed to be the emergence of a new awakening and common struggle epitomised by the rapid development of the Garvey movement, as well as the international influence of DuBois' Pan-African congresses in the post-war period. The fourth congress of the CI implicitly recognised this fact by pledging to organise a 'general Negro conference or Congress in Moscow', and by calling for support for 'every form of Negro movement which tends to undermine or weaken capitalism or imperialism, or to impede its further penetration'.[11]

As a consequence of these policy decisions there were several attempts during the next few years to hold a communist-led Pan-African conference in Berlin, Brussels, Paris or elsewhere in Europe and the European communist parties were urged to make contact with African and Caribbean communities of students and workers living in France, Britain and other countries.[12] Initially, however, the major European parties, which had many other more pressing matters to concern themselves with, paid little heed to CI directives. In the autumn of 1923 the British, French and other major European parties were instructed to submit reports of their work not only in the colonies but also amongst African and Caribbean residents in Europe.[13] This followed admissions by some parties that they had little contact with black workers. The Communist Party of Great Britain (CPGB), for example, admitted with regret and some understatement that it was not optimistic about any international conference of black workers in London because 'there is not sufficient contact between the Party in England and the Negro population'. Instead, it had promised to 'start propaganda among the Negro population', presumably the first time the notion had been considered, even though three of its leading members were part of the Comintern's Negro Commission.[14] In October 1923, the CPGB was again asked what work it had undertaken 'to carry out propaganda amongst the negro (sic) population in the British colonies', and was specifically asked to take up work amongst African sailors who frequented the 'African Natives' Club' in London as well as amongst African sailors in Liverpool, with an aim of also developing work in African ports.[15] Once again the CI received no satisfactory reply.

In February 1924 the *Parti communiste français* (PCF) was being asked by the CI to explain why at its recent congress, 'the question of the Negro was not taken up at all'. One Comintern official remarked that this omission was 'astonishing in view of the fact that the coloured troops are still in France, and that tens of thousands of Negro workers are in France, some of them being used as strike-breakers'. The French Party was again asked 'at least to begin' this work and reminded that 'the Comintern has pointed out to you the necessity of taking up the NEGRO question as a special question and not as part of the colonial problem'(emphasis in original).[16] But the PCF apparently had little interest in this question or, like other parties, was evidently unable to make any headway on it. As a consequence it was impossible at this stage for the CI to convene its 'Negro World Congress'. Indeed, no substantial headway was made in this respect until after the founding of the International Trade Union Committee of Negro Workers (ITUCNW) in 1928.

Despite the criticisms of the Comintern, however, efforts to organise African and Caribbean workers had in fact already begun in France. The first organisation established with the support of the PCF, the Union Intercoloniale (UIC) was an organisation with members drawn from French colonies in Asia, as well as Africa and the Caribbean. Although mainly intellectual in composition it had, by 1924, recruited one of its most celebrated members of proletarian origin, Lamine Senghor.

Senghor, who was born in 1898 in what is today Senegal, came from a family of peasant farmers. He seems to have had little in the way of European education, but he had worked for a time for a colonial trading company before being enlisted in the French army in 1915 and he subsequently saw action on the Somme. There he was wounded and gassed and subsequently awarded the Croix de Guerre. After being demobilised he returned to France in 1921 and worked as a postal clerk before he became involved with the PCF, its trade union organisation the Confédération Générale du Travaille Unitaire (CGTU) and the UIC.[17] In 1925 he stood as a PCF candidate in the municipal elections in Paris, but despite such advances, which compared very favourably with those obtained in Britain, the work of the PCF on the Negro Question was considered extremely weak and was at this stage solely limited to Paris.

In 1926 Senghor led the creation of the Comité de Défense de la Race Nègre (CDRN) a broad Pan-Africanist organisation that included many members of working-class origin, especially those drawn from the French ports of Marseilles, Bordeaux and Le Havre. At least some of its leaders were also workers, including Masse Ndiaye who became the organisation's treasurer, and was like Senghor born in Senegal, and Garan Kouyaté, another African who although already a graduate worked as a clerk in Paris. The working-class membership of the CDRN reflected the fact that it recruited particularly amongst Africans and many Africans in Franc were workers but it also reflected a new political orientation that was clearly influenced by its links with the PCF. It was at first merely sympathetic to the Party but gradually grew much closer and soon some of its activities, and its paper *La Voix des Nègres*, were directly financed by the PCF. The use of the pejorative term 'nègre' rather than 'noire' was itself an indication that the Comité wished to identify itself with the masses.[18] However, the CDRN was not a communist organisation and included some members who were hostile to the PCF and communism. The CDRN was also interested in recruiting Caribbean and especially African seamen in the ports in order to distribute its paper in French West Africa, where it seems to have been read by a wide cross-section of people. It became increasingly strident in its opposition to colonialism and the paper's distribution, as well as the activities of the CDRN in general, were closely monitored by the authorities.

Senghor engaged in a burst of activity from 1926 until his early death at the age of 38 in 1927. He was one of the most notable speakers at the founding conference of the League against Imperialism (LAI) in Brussels in 1927 and was elected to its executive committee. He continued to recruit in the ports, and apparently even amongst African soldiers, and these and other activities led to a short period of imprisonment which probably hastened his death. He was, however, unable to retain unity within the CDRN, which was itself beset by major political disagreements between those who wished to move closer to the PCF and those who did not; between Africans and those from the Caribbean, as well as by major financial problems. As a consequence, Senghor, Kouyaté, and others eventually left the organisation and with PCF support formed the *Ligue de Défense de la Race Nègre* (LDRN) in May 1927.[19]

The LDRN, led by Senghor, Kouyaté and others, produced a publication subsequently entitled *La Race Nègre*, and was established to 'work for the revolutionary education, organisation and complete emancipation of the entire Negro race'.[20] However, it appears that it was mainly African in terms of membership, and often concentrated on matters related to the African continent. Like the CDRN it recruited and utilised African sailors to distribute *La Race Nègre* and membership forms throughout French West Africa and so from its inception established a presence in Africa much to the concern of the colonial authorities. They reported that the LDRN had attempted to establish branches in Senegal, Dahomey and Cameroon, had been responsible for demands for independence and even uprisings in French Congo and others parts of French Equatorial Africa.[21]

The LDRN also had several workers amongst its leadership and it is worth noting that again the organisation employed the word 'nègre' rather than 'noire'. It also took up the plight of the *tirailleurs*, recruited from Africa during the First World War, but discriminated against in terms of pay, conditions and pensions in post-war France. Under the influence of the PCF Senghor in particular began to pay much more attention to recruitment amongst workers in the ports. But the organisation's semi-independent relationship with the PCF and ambivalent political orientation continued even after Senghor's premature death, when the LDRN came under the leadership of Kouyaté.

The task of organising the 'international congress of Negro workers' much discussed in CI circles for many years was finally taken up by the Red International of Labour Unions (RILU or the Profintern), the trade union organisation of the CI, in 1928, after the CI itself had stressed the importance of organising the 'Negro industrial and agricultural workers of the world'.[22] In this period the CI began to put much more emphasis on organisation amongst workers in the colonies and it therefore also encouraged the communist parties in the major colonial countries to do more to work with organisations and individuals who had direct links with the Caribbean and Africa. It was also concerned to tackle the problem of racism and eurocentrism that had an impact even within some communist parties.

In July 1928 a meeting of the leaders of the RILU decided to establish an International Trade Union Committee of Negro Workers (ITUCNW), which was initially led by the African American communist James Ford.[23] One of the main reasons for establishing the ITUCNW was the inability of the 'communist parties of the west' particularly those in Europe to adequately deal with the 'Negro Question'. The ITUCNW was charged with the 'setting up of connections with the Negro workers of the whole world and the unification of the wide masses of the Negro workers on the basis of the class struggle', as well as, preparing and convening 'an International conference of Negro workers' at the end of 1929.[24] Henceforth, the 'Negro Question' would focus on workers and would be addressed mainly through the activities of the RILU and the ITUCNW.

From this time onwards plans for the First International Conference of Negro Workers were made and it was always envisaged that this would be convened somewhere in Europe.[25] From an early stage therefore it was envisaged that the conference would include workers and some other delegates from Britain and France.[26] In 1929 it was decided that the conference would take place in London in July 1930. The preparations for the London conference led to increased activity in regard to the 'Negro Question' by both the CI and RILU. James Ford was engaged in a range of meetings with the communist parties in France, Belgium and Germany and every effort was made to develop and strengthen the 'Negro work' in these areas. The British party too was expected to step up its work, including its activity amongst seamen, 'Negro groups in England', as well as in African and other colonies.[27] Subsequently, William Paterson, another African American member of the ITUCNW, was sent to Paris to hold discussions with the leaders of the PCF concerning its 'very unsatisfactory Negro work.[28] Thus one of the consequences of founding of the ITUCNW and the planned conference was much more concern with organising black workers in France, Britain, Germany and other European countries.

However, although there was renewed concern in Moscow and amongst the members of the ITUCNW almost no preparations for the conference were undertaken by the European communist parties. Even in France where the LDRN was in existence, there were no preparations for the conference, nor in Berlin where a German branch of the LDRN had also already been established.[29] In Europe, in general, preparations for the conference were greatly hampered by what Patterson described as an 'under-estimation of the importance of colonial work', which 'generally become in the case of Negro work because of its present stage of development total neglect'. His explanation for this 'total neglect' was that 'all of the CI resolutions on the Negro Question are regarded here as "Open Letters" to the American Party with no reference to our European parties'.[30]

In Britain where the conference was supposed to take place there was also little activity. Patterson travelled there too and took the opportunity not only to meet with Jomo Kenyatta, who had attended previous meetings where the conference had been planned, but also to travel to Liverpool and Cardiff where he met with what he refers to as a 'group of about 30 Negroes', presumably workers, but about whom no other information has yet been found.[31] At around the same time that Patterson was visiting Liverpool the local branch of the CPGB also began to initiate some work amongst the black community there, although it is not clear if there the two initiatives were connected. In the latter case this initiative was actually taken by Douglas and Molly Walton, two of the leaders of the Communist Party of South Africa, who were in Britain at that time. According to the CI report, the Waltons intervened and 'used their South African experience' but it is not clear if this meant that they were more aware of the significance of black workers than their British comrades. It is clear that Black workers in Liverpool faced many problems, not least the racist *Report on an Investigation into the Colour Problem in Liverpool and other Ports*, issued in 1930.[32] A first meeting of about 80 black workers was held in the premises used by the Nigerian clergyman Daniels Ekarte and several other meetings were subsequently held, although the connection with Ekarte was apparently a deterrent, as was surveillance by the police. A decision was taken to establish 'a Negro Society' with the Waltons and another English communist as the organising committee, although it was also reported that several promising workers had emerged. But although plans were being made to develop the society and take up all the grievances of the '300 Negroes in Liverpool', little more is reported. It is evident, however, that the communists in Liverpool were proposing that a few of the 'Negro comrades', particularly the seamen, should be sent to Moscow for further training, an altogether unusual proposal in the British context.[33]

Subsequently, the Labour government in Britain refused to allow the conference to take place and the venue had to be switched at the last minute to Hamburg. However, Patterson later informed his comrades that while in Britain he worked closely with the National Minority Movement (NMM), the trade union organisation of the CPGB, the LAI and the CPGB itself, and had established a 'Negro liberation society'. It is altogether unclear exactly what this organisation was but presumably the beginnings of what later became known as the Negro Welfare Association.[34] In this regard the conference preparations acted as a catalyst for the organisation of African and Caribbean workers in Britain.

The Hamburg Conference certainly publicly launched the activities of the ITUCNW but there were no representatives there from the black workers of France or Britain. Although Jomo Kenyatta and Kouyaté had attended one of the planning meetings during the LAI congress in Frankfurt, neither made it to Hamburg. The only representative of the 'Negro workers' of Europe was Joseph Bilé of the Berlin branch of the LDRN. In the aftermath therefore there was much criticism of the European communist parties, especially those in France and Britain. In August 1930 a CI report commenced by stating: 'It is impossible to make a report on the Negro work of our French and British Parties. To attempt this would be to infer that concrete work in this sphere of Party activity had been accomplished. In the case of the British Party no such assertion can be made, while with reference to our French Party only a little more may be said'.[35]

However, the greater tempo developed by the CI in regard to 'Negro work' after 1928, especially in connection with the Negro workers' conference, clearly had some impact even in Britain, not least because the CI was demanding of the CPGB that it report on what work it was undertaking amongst 'coloured seamen' as well as other 'Negro groups in England especially London'.[36] African American communists such as Patterson certainly felt that there was a 'good field for Negro work' in Britain but 'extremely little activity of any kind amongst them', and he lamented the fact that the ITUCNW's paper the *Negro Worker* was not widely distributed in Britain. In 1930 he concluded 'no one has conception of what to do or how to do it', but he thought that his presence in Britain and that of other black communists, such as George Padmore who had also visited in preparation for the conference, had been a 'stimulant'.[37]

Following the Hamburg Conference, the visit to Britain of the Nigerian delegate, Frank Macaulay, also acted as a catalyst for more organised activity amongst black workers in Britain and it seems that he was responsible for another attempt to organise a Negro Welfare Association, when he spent a few months in country during the winter of 1930–31. In early 1931 the *Report of the National Conference of the LAI* [League Against Imperialism] (*British Section*) mentioned two significant facts. First that the LAI had established a branch in Liverpool and could report, 'good connections made with coloured workers'. However, it is not clear if these connections were also linked to the meetings held by Patterson and by the Liverpool District Committee of the CPGB some months previously. More importantly, however, it was reported that 'during December a Negro comrade conducted a campaign on behalf of the League amongst Negro and other workers in Liverpool and Cardiff. Meetings were held in Cardiff, where there was some support from Miner's Lodges and individuals'.[38] The 'Negro comrade', was Frank Macauley, the son of the 'father of Nigerian nationalism', Herbert Macaulay, who had attended both the First International Conference of Negro Workers in Hamburg, and afterwards the Fifth Congress of the Profintern in Moscow. On his return from Moscow, via Berlin, he spent several months in Britain and according to his brother's account, had organised a group of 'West African Negroes at Liverpool known as the "Negro Welfare Association"'. Subsequently, in letters to James Ford, Macaulay confirmed that he had 'organised this "Welfare Association"'. Ford initially know nothing more and wrote to the NMM in Britain for further details.[39]

No details of Macaulay's activities in Liverpool have yet come to light, although it appears from other sources that he was able to establish an organisation of workers there, but there was a report by the NMM of one of the meetings Macaulay attended in Cardiff, held in the 'Negro quarter of the docks area' with 'negro seamen'. The report claimed that Macaulay had 'a very remarkable approach to the workers and he was listened to very attentively'. It appears that the meeting was held late in the evening, mostly conducted in what the report refers to as 'native languages', and even after it had concluded Macaulay spent the rest of the night with the seamen. What was said in English seems to have worried the representatives of the NMM who reported that 'the line pursued was that of establishing a kind of Negro Workers organisation'. Although it was difficult for them to say what kind of organisation this might be, they evidently had 'misgivings' and, despite the fact that the seamen were apparently enthusiastic, the NMM accused Macaulay of pursing a 'very narrow and separatist' approach.[40]

Macaulay certainly seems to have played a significant role in both Liverpool and Cardiff. By the close of 1931 Ford reported that 'Negro comrades' were 'working in conjunction with the seamen' in Liverpool, Cardiff and London. He specifically names three of these organisers who worked with the Seamen's Minority Movement (SMM): Arnold Ward in London, Harry O'Connell in Cardiff and 'Comrade Jones', probably the Sierra Leonean seamen Forster-Jones rather than Chris Jones, in Liverpool.[41] E Forster-Jones was a seaman from Sierra Leone, a leader of the Krumen's Seamen's Club, who had apparently formerly been employed as a policeman. He had first come into contact with James Ford in Hamburg, although at this time was partly resident in Liverpool. Ford, and subsequently Padmore who replaced Ford, both had high hopes that he would become a major organiser in West Africa. Jones was for a time a 'contributing editor' to the *Negro Worker*, although only one of his articles appears to have been published. He also evidently organised amongst seamen in Liverpool but was distrusted by SMM officials.

By the end of 1931, as a consequence of the constant prodding of the CI and RILU, and particularly as a result of the activity of the ITUCNW and the convening of its Hamburg conference, African and Caribbean workers were being organised and organising themselves in Britain's ports where the largest black communities were resident. What is more a new organisation, the Negro Welfare Association (NWA), had been established under the auspices of the communist-led LAI. Although the NWA had a diverse membership, much of its activity was subsequently directed towards workers and their families and its secretary and spokesperson was Arnold Ward, a Barbadian of working-class origin. Ward was born in Bridgetown, Barbados, in 1886. Between 1903 and 1906 he is reported to have lived in Trinidad, and from 1907 to 1915 in Germany, where presumably he found employment as a seaman, and where he was interned during World War 1 before being sent to Britain as 'medically unfit'. He seems to have been in touch with the LAI and CPGB before 1931 but did not become a Party member until 1932.[42] In the same year he was also elected to the Executive of the LAI.[43] Since the NWA was the only communist-led African and Caribbean organisation in Britain at that time, it was mainly through the NWA and its contacts that the ITUCNW subsequently tried to organise black workers.

As mentioned above, the NWA was not the only organisation in Britain through which communists attempted to organise 'Negro workers'. The communist-led NMM and Transport Workers Minority Movement undertook some work amongst black seafarers during the late 1920s and after the Seamen's Minority Movement (SMM) was established in 1929 the following year in London it formed what was referred to as, a 'committee of militant coloured seamen' led by the Barbadian Chris Jones (aka Braithewaite) and Jim Headley a seaman from Trinidad. In 1930, the African American James Ford, who initially led the work of the ITUCNW, reported that 'at Liverpool, Cardiff and London, Negro Comrades in cooperation with the SMM have been carrying out work among Negro Seamen for the Negro Committee of the SMM'.[44] But although, in the next few years, work amongst black seamen was also organised under the auspices of the International of Seamen and Harbour Workers (ISH), it appears that in Britain it was mainly undertaken by the ITUCNW, acting through the NWA and its supporters.[45] Communists of Caribbean origin, such as Jones, Headley and others in London, and O'Connell and others in Cardiff were at the forefront of organising amongst black seafarers in Britain's ports, but very little information has emerged about their activities.[46]

When George Padmore became the leading representative of the ITUCNW in Europe in 1931, he attempted to organise a merger between the Negro Committee of the SMM and the NWA. He planned to develop the NWA as a 'strong organisation of all the Negro workers in England', and as the British section of the ITUCNW.[47] The organising skills of Ward were not fully up to this task, although the NWA did make several attempts to turn itself into a 'more effective organisation' of black workers, and the SMM committee in London appears to have met its demise in 1932 when Headley returned to Trinidad.[48] Indeed, there were clearly great difficulties recruiting African and Caribbean seamen to the SMM and in 1932 O'Connell strongly criticised it at the ISH conference in Hamburg.[49] The SMM in Liverpool was also reported by one member to be 'partly broke up' by mid-1932 and 'coloured seamen' reluctant to join it.[50] Nevertheless, Padmore and other representatives of the ITUCNW kept closely in contact with Ward and O'Connell and with others in Liverpool. It is evident that for some years African and Caribbean seamen and other workers had organised themselves in Liverpool, some in connection with the SMM, but again very little information about these individuals and their activities has been found.

The CI viewed organising amongst seamen in Britain as particularly important because of the level of the attacks launched on them by the British government, shipping companies and the National Union of Seamen.[51] It was black seamen who have been amongst those subjected to racist attacks during the riots that had occurred in many British cities in 1919. Following the riots some seamen were deported, while those remaining were subjected to discrimination under the Aliens Acts of 1919 and 1920, the openly racist Special Restriction (Coloured Aliens Seamen) Order of 1925 and, in 1935, the British Shipping Assistance Act. Such legislation was accompanied by a campaign of racist slurs in the press, including remarks made by politicians, leading trade unionists and police chiefs.[52] At the same time, the Comintern recognised that the seamen were an important pivotal link between British communists and Britain's colonial subjects both in Britain and in Africa and the Caribbean, and that therefore it was vital that they were organised.

The attacks on black workers and the hardships they faced during this period also extended to their families. As Arnold Ward expressed it,

> their children are treated as outcasts and "aliens" and they cannot get a decent job. Thus the hardships of hunger misery and squalor combined with segregation make life for our little ones as hard and sorrowful as it is for their parents.[53]

It was for this reason that from the summer of 1932 one of the regular activities of the NWA was a trip for worker's children to one of the seaside towns.

In Cardiff, the black seafarers and their families were often in the front ranks of those who not only bore the brunt of these attacks but also organised resistance alongside other colonial seamen. Harry O'Connell, the main organiser in the port, highlighted some of the problems facing Cardiff's unemployed black population in his letter to the editor of *Negro Worker* in 1933,[54] but *Negro Worker* also reported similar attacks launched in the British press and by the NUS against colonial seamen in Liverpool. According to the press there were some 10,000 'coloured' seamen in these two ports.[55] O'Connell was one of the most important activists during this period, born in British Guiana he came to Britain around 1910. He was a seafarer, a ship's carpenter, who may have founded a 'Cardiff Coloured Association' during the 1920s in the aftermath of the riots.[56] Certainly, he had become involved with the SMM soon after it was established and then with the ITUCNW and the NWA. Whether he met with Patterson and Macaulay in 1930 is not yet clear. In 1935 although the problem of racism still faced the seaman in Cardiff, a Coloured Seamen's Committee had been formed, presumably under O'Connell's leadership and linked to the NWA.[57] Two years later, O'Connell was still writing of the problems facing those in Cardiff, but he also reported that a Colonial Defence Association had been successfully organised, and that it was daily increasing its membership.[58] A year earlier, in 1936, a Colonial Seamen's Association had also been formed at a conference in London, chaired by Chris Jones and with the involvement of the NWA and other organisations.[59] It appears that all of these organisations were communist-led but the precise details are as yet difficult to establish. O'Connell's activism on behalf of the seaman led to questions in Parliament and an investigation and report by the League of Coloured People (LCP).[60] The extent of his influence can perhaps be judged by the comments of Harold Moody, the president of the LCP, who in 1935 told the *Western Mail*, 'the coloured people of Cardiff are mainly Communists, simply because no one else has seen fit to give them a helping hand.[61]

The intervention of communists, and of the ITUCNW in particular, encouraged black workers to organise themselves alongside other workers and only to form separate organisations if they could not join organisations like the SMM and where trade unions discriminated against them. Through the ITUCNW, the LAI and other organisations black workers in Britain were encouraged to have an internationalist outlook, to see themselves as part of the British working class but also to attempt to foster links with individuals and organisations in Africa and the Caribbean, and in particular with colonial workers and political organisations. The 1930s was a period in which workers took part in international campaigns such as those organised in defence of the nine 'Scottsboro Boys' in the United States, or in defence of Ethiopia against fascist aggression. It is noteworthy that the NWA as well as black workers in Cardiff were prominent in both campaigns. Internationalism was also encouraged in the pages of the ITUCNW's *Negro Worker*. Seamen regularly travelled to other ports in Europe but there seem to be few examples of activists travelling abroad to organise, although in 1932 O'Connell travelled to Hamburg and along with Kouyaté was a delegate at the ISH congress. Ward was apparently prevented from travelling abroad by the British government.

During the early 1930s, when the ITUCNW was based in Hamburg, it also managed to make contact with 'Negro workers' in Belgium, Holland, Portugal and Germany, although the two key areas remained Britain and France. In France the membership of the LDRN, was according to Kouyaté, predominantly working class in origin, although it is difficult to know how accurate his figures were.[62] The LDRN was beset by a range of problems, some of them financial and most of which stemmed from its difficult relationship with the PCF. Nevertheless, the founding of the ITUCNW and its intervention in France, as well as the priorities of

RILU and the CI also led to a change in the approach of Kouyaté and the LDRN.

At the beginning of 1930, based on one of the proposals that had been made by the CI, Kouyaté was sent by the PCF to establish sections of the LDRN amongst the seamen and dockers in Bordeaux, Marseilles and Le Havre, although he ended up trying to establish independent unions of black seamen and other workers, contrary to the line and instructions of the PCF and the CGTU, which had been fully discussed with him before he left Paris.[63] Initially, these unions met with some support from black seamen, several hundred attended a meeting in Marseilles and almost a hundred joined in Bordeaux after successful negotiations with the shipping companies. In one sense they build on earlier work that had been carried out by Senghor and to some extent by the CGTU itself, which had established an International Seamen's Club in Marseilles, vividly described by Claude McKay, but which did not appear to have carried out much recruitment amongst black workers.[64] However, initial success was temporarily hampered by the repressive activities of the police, those of the rival trade union centre, the Confédération Générale du Travail (CGT), and even by national divisions between the seamen.[65] Moreover, Kouyaté's unions were based on creating divisions between black and white workers and they were ultimately condemned as divisive by the PCF and 'counter-revolutionary' by the CGTU.[66] The programme of the ITUCNW and the RILU called for the 'opening up of the unions to all workers regardless of race and colour'. However, where a colour bar existed the ITUCNW demanded that 'special unions of Negro workers must be organized'.[67] It seems that Kouyaté simply felt that the CGTU were not organising the seamen and that this was sufficient justification for organising separate unions in the ports.

In the aftermath of this episode there were again CI criticisms of the PCF although also some of Kouyaté. The LDRN clearly faced many problems, including police harassment and infiltration and internal divisions eventually resulted in a split in the organisation, with Kouyaté and his closest comrades launching a new paper, Le Cri des Nègres. In this period Kouyaté came under the wing of James Ford who attempted to again encourage LDRN activity amongst black workers, particularly those in the ports.[68] Ford and Kouyaté held exploratory meetings with seamen in Germany and planned future work with seafarers in Marseilles, through whom they also hoped to develop ITUCNW activities in Africa.[69] On his return to France, Kouyaté was given a position in the Colonial Commission of the CGTU, and from July 1931 he began to organise amongst the black seamen and dockers in Marseilles, as a representative of the ISH and the ITUCNW, as well as of the CGTU. Kouyaté was clearly implementing the programme of the ITUCNW's Hamburg Committee, which had resolved to establish 'sub-committees' amongst seamen and dockers not only in Marseilles but also in other ports including Liverpool, as 'the best avenue to reach the Negro masses in the different countries'.[70] The French Seamen's Federation at this time openly stated 'we refuse to consider the natives of the colonies French citizens having the right to work on our ships', so Kouyaté's main aim was to encourage those unions he had earlier created to join the CGTU.[71] He was briefly imprisoned during the course of this work in August 1931, but continued his organising work in Marseilles in October that year following his release.[72] According to Ford's report this work went well and in one meeting alone Kouyaté was able to recruit over 70 seamen from the Seamen's Federation for the CGTU's International Seamen's club.[73]

The ITUCNW tried to help develop *Le Cri des Nègres* so that it more openly addressed the problems facing black workers. According the ITUCNW the paper should concern itself with educating workers about how to organise themselves against exploitation. In this regard the paper was expected to commence a campaign dealing with the needs and demands of the unemployed, including providing guidance on establishing 'unemployed committees' and combating the chauvinism of the main trade union centre which was seen as 'setting French workers against foreign and colonial workers'. At the same time as stressing the importance of the economic struggles it was emphasised that the paper must also pay attention to the anti-colonial struggle and in particular the attempts of the French government to create a 'huge professional black army' to be used both against French workers and a future war against the Soviet Union.[74]

In short, *Le Cri de Nègres* was expected to play the part of an organiser concerned with the day-to-day life of the 'Negro workers', but also capable of enlightening them about the international situation and the struggles of workers in other countries, especially the Soviet Union. Its work became even more important when the publication of the *Ouvrier Nègre* (the French edition of *the Negro Worker*) was suspended in 1932.[75] Also at this time, because of the splits in the LDRN, in June 1932 Kouyaté and his supporters formed a new organisation, the *Union des Travailleurs Nègres (UTN)*, and by the end of that year established branches, mainly of workers, in Marseilles, Bordeaux and Le Havre.[76]

In May 1932 Kouyaté attended the ISH congress in Hamburg, as leader of the French CGTU delegation, along with O'Connell from Britain and delivered a report in which he stressed the important role of 'Negro workers' in France and estimated that there were between 5000 and 6000

'Negro seamen', who were particularly prominent in Marseilles and Bordeaux, as well as workers in other industries, including the car industry.[77] It is, however, difficult to judge how significant the UTN was in organising these workers. It was again hampered by internal disputes about its relationship with the PCF disputes that ultimately led to the expulsion of Kouyaté in 1933.

The ITUCNW was itself beset by difficulties in that year which eventually led to the expulsion of George Padmore. Although it took several months for it to reestablish its work, and it then because of police repression had to move to various European cities, it eventually managed to continue its activities under the leadership of Otto Huiswoud. Once again there was an emphasis on organising workers, especially seafarers in France and Britain. In Britain, for example, the ITUCNW concentrated on Cardiff, although it was also in contact with 'coloured seamen' in London, Liverpool and North Shields. Some efforts were also made to organise seafarers in Belgium and by the end of 1934 the Belgian press was complaining that the UTN's *Cri des Nègres* was circulating in Belgium. Links were also established with the Surinamech Arbeiders Bund in Holland.[78] The efforts to organise amongst black workers in Europe continued until the struggle against fascism and the response of Africans and the diaspora to the Italian invasion of Ethiopia led to further changes in the policy of the CI and the ITUCNW was itself dissolved in 1937 as part of the cessation of all the activities of the RILU.

The efforts to organise African and Caribbean workers had specific features in both France and Britain. In Britain during the mid-1930s there were efforts to make all 'coloured' seamen bear the brunt of the economic crisis and the problem of mass unemployment. In these circumstances workers and particularly seamen of many different nationalities joined together to form organisations of 'Coloured Seamen' in the major British ports such as London, Liverpool and Cardiff. These organisations included Chinese, Indian, Malay and other seafarers as well as those of African and Caribbean origin. In many cases, these seamen would have been residents in Britain for many years. The need for unity here was not just a Pan-African unity, nor even a unity based on colonial origin. What was always stressed was need for all workers to unite in order to advance their interests. In France the seamen faced similar problems but might organise in a different way. For example, one member of the UTN, Gatien Félix Merlin, originally from Martinique and standing on the communist ticket, even managed to get elected as a local councillor in Paris and became a well-known local politician.[79] However, activists faced similar problems. Senghor, Kouyaté and others were arrested and imprisoned and their organisations were under constant police surveillance and liable to infiltration and repression. In Britain conditions were not quite so severe, although O'Connell was arrested for his activities and sellers of *Negro Worker* and other publications were liable to harassment. In England too police and secret service surveillance of all kinds was ubiquitous. Where there were advances in terms of organising workers there were also great difficulties that had to be overcome.

Until its dissolution in 1937 the ITUCNW constantly complained about the lack of support and work of the European communist parties, suggesting that more could be done and achieved. But it is evident that by this time advances had been made, that workers had been organised and more importantly for the first time had organised themselves. The CI and its affiliates had encouraged these developments and provided an ideology to guide African and Caribbean workers, many of whom now saw themselves as belonging in Europe and as belonging to the working class in their country of employment and residence. This contributed to ushering in a new form of Pan-Africanism, one that not only linked black workers in Europe with Africa and the Caribbean but also with other workers in Europe and with each other. As war clouds gathered what was being demanded was the unity of all workers in Europe against their common foes.

Acknowledgements

Research for this article was carried out with the assistance of a British Academy Small Grant.

Notes

[1] Three exceptions which contain some details in regard to workers in Britain are Ramdin's *The Making of the Black Working Class in Britain*, Tabili's 'We Ask for British Justice' and Frost's, *Work and Community among West African Migrant Workers*.
[2] The most well-known British example was William Cuffay, a tailor who became one of the leaders of the London Chartists in the nineteenth century.
[3] See Geiss, *The Pan-African Movement*.
[4] One recent estimate has suggested that there were at least 8000 workers of African origin in France in the mid-1920s, that is not including those who were serving in the armed forces. There were probably an equal, or even greater, number of workers from the French Antilles. Ndiaye, *La Condition Noire*, 165, 168.
[5] Tabili, *'We Ask For British Justice'*.
[6] Ibid., 81—112.
[7] Adi, 'Pan-Africanism and Communism'.
[8] Daniels, *A Documentary History of Communism*, 89.

[9] From the Small Bureau of the ECCI to Comrades Reed, Fraina, Gurvitch and Jansen Scott n.d., Russian State Archive of Social and Political History (RGASPI) 495/155/1/2.

[10] Wilson, *Russia and Black Africa*, 130.

[11] R. Kanet, 'The Comintern and the "Negro Question', 86—122.

[12] Adi, 'Pan-Africanism and Communism'.

[13] Secretary for Calling Negro Conference to the EC of the CP of France/Portugal/ Italy, 15 November 1923, RGASPI 495/14/19.

[14] Thomas Bell to J. Amter, 17 August 1923. RGASPI 495/155/16/2−3.

[15] Secretary of Negro Conference to CEC, British Communist Party, 24 October 1923. RGASPI 495/155/14/16.

[16] Secretary of Negro Conference to the CC of the CPF, 20 February 1924, RGASPI 495/155/27/6.

[17] Dewitte, *Les Mouvements Nègre*, 127. Unless otherwise indicated this account of workers and their organisations in France is based on Dewitte.

[18] On this issue see Spiegler, 'Aspects of Nationalist Thought'.

[19] For Gothon-Lunion's views on the problems within the CDRN see his *La Verité est en Marche*. The LDRN was formed with members from the UIC but possibly also those from the *Ligue Universelle de Défense de la Race Noire*. Spiegler, 'Aspects of Nationalist Thought', 114.

[20] 'Report', 29 September 1930, RGASPI 495/155/87/396.

[21] Spiegler, 'Aspects of Nationalist Thought', 125−33 and Edwards, *The Practice of Diaspora*.

[22] RGASPI 495/155/53/2.

[23] RILU's International Bureau of Negro Workers was originally composed of Ford, La Guma (South Africa), Ducados (Guadeloupe) and an unnamed Cuban member. The ITUCNW initially had some eight members, including three African Americans, James Ford, William Paterson and Harry Haywood.

[24] RGASPI 495/155/53/1. The ITUCNW immediately issued an 18-point *Trade Union Programme of Action for Negro Workers*. The first edition of the ITUCNW's publication, *Negro Worker* was launched on 16 July 1928.

[25] RGASPI 495/155/53/3.

[26] Ibid.

[27] Report of Comrade Ford to the Negro Bureau, 14 November 1929, RGASPI 534/3/450.

[28] RGASPI 495/155/80/95−6.

[29] RGASPI 534/4/330. On the activities of Bilé and the Berlin LDRN see R. Aitken, 'From Cameroon to Germany and Back'.

[30] Patterson to Dear Comrades, 29 April 1930 and Patterson to Lozovsky, 7 May 1930, RGASPI 534/4/330.

[31] WW (W. Patterson) to Negro Bureau Profintern, 18 April 1930, RGASPI 534/4/330.

[32] See Rich, Race and Empire, 132—36.

[33] 'Report on Work among Negroes in England', 27 August 1930, RGASPI 495/155/83/53−5. Also 495/155/90/73.

[34] Patterson to Negro Bureau, Profintern, 24 May 1930, RGASPI 534/4/330.

[35] RGASPI 495/155/87/277.

[36] 'Report of Comrade Ford to the Negro Bureau' 14 February 1929, RGASPI 534/3/450.

[37] WW (W. Patterson) to the Negro Bureau Profintern, 18 April 1930, RGASPI 534/4/330.

[38] *Report of the National Conference of the LAI (British Section) February 1931*, 15.

[39] 'Report to European Secretariat of RILU on Activities of the ITUCNW at Hamburg', 21 February 1931, RGASPI 534/3/669.

[40] 'Re. Seamen' National M. M., 31 January 1931, The National Archives (TNA) M9/2084. This report was subsequently intercepted by the Special Branch of the Metropolitan Police.

[41] See 'Report of Work of ITUCNW (Hamburg), Covering the Period from December 1930–September 15 1931', RGASPI 534/3/669.

[42] See (TNA) CO 295/606/4.

[43] Bellamy and Saville, *Dictionary of Labour Biography*, 44.

[44] Sherwood, 'The CPGB and Black Britons', 153.

[45] In 1931 the International of Seamen and Harbour Workers appealed to 'Negro Seamen and Dockers' to join its ranks and to attend a congress in Hamburg in 1932. See *Negro Worker NW* 2, no. 4 (April 1932): 20—4.

[46] For some information on O'Connell and Cardiff see Sherwood, 'Racism and Resistance', See also O'Connell to the Editor, *NW* 3, nos. 4–5 (April–May 1933): 24–5. See also *Report of the Annual Conference of the NWA*, 25 October 1935, LOC 301/3943.

[47] Padmore to Ward, 17 December 1931, RGASPI 534/3/668.

[48] On the NWA see Bridgeman to Padmore, 17 February 1932, RGASPI 534/3/754.

[49] *NW* 2, no. 6 (June 1932), 23—25.

[50] William Brown to Padmore, 25 June, 1932, RGASPI 534/3/755.

[51] See, e.g., the LAI's *Colonial News* 1, no.2 (April 1934): 4—5.

[52] Headley, J., 'Let Us Close Ranks'.

[53] *NW* 2, nos. 9–10 (September–October 1932): 22.

[54] O'Connell, H., 'Race Prejudice in England'.

[55] See, e.g., 'Smash the Attacks on Colonial Seamen', *NW* 4, no. 3 (July 1934): 1–5. On the problems of the unemployed in London see, Ward, 'The Negro Situation in England'.

[56] Sherwood, 'Racism and Resistance'. On the Cardiff Coloured Association see also Tabili, '*We Ask for British Justice*', 127.

[57] *NW* 5, no. 9 (September 1935): 10—2.

[58] *Colonial Information Bulletin* 11 (15 September 1937): 10.

[59] *NW* 7, no. 2 (Feburary 1937): 4 and Sherwood, 'Lascar Struggles Against Discrimination'.

[60] Little, *Negroes in Britain*, 75.

[61] Moody is quoted in Evans, 'Regulating the Reserve Army', 98.

[62] Koutaté with a lack of mathematical accuracy claimed that the membership of the LDRN was 80% workers, 5% peasants, 17% professionals and 3% students. 'Report' 29 September 1930, RGASPI 495/155/87/397.

[63] 'Réunion de la Commission Nègre', 2 April 1930, RGASPI 495/18/809/96—7.

[64] Spiegler, 'Aspects of Nationalist Thought', 169. McKay, *A Long Way From Home*, 278—9.

[65] Report on Work of the ITUCNW (Hamburg) Covering the Period from December 1930 to September 15, 1931', 2 October 1931, RGASPI 534/3/669.

[66] Dewitte, *Les Mouvements Nègres*, 197–206. Edwards, *The Practice of Diaspora*, 255.

[67] ITUCNW, 'Trade Union Programme of Action for Negro Workers', 11 March 1929, RGASPI 495/155/74/5.

[68] Padmore to Ford, 17 March 1931, RGASPI 534/3/668.

[69] Ford to Padmore, 31 July 1931, RGASPI 534/3/668.

[70] 'Re. the work of the Colonial Commission of the CGTU and its connection with the sub-committee in Marseilles'. 26 December 1931, and 'Resolution on the Work of the Hamburg Committee'. 18 October 1931, RGASPI 534/3/668.

[71] 'Negro Marine Workers! Organise and Fight Against Exploitation!' 5 November 1931, RGASPI 534/3/668. Also Kouyaté, 'Black and White Seamen Organise for Struggle'.

[72] On Kouyatés arrest see *NW* 1, no. 8 (August 1931): 13—4.

[73] 'Report on the Work of the ITUCNW (Hamburg)', 2 October 1931, RGASPI 534/3/669 and Dewitte, *Les Mouvements Nègres*, 287—8.

[74] 'Practical Decisions on the Discussion of the ITUC', 23–26 May 1932, RGASPI 534/3/753.

[75] 'Practical Decisions on the Discussion of the ITUC', 23–26 May 1932, RGASPI 534/3/753.

[76] Report on the work of the Hamburg Committee for the period 1931–1932', December 1932, RGASPI 534/3/753.

[77] 'Special Report by Kouyaté', n.d. RGASPI 534/3/753.

[78] Report of the ITUCNW, 25 October 1935, RGAPI 495/14/60/39. See *NW* 4 no. 8 (December 1934), 24.

[79] *NW* 5, nos. 7–8 (July–August 1935): 29.

References

Adi, Hakim. "Pan-Africanism and Communism: The Comintern, the 'Negro Question' and the First International Conference of Negro Workers, Hamburg 1930." *African and Black Diaspora* 2, no. 2 (July 2008): 237–55.

Aitken, Robbie. "From Cameroon to Germany and Back via Moscow and Paris: The Political Career of Joseph Bilé (1892–1959), Performer, "Negerbeiter" and Comintern Activist." *Journal of Contemporary History* 43, no. 4 (2008): 597–616.

Bellamy, Joyce and John Saville, eds. *Dictionary of Labour Biography Vol. VII*. London: Palgrave Macmillan, 1984.

Daniels, Robert, V. *A Documentary History of Communism, Vol.1*. New York: Methuen, 1962.

Dewitte, Philippe. *Les Mouvements Nègres en France 1919–1939*. Paris: Harmattan, 1985.

Edwards, Brent, Hayes. *The Practice of Diaspora: Literature, Translation, and the Rise of Black Internationalism*. Cambridge, MA: Harvard University Press, 2003.

Evans, N. "Regulating the Reserve Army: Arabs, Blacks and the Local State in Cardiff, 1919–45." In *Race and Labour in Twentieth Century Britain*, ed. Kenneth Lunn, 68–116. London: Frank Cass, 1985.

Frost, Dianne. *Work and Community among West African Migrant Workers since the Nineteenth Century.* Liverpool: Liverpool University Press, 1999.

Geiss, Immanuel. *The Pan-African Movement: A History of Pan-Africanism in America, Europe and Africa.* New York: Africana Pub, 1968.

Headley, Jim. "Let Us Close Ranks." *Negro Worker* 2, no. 7 (1932): 18–19.

Kanet, Roger. "The Comintern and the "Negro Question": Communist Policy in the United States and Africa, 1921–1941." *Survey* 19, no. 4 (1973): 86–122.

Kouyaté, Garan. "Black and White Seamen Organize for Struggle." *Negro Worker* 1, no. 12 (December 1931): 19–20.

Little, Kenneth. *Negroes in Britain: A Study of Race Relations in English Society.* London: Kegan Paul, 1948.

McKay, Claude. *A Long Way From Home.* (London: Pluto, 1985), 278–9.

Ndiaye, Pap. *La condition noire: Essai sur une minorité française.* Paris: Gallimard, 2008.

O'Connell, H. "Race Prejudice in England." *Negro Worker* 3, nos. 2–5 (April–May 1933): 25–5.

Ramdin, Ron. *The Making of the Black Working Class in Britain.* Aldershot: Gower, 1987.

Rich, Paul, B. *Race and Empire in British Politics.* Cambridge: Cambridge University Press, 1990.

Sherwood, Marika. "Racism and Resistance: Cardiff in the 1930s and 1940s." *Llafur* 4, no. 5 (1991): 51–70.

Sherwood, Marika. "The Comintern, the CPGB Colonies and Black Britons 1920–1938." *Science & Society* (Spring, 1996): 137–63.

Sherwood, Marika. "Lascar Struggles Against Discrimination in Britain 1923–45: The Work of N.J. Upadhyaya and Surat Alley." *The Mariner's Mirror* 90, no. 4, (November 2004): 438–55.

Spiegler, James. "Aspects of Nationalist Thought among French-Speaking West Africans" 1921–1939. Oxford, DPhil diss, 1968.

Tabili, Laura. *We Ask for British Justice" – Workers and Racial Difference in Late Imperial Britain.* Ithaca, NY: Cornell University Press, 1994.

Ward, Arnold. "The Negro Situation in England." *Negro Worker* 4, nos. 6–7 (October–November 1934): 7.

Wilson, Edward. *Russia and Black Africa Before World War II.* London: Holmes and Meier, 1974.

Fighting Racism: Black Soldiers and Workers in Britain during the Second World War

Gavin Schaffer

School of Social, Historical and Literary Studies, University of Portsmouth, Portsmouth, UK

The Second World War led to a substantial increase in the number of black people living and working in Britain. Existing black British communities were bolstered in this period by the arrival of war volunteer workers from the Empire, who came to serve Britain in a variety of military and civilian roles, as well as by the arrival of 130,000 black GIs in the US army's invasion force. This article considers the reception that these communities received from the British government and the British general public, questioning the extent to which racial ideas of white difference and superiority continued to shape white British reactions to black workers and soldiers. Using a variety of sources, including government papers and Mass Observation reports, this article interrogates the roots of changing dynamics of racial thought in wartime Britain, highlighting in particular the extent to which fears of racial mixing continued to undermine white responses to growing black British communities.

In the mid-1980s, pioneering scholars of immigration and minority histories offered a series of important interventions concerning the reception of black people, and the development of black communities, in wartime Britain. In this period, the likes of Marika Sherwood, Ken Lunn, Peter Fryer and Graham Smith provided solid foundations for the developing historical field of black British study, highlighting the experiences of diverse black communities in Britain and offering an enhanced analysis of British racism.[1] The development of black British war history in this period reflected changing currents in broader historical approaches to wartime Britain, in particular, an increasing scholarly willingness to probe more deeply into the nation's war image and engage with less glorious aspects of the British war experience.[2] Pioneering scholars of black history were also no-doubt mindful of the timeliness, amid the nationalistic and often xenophobic atmosphere of Thatcherism, of a history which drew within its scope the long-standing contributions of black people and detailed the complex British history of racism and intolerance.

Twenty years after this burst of scholarship, and despite a generation of historians who have attempted to develop our understanding of the Second World War, key questions remain about the experiences of black people in wartime Britain.[3] In particular, historians continue to debate the extent to which black volunteers were welcomed into the British war effort and the level of government and popular hostility towards the development of black communities in this period. In light of this ongoing debate, this article will focus on the history of both black civilian workers and soldiers during the war in the belief that understanding the reception of soldiers (as well as civilians) is necessary in order to unpick racial sensibilities in a wartime society. To this end, the article will utilise both government papers and the archives of Mass Observation to re-consider the reception of all black volunteers in wartime Britain, questioning the ways in which changing dynamics of racial thought created and conditioned this reception.

At the outset it is important to challenge the idea that black presence or racial conflict was a new phenomenon in wartime Britain. Of course, in the context of this volume, such an idea would not come to the fore. However, government and media outlets during the war repeatedly characterised the black presence in Britain as new. In particular, the idea that the nation had no experience of co-existing with black communities or dealing with racial conflict seems to have been engaged in order to defend, and often defer to, American racial attitudes and policies of segregation. For example, Anthony Eden, the Foreign Secretary, noted in a 1942 memorandum that 'the American point of view' needed to be considered, specifically because Britons 'have not had sufficient experience on a large scale of the colour problem'.[4] The idea of deferring to American expertise on race relations was never universally accepted and was subject to numerous challenges, especially from the Colonial Office.[5] Nonetheless, the notion that black communities posed new problems to a historically white British society remained fairly prominent and has repeatedly entered historical analysis. Smith, for example, has argued that the arrival of black GIs 'caused considerable consternation' precisely because Britain was 'unaccustomed to racial problems'.[6] More black people did though come to Britain because of the Second World War. Volunteers from across the British Empire and black GIs bolstered Britain's existing black communities and played a substantial role in the war effort. Specifically, the war saw the arrival of 1000 technicians and factory workers in Merseyside, 1200 Honduran Foresters in Scotland and the enlistment of over ten thousand Caribbean soldiers by the RAF. More significant in terms of numbers were the one hundred and thirty thousand black GIs of the United States army, which built up in Britain until the attack on the Nazi Continent in 1944.[7]

Fryer has argued that the reception of the black GIs entailed 'a strange mixture of genuine welcome and genuine discrimination'.[8] Similarly, mixed messages seem also to have characterised the reception of black volunteers from the Empire. Many British politicians, perhaps most, were less than happy at the prospect of accepting such volunteers into Britain. As far as the black GIs were concerned, the British government had tried, unsuccessfully, to prevent their arrival in any great numbers. The National Association for the Advancement of Coloured People (NAACP) accused the British government of asking their allies in the United States to station no black troops in Britain. An official at the Foreign Office noted that it was impossible to refute such a statement as there was a 'possibility' that the Prime Minister may have done so. The best answer that could be given, the Official concluded, was that the request had not been to completely stop the sending of black troops but to minimise their number. This nuance, he noted, would do little to reassure the NAACP.[9]

Correspondence between British officials in the United States and the Foreign Office in 1942 indicates the extent to which this reluctant acceptance of black soldiers and volunteers in Britain was entrenched in British policy. A British official in Washington Ronnie Campbell wrote that while he understood that 'coloured' volunteers were 'not desired', any public indication that the British government was operating a policy which discriminated 'on grounds of race ...[was]... likely to give rise to serious trouble with the coloured organisations in this country'. The Foreign Office's reply to Campbell reinforced the idea that, political considerations aside, the recruitment of black volunteers was not on the British agenda. Any such recruitment, it was argued, 'would create most difficult situation (sic) which we are not yet prepared to deal'.[10]

There were two main reasons for British reluctance to host black GIs and other black war volunteers. Firstly, politicians and officials were concerned that an increased black presence might entail negative social consequences. The exact nature of these concerns is not always easy to pin down but they seem to have orientated around fears that a heightened black population might lead to an increase in racial violence and a deep-rooted concern about black and white sexual mixing. The other reason for opposition was a belief that black soldiers and volunteers would not meet the same standards as their white comrades. While British politicians could not act effectively on these fears as regards black GIs, a belief in black inferiority certainly shaped policy towards the use of Empire war volunteers.[11]

The most extreme proponents of the idea of black inferiority resided in the War Office. Here, the Secretary of State, James Grigg, consistently resisted the recruitment and use of black troops. A 1942 report from Grigg to the Cabinet strongly argued the case of black troop inferiority. He argued: 'While there are many coloured men of high mentality and cultural distinction, the generality are of a simple mental outlook ... In short they have not the white man's ability to think and act to a plan'.[12] Throughout the conflict, the War Office maintained its opposition to the use of black troops, and attempted to influence other government departments to minimise black presence in Britain. One 1943 report forcefully argued the case for exclusion. Grigg argued: 'On purely military grounds I am afraid the drawbacks of so employing them, whether as combatant (e.g., anti-aircraft) troops or as labour units outweigh any advantages'.[13]

These attitudes were not shared by everyone. Consistently, the Colonial Office was substantially more supportive of the idea that black volunteers could be used effectively in the war effort. It was on their initiative that the unit of Honduran foresters was brought to Britain in 1941. And when, in 1943, the Ministry of Supply moved to have the Hondurans repatriated, the Colonial Office offered a robust defence of these workers. JL Keith complained that while the men were being labelled as poor workers, the real problem was that they had lacked 'firm and sympathetic leadership' and that there was a case, not to send them home, but instead to improve their terms and conditions. The Colonial Office seemingly considered that prejudice lay at the root of calls for the Unit's disbandment. IG Cummings confided to Keith that it seemed unfair that the Hondurans were to be sent home, while other foreign forestry units (notably from Newfoundland) were not to suffer the same fate. While they could not in the event prevent the disbandment of the Unit, the Colonial Office lobbied and worked hard to place those Hondurans who did not want to leave the UK in new jobs.[14]

Although there were a murkier set of reasons related to 'miscegenation' and the prevalence of VD amongst the foresters, the primary reason given by the Ministry of Supply for the proposed repatriation of the Hondurans was their lack of productivity.[15] Simply, the Ministry of Supply argued that the men did not offer a good service in comparison to other (white) labour. The Royal Navy were similarly unenthusiastic about the Hondurans enlisting for war service with them. In 1943, the Colonial Office attempted to persuade the Navy to consider accepting some of the foresters, who had expressed a wish to join the fight against Hitler. However, despite initial wavering, the Navy soon decided that it did not have a use for these particular volunteers. When Cummings asked whether this was a racial issue the Navy argued that no such considerations had shaped their decision, and reassured him that 'the men were not being kept out on colour bar grounds'. However, it is difficult to see what else can be read into the Admiralty's feeling 'that coloured Colonial volunteers were rather an embarrassment and difficult to place in this country'.[16]

The Navy's stance was similar to that taken by Grigg in the War Office, specifically that the undesirability of engaging black volunteers was not ideological but rooted instead in practical considerations. In this mind frame, black volunteers could be discriminated against within an ostensible atmosphere of non-racialism, under-utilised not because of prejudice but because they were of a poor quality. The effect, as Sherwood has noted, was that anti-racist policy was 'consistently and persistently contravened by various administrative measures'.[17]

Policy towards black volunteers was somewhat more enlightened in the Royal Air Force, though even here there was a fundamental ambivalence towards the idea of mixing black and white troops. The Air Ministry did employ a considerable number of black volunteers in the UK and did not seem to feel that this volunteer labour was as undesirable or substantially inferior as claimed by Grigg and others.[18] With an eye on postwar policy, research was conducted by the RAF in 1945 into the success of black volunteers in their wartime roles. A report was produced by an RAF Wing Commander Shone which considered the performance of 422 West Indian aircrew recruited in Canada and the UK and 3900 black ground personnel recruited from the West Indies. In comparison with the dogmatism of Grigg, this report gave a partially positive analysis of the contribution of black volunteers. In overall conclusion, it noted regarding West Indian aircrew:

> Selected West Indian personnel have on the whole proved themselves fully capable as individuals of holding their own as Pilots and members of aircrew and in the standard of discipline and responsibility required of officers and NCOs.[19]

However, this report was peppered with ambivalence about the recruitment of black volunteers for the RAF. For while it noted that the general quality of the men was comparable to their white peers, it alleged a series of personality flaws which, to the RAF's mind, undermined a future black contribution to the air force. Indian personnel were criticised in the report for a lack of 'power of command' while it was noted that the 'predatory' behaviour of some of the West Indian men had led to the removal of female 'WAAF personnel from duty in Sick Quarters' and an increase of policing in nearby towns 'to prevent disturbances'. The RAF report also criticised the character of West Indians, claiming that their promotion to 'Captain of Aircraft' had created problems as the men had allowed their success to go to their heads:

> A case is known where such an appointment led a coloured airman to regard himself as a privileged person and to show resentment when certain breaches of conduct and behaviour were pointed out to him by superior officers. The difficulties outlined in this sub-para were among the considerations taken into account in reaching the decision to suspend all aircrew recruiting in the Colonies.

Here, a seemingly trivial and individual problem seems to have been extrapolated into a policy of not recruiting further black personnel, serving as another example of Sherwood's idea that non-racial issues were used to continue racial restriction.

Some historians have taken the view that while the government may have been keen to minimise the black presence in wartime Britain, the general public were more welcoming. In particular, this argument has been made by some of the leading scholars of the US military presence in Britain. For example, David Reynolds has argued: 'To a degree that may seem surprising today, British people transcended the stereotypes about "negroes" and welcomed the black GIs'.[20] These arguments are built upon numerous examples of good neighbourliness between black GIs and their British hosts and, in particular, on the fairly numerous displays of grass-roots British hostility towards the racist behaviour of white American soldiers. Although the British government issued secret instructions to British troops to respect the American colour bar, it is clear that many British soldiers and civilians felt outraged on behalf of black GIs, and often became embroiled in fights to defend them from aggressive white American behaviour.[21] However, these instances cannot be used easily as evidence of broader enlightened British attitudes towards 'race'. Often the (white) British defence of black people seems to have stemmed from a disinclination to have policy and values in Britain dictated by the US military. In this way, the oft-cited tendency of British publicans and retailers to ban white GIs (when faced with demands from US soldiers to segregate) is probably as well explained by anti-Americanism as by anti-racism.[22] Indeed, records held in the Mass Observation archive indicate a popular British ambivalence towards black people in wartime Britain, not dissimilar to the views held by the government and military leadership.

Mass Observation (MO) papers do not give perfect insight into popular views in wartime Britain. MO diarists and directive respondents were self-selecting and thus never comprised any kind of sociologically sound representative sample group.[23] Observers were disproportionately liberal/left wing, middle class and middle aged. Nonetheless, used with caution, the MO Race Directives of 1939 and 1943 offer unparalleled access into white British thinking about black people in this period.[24] Directives were monthly questionnaires given out to MO's volunteers who could decide for themselves if they wanted to answer them. During the war (as MO developed a formal working relationship with the Ministry of Information) directives frequently posed questions with the goal of revealing the wartime civilian state of mind and the race directives should be seen in this context. These directives asked Observers to give their feelings about different foreign groups, in categories which were sometimes national (like the 'French' and the 'Germans') and sometimes racial ('Jews', 'Negroes' and 'Asiatics').

While Mass Observers never wrote without the recognition that their responses would be read, they knew that the views they expressed would neither be challenged nor publicised. Thus, to a certain extent, they seem to have felt free to express themselves. Although it is impossible to over-simplify the diversity of MO responses that are evident in the 1939 and 1943 Race Directives, this body of data makes clear that most of those questioned tended to perceive colour as denoting essential difference, otherness and inferiority. As Kushner has noted: 'Rather than open up the possibility of being Black and British, experiencing those of colour in a domestic arena caused many Observers deep unease'.[25]

In both directives, many Observers disclosed a belief that black men were essentially different and inferior to white Britons. Asked to give their opinion on 'Negroes', Observers frequently fell into highly racialised language and thinking, volunteering the idea that black people were a different species or type of human, essentially unlike white Britons. One Observer wrote, Negroes 'seem to me to be of an entirely different type to white men' while another argued that 'it is hard to feel that they are completely human with their shiny black skins, woolly hair and general appearance of missing linkness'. To many writers, 'blackness' betrayed a total difference. Black people came, according to a third contributor, from 'another order of things'.[26]

Observers mostly had little doubt that this 'other' type was inferior and primitive compared to the white Briton. Black people were described as 'a biologically inferior race, [with] mental and physical processes ... on a much lower plane than ours'. Another Observer said that he thought of them as '100, 000 years behind in mental evolution' and a third offered this similar opinion.

> I consider negroes on the whole to be at an earlier stage of civilisation than white races, and because of that, I consider that except in the cases of exceptionally advanced negroes, association between the negro and white races cannot be on an exactly level footing but rather that of a school master and middle school or senior boy.[27]

The idea that the inferiority of black people was similar to that of white children was a common one in Observers' answers. One described Negroes as a 'child like race with elemental passions'; another said that the black men that he had encountered were 'rather like children of 10 or so'.[28]

Children, however, could learn and grow and many other Observers did not believe that black people could ever master white civilisation. Often, therefore, comparisons were made not with children but animals. When considering if he would live under the same roof as a black person, one Observer answered: 'Would I willingly share a bedroom, a dinner table, or a change of clothes with a Negro? No, no more than I would admit my dog to such intimacy'. Another recorded: 'I feel like patting the Negro on the back or head, like a big black docile dog or pony'.[29] As black people were not perceived as equally human, it stood to reason for many Observers that any attempt to bring them to Britain or another 'civilised' country would be disastrous. One contributor noted: 'I don't think Negroes are "responsible" people somehow ... those who visit English universities acquire only a superficial veneer of white conduct and civilisation'. Another concluded:

> Driven by their emotions. Intellectually different from the white man, and almost certainly needs to develop an individual system of education fitted to their mental capacities. Unless they are extraordinary, 'western' education makes them into misfits.[30]

The 1943 records of Mass Observation do reveal substantial British opposition to US army influence on race relations in Britain. When asked about their feelings towards the colour bar in a questionnaire, 75% of polled Observers said that they opposed it.[31] However, this opposition does not seem to have been triggered by any radical change of racial views. The summary of the 1943 Race Directive by Mass Observation revealed that only one in five of those polled believed in racial equality, even as a quarter of Observers who completed the directive thought that the war had changed racial attitudes for the better.[32]

Taken as a whole, what the Mass Observation 'race' data seem to indicate is a British ambivalence towards black people which cannot be explained by simple differences of opinion between those of a racist, and those of a non-racist, disposition. This popular ambivalence towards, and lack of confidence in, black people in Britain seems to have reflected high political attitudes, challenging historical notions of a division between governors and the governed as regards racial matters. Of course, society and government were comprised from a spectrum of differing racial viewpoints, but the preponderance of British opinion during the war seems to have been dominated by hostility towards both racism and black people. This led to an atmosphere where, as we have seen, the military attempted to restrict black enlistment while denying that any racial rationale was operating, where black Empire volunteers were rejected because of their 'lack of productivity', and Mass Observers expressed an apologetic continuing belief in racial difference, one typically noting in the 1939 Race Directive: 'I have a certain "feeling" against Negroes. I realise this is irrational and must be resisted'.[33]

Peter Fryer has analysed this confused British attitude towards racism as a display of hypocrisy, a view mirrored by Neil Wynn who has highlighted a gap between what was 'professed' and what was 'practised' in terms of Allied racial values. In a convincing consideration of British national identity during the war, Rose has explained the internal contradictions of British racial thinking in terms of a clash between a long-standing perception of white superiority and opposition to the extreme racial stances of the Nazis and the US military, views that were not seen to be conducive with British liberal Empire ideology: 'Being British in Great Britain meant being white. It also meant being tolerant, at least more tolerant than white Americans and less racist than the Nazis'.[34]

It certainly seems arguable that the war pressurised long-standing assumptions and beliefs in British society, and that in this period Britons increasingly articulated their racial values in negative terms, defining their own views in opposition to more extreme positions. This did not mean, as we have already seen, that British racism died as a result of abhorrence towards American or Nazi racial policy. But it would be naïve to fail to see that British opposition to racial extremism (especially towards Nazi anti-Semitism) did have some impact on British racial thinking, an impact which is most obvious in the output of Britain's leading 'race' experts in this period.

Most British 'race' experts were outspoken in their opposition to Nazi racial theory from the mid-1930s.[35] The increased influence of genetics and the decline in credibility of older anthropological racial beliefs had been causing a methodological pressure on ideas of racial difference since the 1920s but there is little doubt that the ascendance of Hitler galvanised scientific challenges to the idea of 'race'. By the time of the Second World War, Britain's leading race experts had consciously created a body of work which opposed the idea of racial prejudice and argued for equal rights. This, to eminent biologist and popular broadcaster JBS Haldane, was part of the war effort itself because, as he noted, it was crucial to 'prevent the teaching of bogus biology which can be used as the theoretical basis of British fascism'.[36]

While there was a great quantity of research in this area, across a range of disciplines, perhaps the most prominent British offering in this context was Alfred Cort Haddon's and Julian Huxley's *We Europeans: A Survey of Racial Problems*, published in 1935. Like Haldane, Huxley and Haddon saw a need to produce anti-racist scholarship in opposition to the Third Reich; to place, as Huxley put it in his first autobiography, 'a spoke into Hitler's wheel'.[37] *We Europeans* argued that modern populations were 'melting pots of race', that pure 'races' did not exist, and that 'all that exists today is a number of arbitrary ethnic groups, intergrading into each other'. Most of all, *We Europeans* repeatedly made the case that racial prejudice was not justified by fact. Indeed, the authors' argued: 'In the circumstances, it is very desirable that the term race as applied to human groups should be dropped from the vocabulary of science'.

But looking in more depth at the views of these experts concerning black people seems to reveal similar ambivalence as has been seen in broader British thinking on 'race' in this period. For while scholars like Huxley and Haldane were determined to fight the racial extremism of the Third Reich they remained largely convinced of the inferiority conferred by blackness. The ambiguities of the British scientific challenge to racism were even evident in *We Europeans* itself. For example, in this text the authors argued that popular fears about the psychological effects of 'racial crossing' might well 'have some validity'.[38]

Similarly, J.B.S Haldane continued even in the wake of the war and the Holocaust to assert that racial differences did exist and matter, even if the Nazis had exaggerated their importance. He argued:

> ... I don't believe in racial superiority, in the sense that some races lack capacities present in others, but I am inclined to think that certain inborn capacities may be commoner in some races than in others.[39]

These ongoing scientific beliefs led to a specific expert intervention in British politics in this period. Numerous attempts were made to discredit Nazi racial science. However, these same experts declined to support the development of black communities in Britain. In science, as in broader society, a picture emerges of a majority of Britons who were willing to oppose racial extremism but, for the most part, unwilling to infer from this opposition that 'race' was a meaningless concept, or that there were not important racial differences between white and black people.

Understanding this persistence of racist thinking in wartime Britain is no easy matter. Why, historians need to ask, did the fight against Hitler and the growing tide of international anti-racism (epitomised in the drawing up of the UNESCO First Statement on Race in 1950) not do more to erode British racist attitudes towards Britain's growing black communities? In answering this question, many scholars of interwar and wartime Britain have emphasised the continuing importance of material considerations in shaping racial views at all levels. Most notably Ken Lunn and Laura Tabili have concluded that opposition to the development of black communities in Britain can only be understood with reference to broader social conflicts, in which the idea of 'race' became frequently embroiled. In Tabili's words:

> In interwar Britain, the definition of who was Black and to what this entitled him was shaped by domestic, labor, and imperial politics. This history might encourage us to seek material, institutional, and historical bases for racial conflict. We must understand racial conflict as a product of structural inequality and racial conflict as one of many forms of conflict ... that result from inequality rather than create it.[40]

Most of all, the ideology which justified the British Empire, however liberal and benign many of its adherents in this period believed it to be, was always and necessarily underwritten by a racial ideology which surely shaped significantly British engagement with black people at home in this period.[41]

However, the racist beliefs of Marxist scientists like JBS Haldane (who was vehemently opposed to Empire) seem to point to an additional foundation stone of British racial views; namely the long-standing influence of scientific racism and eugenics. Whilst the roots of these academic terrains were also undoubtedly shaped by imperialism and all it entailed, by this period racial science seems to have exercised an influence on social and political thinking on race in its own right.[42] Put simply, generations of expert pronouncements on the subject of racial difference created a widespread social belief in the need to maintain racial type. This belief was not consciously related to the material world in any sense, but instead had become an unchallengeable (scientifically legitimised) truth in the belief system of many Britons. Ongoing anxiety about the dangers of 'miscegenation' seems to demonstrate the power and persistence of these concerns about racial type and quality. For even when conscious minds could be made to accept the principle of racial equality, fears of 'miscegenation' continued to provoke a deep reservoir of opposition to the presence of black people in wartime Britain.

Fears about racial mixing lay at the heart of the concerns of many Mass Observers in this period. Even those Observers who held generally positive views about the presence of black people in the UK often could not escape from a squeamish backtracking when it came to the subject of inter-racial sex and marriage.[43] One recorded on the subject of Negroes: 'I admire those who come to this land to study medicine, etc. They should not be used as slaves. Nevertheless, I do not approve of white marrying colour'. Another similarly remarked:

> I have met only one in my life, and he struck me as particularly charming. I feel that their association with white women is revolting, but I have nothing against them as a class, and have every sympathy with them as regards the treatment which is meted out to them by the Americans.[44]

Reading the Race Directive of 1939, one cannot help but be overwhelmed by levels of anxiety about mixed-'race' relationships, concerns which are also recalled in several of the auto-biographical accounts of black Britons living in wartime Britain.[45] These views were expressed perhaps more frequently than any other and dominate Observers' responses about black people. Most often concerns of this nature were focused on sexual intercourse, as Observers argued that mixed 'race' sex was naturally abhorrent to a healthy, moral citizen. This belief fuelled a corresponding assumption that those who engaged in such sexual encounters were deviant or disturbed.[46] One Observer asserted that mixed-'race' sex would be virtually impossible to carry out. 'Such close intimacy, as say, sexual with a Negress would not in normal circumstances be possible because of an innate feeling of revulsion'. Another commented: 'Negresses disgust me and whenever I see a white woman and a coloured man I feel like shooting both'.[47] Some Observers felt that black people exuded an odour that, to white noses, was too repulsive to even allow mixed-'race' dancing. 'I got a Negro in a spoon dance once. They smell: I am sorry but that is my strongest feeling about them'. Another was sure that even contact without sight would not leave her in any doubt as to the 'race' of the person with whom she was associating. 'I could tell from the feel of the skin that he was a Negro'.[48]

As indicated by these responses, a wide group of Observers seem to have believed in the existence of significant physical 'racial' differences between white and black people, which fuelled their fears about 'miscegenation'. One wrote that 'marriage between white and coloured people should, I think, be discouraged because between our races and the Negroes there are physical differences'. Other Observers voiced fears that 'miscegenation' would lead to the deterioration of British 'racial' stock. 'Intermarriage should be forbidden by law as marriage between white and black results in white race deterioration'. Another asserted that black 'intermarriage and intercourse with Europeans should be discouraged, because half-castes generally are below a favourable standard'.[49]

These deep-rooted concerns often boiled to the surface in the form of highly charged constructions of black sexuality. One female Observer offered the following answer to a question about what came into her mind when she thought of 'Negroes':

> A black shining figure of fine physique, wearing only a loin cloth, and with a wide smile showing white, even teeth ... in his fine body and open expression, he is superior to many other men. His sexual attraction is quite strong, more so than in white men – though remember this is a mind picture, not reality.

Similarly, a male Observer commented that black men 'shine in the world of Hot music ... the grosser the cacophony of sound the greater the attraction to women and cissyfied men'.[50]

Fears about the sexual differences of black people (especially black men) seem to have translated into a heightened media sensitivity towards reports of intimate relationships between white British women and black soldiers and volunteers. While much of the press did not play to these concerns, some coverage reveals the extent of social fascination with this kind of sexual activity. One local paper told its readers of the problem of 'white girls and coloured men meeting clandestinely and making love to one another in shop doorways, quiet side streets, open spaces and in some instances in vehicles drawn up at the side of the pavement'.[51] Michael Banton's analysis of host–immigrant relations in the immediate postwar period reinforces this picture of an ongoing and entrenched interest and belief in black and white sexual difference, relating in Banton's mind to the construction of both black men and women:

> There are widespread beliefs among Englishmen that a coloured woman is more satisfying sexually and corresponding ideas occur among Englishwomen, often supplanted by the belief that the Negro male's genitals are larger (I understand that physiological research has failed to substantiate this).[52]

During the war, it seems beyond doubt that these kinds of sexual constructions shaped thinking at high levels of government. Unsurprisingly, Grigg was at the centre of them, arguing to Churchill that 'the natural propensities of the coloured man' created a threat to British women which was 'twice as heavy' as it would have been with white troops.[53] Indeed, the management of black troops when they arrived for service indicates that Grigg's perspective was certainly taken into account.

For example, when the Duke of Buccleuch allowed the Honduran foresters to work on his land, he did so only on the understanding that their housing was located well away from local communities, and the opportunities that these communities might provide for inter-racial sexual contact. In fact, the Duke was sufficiently concerned to write to the government to ask what could be done to prevent sexual mixing taking place. The response which he received reveals much about a government which was as concerned as him about sexual mixing but unprepared (in the political climate) to speak publicly on the subject. Harold Macmillan, then the Parliamentary Secretary to the Minister of Supply, wrote to the Duke that while the Hondurans' presence may indeed lead to 'some undesirable results ... All we can do is mitigate the evil'. As on other occasions, government action involved using a bizarre range of existing laws to try to manage the situation without compromising core anti-racist principles. Sherwood has noted in this context that police raided the Hondurans' camps in 1942 and removed white women, not on any racial charge, but because they were trespassing; a policy of policing black volunteers and soldiers which has also been emphasised by Reynolds in his research into British social relations with Black GIs.[54]

Always at the extremes of government racial policy, Grigg wanted to enact laws which would prevent 'miscegenation'. While his fears on this subject probably had deeper roots, ostensibly his case was that inter-racial infidelities at home could have a disastrous impact on the morale of British troops abroad.[55] Grigg's proposed legislation would have totally undermined Britain's projected war image and it is unsurprising that the government did not enact any such law. However, the research of Sherwood and others into the numerous non-legislative measures that were taken to prevent 'miscegenation' indicates that considerable sympathy for Grigg's position existed within the British government. Their middle position, fuelled both by racism and the desire not to be perceived as racist, seems to sum up British policy in this period more generally.

Conclusion

Attitudes towards 'race' in Britain were changing in this period and there is little doubt that the visible black contribution to the war effort played an important role in this process. Similarly, there is considerable evidence that the racial extremism of the US army and the fight against the Nazi racial state did catalyse white Britons to re-think their relationship to racism during the war. But neither the utility of black manpower in wartime Britain nor opposition to Nazi racism could do much to erode long-standing beliefs in black difference and inferiority which, to many British people, seemed little more than a natural deference to common sense. Thus the reception of black workers in wartime Britain was persistently dogged by racist concerns about black intelligence and reliability, and most of all by the belief that 'miscegenation' would lead to the contamination of British racial stock.

These prejudices did not stop the growth of black working communities in Britain but they did frequently limit the work opportunities that were afforded to black people and served to create a climate where black war volunteers often felt unwanted and under threat.[56] In a fight against the political racism of Nazism, British attitudes and policy were constrained by long-standing, home-grown beliefs about racial difference and inferiority. Racial thinking was certainly changing in this period but its longevity would go on to cast a shadow over postwar labour relations in Britain.

Acknowledgements

I would like to thank Mass Observation for allowing me access to their archive.

Notes

[1] The term 'black' is used in this chapter to encompass Caribbean, African and Asian workers in Britain, interspersed with references to specific geographical locations where these are significant. The term is used in recognition that in many cases African, Caribbean and sometimes Asian workers were lumped together as a category in the thinking of many officials and much of the public, as we shall see below. For the reception of Black people in Britain see Sherwood, *Many Struggles*; Lunn, 'Race Relations or Industrial Relations?'; Fryer, *Staying Power* and Smith, *When Jim Crow Met John Bull*. Also see Gilroy, *There Ain't No Black in the Union Jack*.

[2] See, for example, the development in the wake of the Thatcher period of research which attacked war myths of unity and national solidarity. In particular, see Calder, *The Myth of the Blitz* and Ponting, *1940: Myth or Reality*.

[3] In particular, see Adi, *West Africans in Britain 1900–1960*; Reynolds, *Rich Relations: The American Occupation of Britain 1942–45*; Rose, *Which People's War?* and Spencer, *British Immigration Policy since 1939*.

[4] Specifically, British experiences of racial rioting in 1919 certainly seem to have influenced responses to the heightened black presence in the Second World War. See Rich, 'Philanthropic Racism in Britain', Flint, 'Scandal at the Bristol Hotel' and Marke, *In Troubled Waters*, 145–6. National Archives of the United Kingdom (NA), Kew, Surrey, CO 876/14, Memorandum from the Home Secretary, 10/10/42.

[5] John L Keith, amongst other Colonial Office officials, repeatedly voiced opposition to the idea that the British should adopt American attitudes towards black people. For example, in one 1942 memorandum he noted: 'We should not allow any nonsense about rape, VD, etc., to deter us from sticking to our principles and resisting the so-called Southern American attitude towards Negroes'. NA, CO876/14, 12/9/42.

[6] Smith, *When Jim Crow*, 217.

[7] Figures on British Empire volunteers from Spencer, *British Immigration Policy*, 17. Sherwood's research, in *Many Struggles*, suggests that numbers were smaller. Also see Wynn, '"Race War"', 324–66. For Black GIs see Smith, *When Jim Crow*, 20–36 and Reynolds, *Rich Relations*, 216–17.

[8] See Fryer, *Staying Power*, 359.

[9] NA, FO371/30680, Malcolm to Butler, December 1942. For analysis see Smith, *When Jim Crow*, 45–52.

[10] NA, FO371/32530, Campbell to Steele, 30/7/42 and FO371/32530, Steel to Campbell, 12/8/42.

[11] On sexual fears see Rose, 'Race, empire and British wartime national identity, 1939–45', 237 and Schaffer, *Racial Science and British Society 1930–62*, 86–9. For in-depth analysis of British attitudes towards Black GIs see Wynn, "Race War", Reynolds, *Rich Relations* and Smith, *When Jim Crow*.

[12] NA, PREM4/29/6, Report by Grigg for the War Cabinet, September 1942.

[13] NA, CO968/17/5, Letter from Grigg to Stanley, 23/9/43.

[14] See Sherwood, *Many Struggles*, 99. For Colonial Office defence of the Hondurans see NA, CO876/42, Keith to Ministry of Supply, 17/8/43. The Colonial Office felt that the problems of the Hondurans stemmed from the poor leadership of General Harold Carrington. In another memorandum, RH Whitehorne agreed that Carrington was 'the villain of the piece'. Also see NA, CO 876/42, Note by Whitehorne, 23/8/43 and CO876/42, Note by IG Cummings to JL Keith, 3/9/43. For efforts from the Colonial Office to place the Hondurans in new jobs see NA, CO876/68. The Colonial Office attempted to secure roles for Hondurans in the Rolls Royce plant in Glasgow, 9/12/43, in the Royal Navy, 10/12/43 and in Lochaber Camp and Works, British Aluminium Co, 22/12/43.

[15] NA, CO876/42, Note by IG Cummings to JL Keith, 3/9/43.

[16] NA, CO876/68. IG Cummings, at the Colonial Office, wrote a memorandum noting: 'Quite naturally, some of the men have expressed an option to serve in His Majesty's Forces, and in particular a few of them have said they would like to be considered for service in the Royal Navy', 9/12/43. The Navy confirmed that the rejection of the Hondurans was not related to colour, NA, CO876/68, Cummings to Keith, 9/12/43.

[17] Sherwood, *Many Struggles*, 15.

[18] For one account of Caribbean recruitment and service in the Royal Air Force see Noble, *Jamaica Airman*.

[19] NA, AIR2/6876, Report of Wing Commander Shone, circa May 1945.

[20] See Reynolds, *Rich Relations*, 302–24 and Smith, *When Jim Crow*, 20–36 and 218–27. Also see Wynn, '"Race War"', 328–9; Fryer, *Staying Power*, 359 and Rose, 'Race, Empire . . .', 225.

[21] The instructions to British troops to respect the US colour bar were written down by General Arthur Dowler, Senior Administrative Officer in Southern Command. See Reynolds, *Rich Relations*, 224–6 and Smith, *When Jim Crow . . .* , 56–60.

[22] For one famous example of such an incident see Toole, *GIs and the Race Bar in Wartime Warrington*.

[23] On the merits of using Mass Observation in war research see Calder, 'Mass-Observation 1937–1949', 121–36; Hubble, *Mass-Observation and Everyday Life*; Kushner, *We Europeans?* and Sheridan, Street and Bloome, (eds.), *Writing Ourselves: Mass-Observation and Literary Practices*.

[24] Calder has rightly criticised the use of inconsistent language in this directive, while acknowledging the importance of its results. See Calder, *Mass Observation . . .* ,133–5.

[25] Kushner, *We Europeans*, 128.

[26] M-OA, 'Race Directive 1939', D1129, D2151 and D1939.

[27] Ibid., D1423, D1460 and D1346. Also see Reynolds, *Rich Relations*, 304–308. These views regarding the immaturity of black peoples corresponded with some high-ranking expert opinion in this period. See scientific support for the idea of Britain taking a 'parental' stance towards its black Empire in Huxley, *Democracy Marches*, 86–95.

[28] M-OA, 'Race Directive 1939', D2091 and D2007.

[29] Ibid., D1403 and D1529.

[30] Ibid., D1379 and D1423. Alibai Brown's records of attitudes amongst British soldiers in India during the war have highlighted the commonness of positive constructions of Black troops which were nonetheless framed within a discourse of inferiority. Recalling the attitudes of his colleagues and himself towards 'native' Indian troops, one retired, white soldier said: 'To be honest, we regarded these soldiers very highly but never as our equals', Alibai Brown, Y, recorded in the Black Cultural Archives, Coldharbour Lane, Brixton, File for 1991. Also see Wilson, '"In their own words"', 71–87.

[31] M-OA: FR 2021.

[32] M-OA: FR 1885. For analysis of these data see Kushner, *We Europeans*, 129–33.

[33] M-OA, Race Directive 1939, D2145.

[34] See Fryer, *Staying Power*, 363, Wynn, '"Race War"', 325 and Rose, 'Race, Empire. . .', 226.

[35] See Schaffer, *Racial Science and British Society*, 39–48. Also see Barkan, *The Retreat of Scientific Racism*, 279–340 and Stepan, *The Idea of Race in Science*, 140–69.

[36] JBS Haldane, *Science Advances* (London: George Allen and Unwin), 1947, 236.

[37] In actuality, *We Europeans* was not just the work of Huxley and Haddon, but was team-written by a larger group of scholars including Charles Singer, Alexander Carr-Saunders and Charles Seligman. For analysis see Barkan, *The Retreat of Scientific Racism*, 296–310 and Schaffer, *Racial Science and British Society*, 32–5. For Huxley's agenda see Huxley, *Memories I*, 207.

[38] Huxley and Haddon, *We Europeans: A Survey of Racial Problems*, 107 and 282–3.

[39] Haldane MSS, 20549. 'Our Men and Women', *Reynolds News*, November 1950.

[40] Tabili, 'The Construction of Racial Difference in Twentieth-Century Britain', *Journal of British Studies*, 98. Also see Lunn, 'Race Relations or Industrial Relations'.

[41] Rose, 'Race, Empire . . .', 237.

[42] For an analysis of the influence of social and political issues in shaping British racial science see Mazumdar, *Eugenics, Human Genetics and Human Failings*, Jones, 'Eugenics and Social Policy Between the Wars', 717–28 and Hawkins, *Social Darwinism in European and American Thought*.

[43] Smith has cited this tendency, noting that '. . . few people saw any intellectual gulf between their broad acceptance of Blacks and their particular dislike of miscegenation' in Smith, *When Jim Crow Met John Bull*, 199.

[44] M-OA, 'Race Directive', 1939, D1456 & D1119.

[45] See Noble, *Jamaica Airman*, 60–1 and Marke, *In Troubled Waters*, 140–1.

[46] Michael Banton noted the common belief that only 'rebels' or 'those whom the white group have rejected' had relationships with immigrants in *The Coloured Quarter*, 150.

[47] M-OA, 'Race Directive', 1939, D1264 and D2094.

[48] Ibid., D1077 and D1563.

[49] Ibid., D1656, D1423 and D1559.

[50] Ibid., D1047 and D1616.

[51] *Huddersfield Daily Examiner*, 20/9/40.

[52] Banton, *The Coloured Quarter*, 151. Banton's findings echo the research of other pioneering sociological studies of black communities in Britain. See, for example, Richmond, *Colour Prejudice in Britain*, 78.

[53] NA, PREM 4/26/9, Marlborough to Churchill, (Undated), 1943 and PREM 4/26/9, Grigg to Churchill, 2/12/43.

[54] See Reynolds, *Rich Relations*, 229.

[55] NA, PREM 4/26/9, Grigg told Churchill that there was a necessity 'for measures more stringent than education', Grigg to Churchill, 21/10/43.

[56] See Marke, *In Troubled Waters*, 142–6 and Noble, *Jamaica Airman*, 64–5.

References

Adi, Hakim. *West Africans in Britain 1900–1960: Nationalism, Pan-Africanism and Communism*. London: Lawrence and Wishart, 1998.

Banton, Michael. *The Coloured Quarter: Negro Immigrants in an English City*. London: Jonathon Cape, 1955.

Barkan, Elazar. *The Retreat of Scientific Racism: Changing Concepts of Race in Britain and the United States between the World Wars*. Cambridge: Cambridge University Press, 1992.

Calder, Angus. "Mass-Observation 1937–1949." In *Essays on the History of British Sociological Research*, edited by M. Bulmer. Cambridge: Cambridge University Press, 1985.

Calder, Angus. *The Myth of the Blitz*. London: Jonathan Cape, 1991.

Flint, John. "Scandal at the Bristol Hotel: Some Thoughts on Racial Discrimination in Britain and West Africa and its Relationship to the Planning of Decolonisation, 1939–47." *Journal of Imperial and Commonwealth History* 12, no. 1 (1983): 74–93.

Fryer, Peter. *Staying Power: The History of Black People in Britain.* London: Pluto, 1984.

Gilroy, Paul. *There Ain't No Black in the Union Jack: The Cultural Politics of Race and Nation.* London: Unwin Hyman, 1987.

Haldane, John Burdon Sanderson. *Heredity and Politics.* London: Allen and Unwin, 1938.

Haldane, J. B. S. *Science Advances.* London: Allen and Unwin, 1947.

Hawkins, Mike. *Social Darwinism in European and American Thought: Nature as Model and Nature as Threat 1860–1945.* Cambridge: Cambridge University Press, 1997.

Hogben, Lancelot. *Dangerous Thoughts.* London: Allen and Unwin, London, 1939.

Hubble, Nick. *Mass-Observation and Everyday Life: Culture, History, Theory.* Basingstoke: Palgrave Macmillan, 2006.

Huxley, Julian. *Memories I.* London: Allen and Unwin, 1970.

Huxley, Julian and Haddon Alfred. *We Europeans: A Survey of Racial Problems.* London: Jonathon Cape, 1935.

Jones, Greta. "Eugenics and Social Policy between the Wars." *The Historical Journal* 25, no. 3 (1982): 717–28.

Kushner, Tony. *We Europeans?: Mass-Observation, 'Race' and British Identity in the Twentieth Century.* Aldershot: Ashgate, 2004.

Lunn, Ken. "Race Relations or Industrial Relations? Race and Labour in Britain, 1880-1950." *Immigrants and Minorities* 4, no. 2 (1985): 1–29.

Marke, Ernest. *In Troubled Waters: Memoirs of Seventy Years in England.* London: Karia, 1986.

Mazumdar, Pauline. *Eugenics, Human Genetics and Human Failings: The Eugenics Society, its Sources and its Critics in Britain.* London and New York: Routledge, 1992.

Noble, E. Martin. *Jamaica Airman: A Black Airman in Britain 1943 and After.* London: New Beacon, 1984.

Ponting, Clive. *1940: Myth or Reality.* London: Hamilton, 1990.

Reynolds, David. *Rich Relations: The American Occupation of Britain 1942–45.* New York: Random House, 1995.

Rich, Paul. "Philanthropic Racism in Britain: The Liverpool University Settlement, the Anti-Slavery Society and the Issue of 'Half-Caste' Children, 1919–51." *Immigrants and Minorities* 3, no. 1 (1984): 69–88.

Richmond, Anthony. *Colour Prejudice in Britain: A Study of West Indian Workers in Liverpool 1941–51.* London: Routledge and Kegan Paul, 1954.

Rose, Sonya. *Which People's War? National Identity and Citizenship in Britain 1939–45.* Oxford: Oxford University Press, 2003.

Schaffer, Gavin. *Racial Science and British Society 1930–62.* Basingstoke and New York: Palgrave, 2008.

Sheridan, Dorothy, Street Brian, and Bloome David, eds. *Writing Ourselves: Mass-Observation and Literacy Practices.* Cresskill, NJ: Hampton Press, 2000.

Sherwood, Marika. *Many Struggles: West Indian Workers and Service Personnel in Britain 1939–45.* London: Karia Press, 1985.

Smith, Graham. *When Jim Crow Met John Bull.* London: IB Tauris, 1987.

Spencer, Ian. *British Immigration Policy Since 1939: The Making of Multi-Racial Britain*. London: Routledge, 1997.

Stepan, Nancy. *The Idea of Race in Science: Great Britain 1800–1960*. London: Macmillan, 1982.

Tabili, Laura. "The Construction of Racial Difference in Twentieth-Century Britain: The Special Restriction (Coloured Alien Seamen) Order, 1925." *Journal of British Studies* 33 (1994): 54–98.

Toole, Janet. "GIs and the Race Bar in Wartime Warrington." *History Today* 43, no. 7 (July 1993): 22–8.

Wilson, C. "'In Their Own Words': West Indian Technicians in Liverpool during World War Two." *Journal of Caribbean Studies*, 5, Winter/Summer (1990/1991): 71–87.

Wynn, Neil. "Race War: Black American GIs and West Indians in Britain during the Second World War." *Immigrants and Minorities* 24, no. 3 (2006), 324–66.

Index

Page numbers in **Bold** represent figures.

Routledge
Taylor & Francis Group

The European Legacy

Listed in the Thomson Reuters Arts & Humanities Citation Index®

The Official Journal of the International Society
for the Study of European Ideas

FOUNDING EDITOR:
Sascha Talmor 1925 - 2004

EDITORS:
Ezra Talmor, *Haifa University, Israel*
David W. Lovell, *Australian Defence Force Academy, Australia*
Edna Rosenthal, *The Kibbutzim College of Education, Israel*

The European Legacy is a multidisciplinary journal devoted to the
study of European intellectual and cultural history and the new
paradigms of thought evolved in the making of the New Europe.

The European Legacy publishes articles, reviews, and book
reviews on the main aspects of 'The European Legacy' in the
following disciplines: philosophy, philosophy of science, literature,
politics, history of religion, science, education, law, European
studies, war studies, women's studies, sociology, art, music,
economics and language.

To sign up for tables of contents, new publications and citation alerting services visit **www.informaworld.com/alerting**

updates
Taylor & Francis Group

Register your email address at **www.tandf.co.uk/journals/eupdates.asp** to receive information
on books, journals and other news within your areas of interest.

Powered by
informaworld

For further information, please contact Customer Services at either of the following:
T&F Informa UK Ltd, Sheepen Place, Colchester, Essex, CO3 3LP, UK
Tel: +44 (0) 20 7017 5544 Fax: 44 (0) 20 7017 5198
Email: subscriptions@tandf.co.uk

Taylor & Francis Inc, 325 Chestnut Street, Philadelphia, PA 19106, USA
Tel: +1 800 354 1420 (toll-free calls from within the US)
or +1 215 625 8900 (calls from overseas) Fax: +1 215 625 2940
Email: customerservice@taylorandfrancis.com

View an online sample issue at:
www.tandf.co.uk/journals/cele